Carl T. Berkhout and Jeffrey B. Russell

Medieval Heresies: A Bibliography 1960-1979

The two decades from 1960 to 1980 have witnessed a great surge in historical interest in medieval heresy; during this period well over 2,000 books and articles have appeared. Intellectual, social and institutional historians and theologians have all contributed to this growing interest, and interpretations of various kinds, from idealist to nationalist to Marxist, have been presented. Owing to the quantity and the variety of these works it has not always been possible to obtain a full prospect on the current state of the subject, especially since many of the articles have appeared in difficult-to-find journals. This bibliography lists virtually all these works.

The focus of the bibliography is on the social, popular heresies of western Europe from 700 to 1500. Intellectual and doctrinal heresies are covered where they produced a popular following, and eastern heresies are covered where (as with the Bogomils) they exerted substantial influence on the West. The scheme of classification employs categories in general use among historians: general works on heresy; heresy and reforms to 1140; the Bogomils; the Cathars; Valdes and the Waldensians; heresies of poverty; Beguines and Beghards; Joachim and Millenarianism; the Franciscan heretics; the heresy of the Free Spirit; Wyclif and the Lollards; Hus and the Hussites; other popular heresies; witchcraft; and the repression of heresy.

A full bibliographic citation is provided for each entry, including reviews of the books. The entries are thoroughly indexed in three sections: a general index forms a guide to subjects, heresies, heretics and place names; an author index provides the full name of each author or reviewer; a manuscript index lists by city the manuscripts used as important sources in the works themselves.

SUBSIDIA MEDIAEVALIA 11

MEDIEVAL HERESIES
A BIBLIOGRAPHY 1960-1979

BY

CARL T. BERKHOUT

AND

JEFFREY B. RUSSELL

PONTIFICAL INSTITUTE OF MEDIAEVAL STUDIES

TORONTO   1981

Canadian Cataloguing in Publication Data

Berkhout, Carl T., 1944-
  Medieval heresies

(Subsidia mediaevalia ; 11 ISSN 0316-0769)
Includes indexes.

ISBN 0-88844-360-9

1. Heresies and heretics - Middle Ages, 600-1500 - Bibliography. I. Russell,
Jeffrey Burton 1934- II. Pontifical Institute of Mediaeval Studies. III. Title.
IV. Series.

Z7777.B47   016.262´8   C80-094544-1

Pontifical Institute of Mediaeval Studies
59 Queen's Park Crescent East
Toronto, Ontario, Canada M5S 2C4

PRINTED BY UNIVERSA, WETTEREN, BELGIUM

For
C. Warren Hollister
and
John R. Sommerfeldt

Contents

Preface

Serious historical study of medieval heresies has been continuing for nearly a century, and the past two decades have been especially prolific in ideas, research, and publications. Two general bibliographies of medieval heresy appeared in the 1960s: Zsuzsánna Kulcsár's *Eretnekmozgalmak a XI-XIV. században* (Budapest, 1964) and Herbert Grundmann's *Bibliographie zur Ketzergeschichte des Mittelalters* (Rome, 1967). The need for another bibliography at this time attests to the extraordinarily large amount of scholarship in the 1960s and 1970s. Our original intent was to offer a supplement to Grundmann, but we found that he had omitted a substantial number of works, particularly in the period after 1960, and we also discovered that scholarly production in the period has been even more prodigious than we had imagined. Where Grundmann's bibliography covering the period 1900 to 1966 lists 775 entries, this bibliography covering the two decades 1960 to 1979 lists over 2000, not including reviews. Though works on heresy continue to appear at a rapid rate, the crest may have passed, and it is a good time to review the work accomplished. We have tried to make this bibliography as nearly complete as possible. We cite without judgment of value books and articles published from 1960 to 1979 that relate substantially to heresy. We also include reviews of major monographs, and we cite (without reviews) titles originally published before 1960 but reprinted in these two decades. With Wazo of Liège, we prefer to let the tares grow with the wheat until the day of harvest.

We have set the following limits: (1) We list only those works in which the subject of heresy is prominent, as for example in a broad textbook or essay in church history. (2) We have not included encyclopaedia articles. (3) We provide entries only for that part of Europe where Latin was the usual language of learning and where churches were generally subject to the authority of Rome. Heresies in other parts of the world are included only insofar as they directly influenced those of the West, Bogomilism being the most notable example. In this we have followed Grundmann, Kulcsár, and most recent histories of heresy, notably the standard work of

Malcolm Lambert, *Medieval heresy* (London and New York, 1977).
(4) We treat only the period from the eighth through the fifteenth century.
Earlier heresies were generally doctrinal in nature, and after the fifteenth
century the lines between heresy and Reformation are often indistinct.
Only the period from 700 to 1500 exhibits the typical characteristics of
medieval heresy: its social character, its moral emphasis upon reform, and
its ground of being in the Western church. (5) We cover only the popular,
social heresies as opposed to intellectual and doctrinal disputes. But we
have included intellectuals such as Amalric of Bena who appear to have
had a substantial popular following, and that is true *a fortiori* of Wyclif
and Hus. In border areas we have accommodated scholarship by
including works that might otherwise have been barred by an undue
respect for consistency. For example, we have included Peter Olivi
because of his ties with Joachim and with the Fraticelli, and in so doing
we have listed a number of works dealing with teachings of Olivi not
directly relevant to heresy.

The scheme of classification employs categories in general use among
historians. We have attempted to achieve a middle ground between over-
analysis and underanalysis. We hope that the reader will find in the
indexes a remedy for categorical ills. Entries are listed alphabetically by
author in each category, except for the "Hussitism: individuals" category,
where entries are listed alphabetically first by the name of the individual
and then by that of the author. This category includes both Hussites and
other individuals involved in Hussite controversies.

The general index is a guide to subjects, names of heresies and heretics,
and place names. We have chosen the index entries on the basis either of
their general importance or of their prominence in an individual book or
article. In the arrangement of Christian names and surnames, particularly
unsettled for the transitional fifteenth century, we have followed most
recent general usage. When the Christian name is placed first, we have
generally preferred the English form to the Latin or the vernacular. When
the surname is placed first, we have generally preferred the vernacular.
Where common usage has suggested departures from this procedure, we
have generally provided cross-references. The author index provides the
full name of each author including reviewers. The manuscript index lists
in alphabetical order by city the manuscripts that have been used as
sources.

We have attempted to see and verify each work entered. Where after all
efforts this remained impossible, we have established the entry by cross-

checking secondary references. In such instances we have placed a dash after the entry.

In preparing this bibliography we have used the resources of a number of libraries throughout Europe and North America. We should like particularly to thank the Bibliothèque Nationale, the British Library, the Vatican Library, and the libraries of the University of California at Los Angeles, the University of California at Santa Barbara, the University of Chicago, the University of Dallas, the University of Michigan, the University of Notre Dame, the Pontifical Institute of Mediaeval Studies, the University of Texas at Austin, and Yale University. We are also especially grateful for the kind assistance and advice of Jeanette Jones, Christopher Kleinhenz, James Landis, Robert E. Lerner, Bernard McGinn, Ann M. Repetto, Jennifer Russell, Brian Stock, and Jarold Knox Zeman.

Abbreviations

AB	*Analecta bollandiana*
AER	*The American ecclesiastical review*
AFH	*Archivum franciscanum historicum*
AFP	*Annuarium fratrum praedicatorum*
AHC	*Annuarium historiae conciliorum*
AHP	*Archivum historiae pontificae*
AHR	*The American historical review*
AKG	*Archiv für Kulturgeschichte*
AKK	*Archiv für katholisches Kirchenrecht*
AM	*Annales du midi*
Annales	*Annales: économies, sociétés, civilisations*
ARG	*Archiv für Reformationsgeschichte*
ASI	*Archivio storico italiano*
ASR	*Archives de sociologie des religions* [title changed to ASSR in 1973]
ASSR	*Archives de sciences sociales des religions* [formerly ASR]
AST	*Analecta sacra tarraconensia*
ATR	*Anglican theological review*
AUC Hist	*Acta universitatis carolinae, Historia universitatis carolinae pragensis*
BEC	*Bibliothèque de l'École des chartes*
BIHR	*Bulletin of the Institute of historical research*
Bijdragen	*Bijdragen: tijdschrift voor filosofie en theologie*
BISIM	*Bullettino dell'Istituto storico italiano per il medio evo e Archivio muratoriano*
BLE	*Bulletin de littérature ecclésiastique*
BPH	*Bulletin philologique et historique (jusqu'à 1610) du Comité des travaux historiques et scientifiques = Actes du Congrès national des sociétés savantes*
BSSV	*Bollettino della Società di studi valdesi*
BTAM	*Bulletin de théologie ancienne et médiévale*
ČČH	*Československý časopis historický*
CCM	*Cahiers de civilisation médiévale*
CD	*La ciudad de Dios*
CEC	*Cahiers d'études cathares*
CF	*Collectanea franciscana*
CH	*Church history*

CHR	*The Catholic historical review*
CQR	*The church quarterly review*
CV	*Communio viatorum*
DAEM	*Deutsches Archiv für Erforschung des Mittelalters*
DAI	*Dissertation abstracts international*
DLZ	*Deutsche Literaturzeitung*
EHR	*The English historical review*
ELN	*English language notes*
ETL	*Ephemerides theologicae lovanienses*
ETR	*Études théologiques et religieuses*
FČ	*Filosofický časopis*
FS	*Franciscan studies*
FSt	*Franziskanische Studien*
HibbJ	*The Hibbert journal*
HJ	*The Heythrop journal*
HZ	*Historische Zeitschrift*
IER	*The Irish ecclesiastical record*
JAAR	*Journal of the American academy of religion*
JCS	*Journal of church and state*
JEH	*The journal of ecclesiastical history*
JIH	*The journal of interdisciplinary history*
JR	*The journal of religion*
JRH	*The journal of religious history*
JSH	*Jihočeský sborník historický*
JTS	*The journal of theological studies*
KR	*Křesťanska revue* [see also *TPKR*]
LF	*Listy filologický*
LW	*Lutheran world*
MA	*Le moyen âge*
MÆ	*Medium Ævum*
MB	*Mediaevalia bohemica*
MH	*Medievalia et humanistica*
MIÖG	*Mitteilungen des Instituts für österreichische Geschichtsforschung*
MS	*Mediaeval studies*
MSR	*Mélanges de science religieuse*
N&Q	*Notes and queries*
NRT	*Nouvelle revue théologique*
PH	*Przegląd historyczny*
RAM	*Revue d'ascétique et de mystique* [later *RHS*]
RB	*Revue bénédictine*
RBPH	*Revue belge de philologie et d'histoire*
RES	*The review of English studies*

RESEE	Revue des études sud-est européennes
RH	Revue historique
RHDFE	Revue historique de droit français et étranger
RHE	Revue d'histoire ecclésiastique
RHEF	Revue d'histoire de l'église de France
RHPR	Revue d'histoire et de philosophie religieuses
RHR	Revue de l'histoire des religions
RHS	Revue d'histoire de la spiritualité
RS	Religious studies
RSCI	Rivista di storia della chiesa in Italia
RSI	Rivista storica italiana
RSLR	Rivista di storia e letteratura religiosa
RSPT	Revue des sciences philosophiques et théologiques
RSR	Recherches de science religieuse
RSyn	Revue de synthèse
RTAM	Recherches de théologie ancienne et médiévale
SEER	The Slavonic and East European review
SF	Studi francescani
SM	Studi medievali
SN	Studia neophilologica
SZG	Schweizerische Zeitschrift für Geschichte
TG	Tijdschrift voor geschiedenis
TLS	The Times literary supplement
TLZ	Theologische Literaturzeitung
TPKR	Theologická příloha Křesťanské revue [see also KR]
TPQ	Theologisch-praktische Quartalschrift
TR	Theologische Revue
TS	Theological studies
TZ	Theologische Zeitschrift
WS	Die Welt der Slawen
WW	Wissenschaft und Weisheit
ZDADL	Zeitschrift für deutsches Altertum und deutsche Literatur
ZG	Zeitschrift für Geschichtswissenschaft
ZKG	Zeitschrift für Kirchengeschichte
ZOF	Zeitschrift für Ostforschung
ZRGG	Zeitschrift für Religions- und Geistesgeschichte
ZSKG	Zeitschrift für schweizerische Kirchengeschichte
ZSSRG	Zeitschrift der Savigny-Stiftung für Rechtsgeschichte
ZTK	Zeitschrift für Theologie und Kirche

Part One

General

ENTRIES 1 TO 144

1 Angelov, D. "Conférences scientifiques sur les hérésies à l'époque médiévale." *Bulgarian historical review*, 1, no. 4 (1973), 135-140.

2 Argentré, C. du Plessis d', éd. *Collectio judicorum de novis erroribus, qui ab initio duodecimi seculi post Incarnationem Verbi usque ad annum 1632 in ecclesia proscripti sunt & notati.* Paris, 1728-1736. Rpt. Brussels: Culture et Civilisation, 1963. 3 v.

3 Arnold, G. *Unparteiische Kirchen- und Ketzerhistorie.* Sel. and ed. R. Riemeck. Leipzig: Koehler and Amelang, 1975. 365 p.

4 ———. *Unparteiische Kirchen- und Ketzerhistorie vom Anfang des Neuen Testaments bis auf das Jahr Christi 1688.* Frankfurt am Main, 1729. Rpt. Hildesheim: Olms, 1967. 4 v. in 2.

5 Babić, A. "Srednjovjekovni heretici." *Pregled* (Sarajevo), 1962, no. 3, p. 141-153. Rpt. in his *Iz istorije srednjovjekovne Bosne* (Sarajevo: Svjetlost, 1972), p. 178-194. [Medieval heresies]

6 Barbero, A. "Fermenti ereticali nel Piemonte alla fine del trecento." Diss. Università di Torino, 1966. 2 v. ———

7 Becquet, J. "Érémitisme et hérésie au moyen âge." With discussion. *Hérésies et sociétés* (1968). p. 139-145. See 65.

8 Bonet-Maury, G. *Les précurseurs de la réforme et de la liberté de conscience dans les pays latins du xiie au xve siècle.* Paris, 1904. Rpt. Geneva: Slatkine, 1969. viii, 268 p.

9 Borst, A. "La transmission de l'hérésie au moyen âge." With discussion. *Hérésies et sociétés* (1968). p. 273-280. See 65.

10 Bossy, J. "The sacred and profane history machine: the middle ages." *Encounter,* 49, no. 5 (November 1977), 70-75. [Essay-review of recent studies]

11 [Broëns, M.] "Luciférianisme médiéval et tradition chthonienne." *Chthonia,* 4 (1964), 1-13.

12 ——. "Le paganisme médiéval en Germanie danubienne, d'après ses cata-
combs – 'Erdställe', 'Heidenlöcher', etc. – et les écrits qui s'y rapportent."
Chthonia, 5/6 (1965), 1-42, ill., maps.

13 Brooke, C. N. L. "Heresy and religious sentiment: 1000-1250." *BIHR*, 41 (1968),
115-131.

14 Brusa, A. "Eretici in Italia meridionale dall'età normanna all'età angioina."
Quaderni medievali, 1 (1976), 45-61.

15 Buonaiuti, E. "Scisma ed eresia alle soglie del medioevo." *Quaderni medievali* 3
(1977), 11-29. ——

16 Bussell, F. W. *Religious thought and heresy in the middle ages*. London, 1918.
Rpt. Port Washington, N.Y.: Kennikat, 1971. 3 v. (xiii, 873 p.).

17 Capitani, O., ed. *L'eresia medievale*. Bologna: Mulino, c1971; 3rd ed., 1974.
204 p.

18 Carrasco, S. "Herejes e infieles en la ciudad medieval (notas para el estudio de la
actitud de Santo Tomás ante la inquisición de su tiempo)." *Escritos del
Vedat*, 4 (1974), 699-708.

19 Cassell, A. K. "Dante's Farinata and the image of the *arca*." *Yale Italian studies*, 1
(1977), 335-370, ill.

20 Chenu, M.-D. "Orthodoxie et hérésie: le point de vue du théologien." *Annales*, 18
(1963), 75-80. Rpt., with discussion, in *Hérésies et sociétés* (1968), p. 9-17.
See 65.

21 Christie-Murray, D. *A history of heresy*. [London]: New English Library, c1976.
viii, 243 p.
Rev. A. Patschovsky, *DAEM*, 34 (1978), 637-638.

22 Clasen, C. P. "Medieval heresies in the reformation." *CH*, 32 (1963), 392-414.

23 Classen, P. "Der Häresie-Begriff bei Gerhoch von Reichersberg und in seinem
Umkreis." *The concept of heresy in the middle ages* (1976). p. 27-41.
See 25.

24 Cohn, N. *The pursuit of the millennium: revolutionary millenarians and mystical
anarchists of the middle ages*. Rvsd. ed. London and New York: Oxford
University Press, 1970. 412 p. [Orig. publ. 1957; 2nd ed. 1961.] Trans. S.
Clémendot, M. Fuchs, and P. Rosenberg, *Les fanatiques de l'apocalypse*
(Paris: Julliard, 1962). Trans. R. Alaix Busquets, *En pos del milenio*
(Barcelona: Barral, 1972). Trans. E. Thorsch, *Das Ringen um das
tausendjährige Reich* (Bern: Francke, 1961). Trans. A. Guadagnin, *I
fanatici dell'apocalisse* (Milan: Edizioni di Comunità; Vicenza: Arti
grafiche delle Venezie, 1965). [Numerous other imprints of English
editions.]
Rev. W. H. C. Frend, *EHR*, 87 (1972), 396 ; *TLS*, 11 June 1970, p. 644; P.
Porter, *New statesman*, 79 (1970), 661-662.
Rev. (Fr. trans.) P. de Vooght, *RHE*, 59 (1964), 159-160; F. Lovsky, *Foi et
vie*, 62 (1963), 275-276.

Rev. (Span. trans.) E. Mitre Fernández, *Hispania*, 33 (1973), 161-164; J. Retamal Favereau, *Historia* (Universidad Católica de Chile), 12 (1974-75), 411-413.

Rev. (Ger. trans.) H. Grundmann, *HZ*, 196 (1963), 661-666; G. Müller, *TZ*, 19 (1963), 147-148; E. Winter, *DLZ*, 83 (1962), 998-1001.

Rev. (Ital. trans.) R. Manselli, *RSLR*, 3 (1967), 532-538.

25   *The concept of heresy in the middle ages (11th-13th c.)*. Proceedings of the International conference, Louvain, May 13-16, 1973. Ed. W. Lourdaux and D. Verhelst. Mediaevalia lovaniensia, ser. 1, studia 4. Louvain: University Press; The Hague: Nijhoff, 1976. viii, 232 p.

Rev. A.-D. v. den Brincken, *HZ*, 225 (1977), 688-689; J. B. Russell, *Speculum*, 53 (1978), 161-163; A. García y García, *Revista española de derecho canónico*, 33 (1977), 539-541; C. M. D. Crowder, *The humanities association review*, 28 (1977), 272-273; C. C. de Bruin, *TG*, 91 (1978), 94-95; A. Patschovsky, *DAEM*, 34 (1978), 638-639; M. Pacaut, *RH*, 261 (1979), 214-216.

26   Contreni, J. J. "Haimo of Auxerre, abbot of Sasceium (Cessy-les-Bois), and a new sermon on I John v, 4-10." *RB*, 85 (1975), 303-320.

27   Crowder, C. M. D., ed. and trans. *Unity, heresy and reform, 1378-1460: the conciliar response to the Great Schism*. London: Arnold; New York: St. Martin's, 1977. [x], 212 p.

28   Cueto Alas, J. *Los heterodoxos asturianos*. Colección popular asturiana, 33. Salinas: Ayalga, 1977. 288 p. ill. —

29   Dando, M. "Petite histoire des hérésies pré-cathares en occident." *CEC*, 28, no. 76 (1977), 3-37.

30   Delaruelle, E. "Dévotion populaire et hérésie au moyen âge." With discussion. *Hérésies et sociétés* (1968). p. 147-157. See 65.

31   ———. *La piété populaire au moyen âge*. Preface by P. Wolff; Introduction by R. Manselli and A. Vauchez. Turin: Bottega d'Erasmo, 1975. xxviii, 561 p. Collected essays.

Rev. J. Séguy, *ASSR*, 41 (1976), 217.

32   Döllinger, I. von. *Beiträge zur Sektengeschichte des Mittelalters*. Pt. 1: Geschichte der gnostisch-manichäischen Sekten im früheren Mittelalter. Pt. 2: Dokumente vornehmlich zur Geschichte der Valdesier und Katharer. Munich, 1890. Rpt. New York: Burt Franklin [1960]. 2 v. See 38.

33   Donini, A. "Un inedito di Ernesto Buonaiuti sulle eresie medievali." *Quaderni medievali* 3 (1977), 5-10. See 15.

34   Dontenville, H. "Hétérodoxies médiévales et souterrains refuges." *Bulletin de la Société de mythologie française*, 64 (1966), 143-149.

35   Dupré Theseider, E. *Mondo cittadino e movimenti ereticali nel medio evo*. Bologna: Pàtron, 1978. 454 p. —

36   Duvernoy, J. "La contribution des ouvrages critiques récents à l'histoire de l'héré-

sie méridionale." *Société ariégeoise, sciences, lettres et arts: bulletin annuel*, 24 (1968), 231-247.

37 ——. "Note relative à la terminologie des hypogées et autres retraites des hérétiques, d'après les registres de l'inquisition toulousaine." *Chthonia*, 4 (1964), 14-18.

38 ——. "Une source familière de l'hérésiologie médiévale: le tome II des *Beiträge* de Döllinger." *RHR*, 183 (1973), 161-177. See 32.

39 Erbstösser, M. "Publikationen zu den sozial-religiösen Bewegungen in Westeuropa und Deutschland während des Mittelalters." *ZG*, 8, suppl. (1960), 105-115.

40 ——. *Sozialreligiöse Strömungen im späten Mittelalter: Geißler, Freigeister und Waldenser im 14. Jahrhundert*. Forschungen zur mittelalterlichen Geschichte, 16. Berlin: Akademie-Verlag, 1970. 174 p.
     Rev. H. Mohr, *ZG*, 8 (1975), 973.

41 Evans, G. R. "Duo principia: an old problem resolved. Christians, philosophers and heretics in the twelfth century." *Antike und Abendland*, 24 (1978), 85-97.

42 Falbel, N. *Heresias medievais*. Coleção Kronos, 9. São Paulo: Perspectiva, 1977. 117 p.
     Rev. F. Flaksberg, *Revista de história* (São Paulo), 56 (1977), 606-609.

43 Fearns, J., ed. *Ketzer und Ketzerbekämpfung im Hochmittelalter*. Historische Texte / Mittelalter, 8. Göttingen: Vandenhoeck und Ruprecht, c1968. 80 p.

44 Foucault, M. "Les déviations religieuses et le savoir médical." With discussion. *Hérésies et sociétés* (1968). p. 19-29. See 65.

45 Francastel, P. "Art et hérésie." With discussion. *Hérésies et sociétés* (1968). p. 31-50. See 65.

46 Gieysztor, A. "Mouvements para-hérétiques en Europe centrale et orientale du 9ᵉ au 11ᵉ siècle: apostasies." With discussion. *Hérésies et sociétés* (1968). p. 159-169. See 65.

47 Gonnet, G. "Un decennio di studi sull'eterodossia medioevale." *Protestantesimo*, 17 (1962), 203-239. ——

48 ——. "La Donazione di Costantino presso gli eretici medievali." *BSSV*, 132 (1972), 17-29. Rvsd. version, "La Donazione di Costantino in Dante e presso gli eretici medievali," in *Dante nel pensiero e nella esegesi dei secoli XIV e XV: Atti del III congresso nazionale di studi danteschi* (Florence: Olschki, 1975), p. 237-259.

49 Graus, F. "Ketzerbewegungen und soziale Unruhen im 14. Jahrhundert." *Zeitschrift für historische Forschung*, 1 (1974), 3-21.

50 Grundmann, H. *Ausgewählte Aufsätze, 1: Religiöse Bewegungen*. Schriften der Monumenta Germaniae historica, 25, 1. Stuttgart: Hiersemann, 1976. xxviii, 448 p.

Rev. J. B. Freed, *AHR*, 83 (1978), 141-142; H. Fichtenau, *MIÖG*, 86 (1978), 247; W. Ullmann, *JEH*, 29 (1978), 217-219; K.-V. Selge, *ZKG*, 90 (1979), 117-120.

51 ——. *Bibliographie zur Ketzergeschichte des Mittelalters (1900-1966).* Sussidi eruditi, 20. Rome: Storia e Letteratura, 1967. 95 p. Earlier, shorter version publ. as "Bibliographie des études récentes (après 1900) sur les hérésies médiévales" in *Hérésies et sociétés* (1968), p. 407-479. See 65.

Rev. J.-P. Massaut, *MA*, 75 (1969), 596-599; A. Molnár, *CV*, 13 (1970), 215-216, and *RSLR*, 7 (1971), 186-187; E. Segatti, *RSLR*, 6 (1970), 438; Y. Dossat, *CCM*, 11 (1968), 233; A. C. Shannon, *CHR*, 57 (1971), 327.

52 ——. "Hérésies savantes et hérésies populaires au moyen âge." With discussion. *Hérésies et sociétés* (1968). p. 209-218. Rpt. in H. Grundmann, *Ausgewählte Aufsätze*, I (Stuttgart: Hiersemann, 1976), 417-422. See 65.

53 ——. *Ketzergeschichte des Mittelalters.* Die Kirche in ihrer Geschichte, 2, fasc. G, pt. 1. Göttingen: Vandenhoeck und Ruprecht, c1963. 66 p. 3rd ed. publ. 1974.

Rev. T. Bergsten, *Kyrkohistorisk årsskrift*, 63 (1963), 291-293; V. Mudroch, *Speculum*, 40 (1965), 509-512; W. Kühnert, *ZKG*, 74 (1963), 375-376; H. Fichtenau, *MIÖG*, 72 (1964), 455-456; E. Dupré-Theseider, *HZ*, 207 (1968), 643-646; F. Merzbacher, *ZSSRG*, kan. Abt., 81 (1964), 313-315.

54 ——. "Neue Beiträge zur Geschichte der religiösen Bewegungen im Mittelalter." *AKG*, 37 (1955), 129-182. Rpt., with updated bibl. notes and without prelim. note, in his *Religiöse Bewegungen im Mittelalter*, 2nd ed. (Hildesheim: Olms, 1961), p. 487-538, 542-543; and, with updated bibl. notes, in his *Ausgewählte Aufsätze*, I (Stuttgart: Hiersemann, 1976), 38-92.

55 ——. "*Oportet et haereses esse*: das Problem der Ketzerei im Spiegel der mittelalterlichen Bibelexegese." *AKG*, 45 (1963), 129-164. Rpt. in H. Grundmann, *Ausgewählte Aufsätze*, I (Stuttgart: Hiersemann, 1976), 328-363. Trans. L. Tosti, "*Oportet et haereses esse*: il problema dell'eresia rispecchiato nell'esegesi biblica medievale," *L'eresie medievale*, ed. O. Capitani (Bologna: Mulino, c1971), p. 23-60.

56 ——. *Religiöse Bewegungen im Mittelalter: Untersuchungen über die geschichtlichen Zusammenhänge zwischen der Ketzerei, den Bettelorden und der religiösen Frauenbewegung im 12. und 13. Jahrhundert und über die geschichtlichen Grundlagen der deutschen Mystik.* Historische Studien, 267. Berlin, 1935. 511 p. Rpt. Vaduz: Kraus, 1965. Rvsd. rpt. (= 2nd ed.), with suppl., "Neue Beiträge...," Hildesheim: Olms; Darmstadt: Wissenschaftliche Buchgesellschaft, 1961 (vi, 580 p.). Rpt. Millwood, N.Y.: Kraus, 1975. Trans. M. Ausserhofer and L. Nicolet Santini, *Movimenti religiosi nel medioevo*, with intro. by R. Manselli (Bologna: Mulino, 1974) [xx, 528 p.].

Rev. (of Ital. trans.) F. Cardini, *ASI*, 131 (1973 [1975]), 289-291; P. Golinelli, *RSLR*, 12 (1976), 442-448; J. C. Schmitt, *ASSR*, 44 (1976), 242.

57 ——. "Der Typus des Ketzers in mittelalterlicher Anschauung." *Kultur- und Universalgeschichte: Walter Goetz zu seinem 60. Geburtstage.* Leipzig, 1927. p. 91-107. Rpt. in his *Ausgewählte Aufsätze,* I (Stuttgart: Hiersemann, 1976), 313-327.

58 Guitton, J. *Le Christ écartelé: crises et conciles dans l'église.* Paris: Perrin, 1963. 279 p. Trans. F. D. Wieck, *Great heresies and church councils* (New York: Harper and Row; London: Harvill, c1965); rpt. Freeport, N.Y.: Books for libraries, 1971. Trans. C. De Piaz, *Il Cristo dilacerato: crisi e concili nella chiesa* (Milan: Il Saggiatore; Bologna: STEB, 1964).
Rev. (Eng. trans.) B. C. Butler, *The tablet,* 219 (1965), 264; H. Graef, *Eastern churches review,* 1 (1966), 84-85; J. J. Healy, *America,* 112 (1965), 786; C. L. Hohl, *Cross currents,* 18 (1968), 374-375; K. W. Kleinz, *TS,* 26 (1965), 513-514; L. L. Rummel, *AER,* 154 (1966), 212-213; A. C. Shannon, *CHR,* 53 (1968), 682-683; S. P. Theisen, *Ave Maria,* 102 (4 September 1965), 27-28; E. Yarnold, *The month,* 34 (1965), 118; E. I. Watkin, *The Downside review,* 83 (1965), 375-377.

59 Gutnova, E. V. "Srednevekovoe krest'ianstvo i eresi." *Srednie veka,* 38 (1975), 28-38. [Incl. summary, "Medieval peasantry and heresies in the 11th to 15th centuries".]

60 Hahn, C. U. *Geschichte der Ketzer im Mittelalter, besonders im 11., 12. und 13. Jahrhundert.* 3 v. Stuttgart, 1845-1850. Rpt. Aalen: Scientia, 1968.

61 Hasenhüttl, G., and J. Nolte. *Formen kirchlicher Ketzerbewältigung.* Texte zur Religionswissenschaft und Theologie, historische Sektion, II, 1. Düsseldorf: Patmos, c1976. 149 p.
Rev. F. de Grijs, *Bijdragen,* 39 (1978), 335; H. Kirchner, *TLZ,* 103, 598.

62 Heath, C. *Social and religious heretics in five centuries.* London, 1936. Rpt., with new intro. by S. Strauss, New York and London: Garland, 1972. 158 p.

63 Heinemann, H. *Die rechtliche Stellung der nichtkatholischen Christen und ihre Wiederversöhnung mit der Kirche.* Münchener theologische Studien, kan. Abt., III, 20. Munich: Hueber, 1964. xx, 222 p.

64 Heitmeyer, H. *Sakramentenspendung bei Häretikern und Simonisten nach Huguccio, von den "Wirkungen" besonders der Taufe und Weihe in der ersten Causa seiner "Summa super Corpore decretorum."* Analecta Gregoriana, 132. Rome: Pontificia Universitas Gregoriana, 1964. xvi, 173 p.

65 *Hérésies et sociétés dans l'Europe pré-industrielle, 11e-18e siècles.* Communications et débats du Colloque du Royaumont présentés par J. Le Goff. École pratique des hautes études – Sorbonne, VIe section: Sciences économiques et sociales, Centre de recherches historiques, Civilisations et sociétés, 10. Paris and The Hague: Mouton, 1968. 484 p.

Rev. L. Gaillard, *RHE*, 65 (1970), 276-278; D. Bigalli, *Studi storici*, 13 (1972), 395-403; F. Rapp, *RHEF*, 57 (1971), 107-109; C. Frova, *RSI*, 82 (1970), 755-758; Y. Congar, *RSPT*, 54 (1970), 404-406; M. de Certeau, *Études* (Paris), 330 (mars 1969), 461; G. Michiels, *BTAM*, 11 (1970), 143-145; A. Vauchez, *ASR*, 27 (jan.-juin 1969), 194-195.

66   Hösch, E. *Orthodoxie und Häresie im alten Rußland*. Schriften zur Geistes-geschichte des östlichen Europa, 7. Wiesbaden: Harrassowitz, 1975. 321 p.

67   ——. "Sowjetische Forschungen zur Häresiengeschichte Altrußlands: metho-dologische Bemerkungen." *Jahrbücher für Geschichte Osteuropas*, 18 (1970), 279-312.

68   Jundt, A. *Histoire du panthéisme populaire au moyen âge et au seizième siècle*. Paris, 1875. Rpt. Frankfurt am Main: Minerva, 1964. 310 p.

69   Kühner, H. *Nur grosse Menschen können Ketzer sein*. Basel: National-Zeitung, c1975. [31] p., ill.

70   Kulcsár, Z. *Eretnekmozgalmak a XI-XIV. században*. A Budapesti Egyetemi Könyvtár kiadványai, 22. Budapest: Tankönyvkiadó, 1964. 335 p. [Heretical movements from the 11th to the 14th century: a bibliography] Rev. G. Constable, *Speculum*, 40 (1965), 735-736; J. Paquet, *MA*, 72 (1966), 604-608.

70A Kurze, D. "Häresie und Minderheit im Mittelalter." *HZ*, 229 (1979), 529-573.

71   Lambert, M. *Medieval heresy: popular movements from Bogomil to Hus*. London: Arnold, c1976; New York: Holmes and Meier [1977]. xvi, 430 p. ill. Rev. G. Leff, *TLS*, 1 July 1977, p. 811; F. L. Cheyette, *History: reviews of new books*, 6 (1977), 22-23; E. Werner, *ZG*, 25 (1977), 1486-1487; J. H. Mundy, *AHR*, 83 (1978), 142-143; W. Ullmann, *JTS*, 29 (1978), 253-255; B. McGinn, *CH*, 47 (1978), 221-223; M. Erbstösser, *DLZ*, 99 (1978), 48-50; B. Stock, *The historian*, 40 (1978), 530-531; G. Shriver, *Religious studies review*, 4 (1978), 51; R. I. Moore, *EHR*, 93 (1978), 381-383; M. J. Walsh, *HJ*, 20 (1979), 101-102; M. Aston, *History*, 64 (1979), 81-82; A. Uña, *CD*, 191 (1978), 496; J. B. Russell, *CHR*, 65 (1979), 350-352; J. Jolivet, *RHR*, 195 (1979), 96-97; J. Bossy, *Encounter*, 49, no. 5 (1977), 73-75; A. Patschovsky, *DAEM*, 35 (1979), 300-301; P. L. Nyhus, *Canadian journal of history*, 14 (1979), 98-99.

72   Leclercq, J. "L'hérésie d'après les écrits de S. Bernard de Clairvaux." *The concept of heresy in the middle ages* (1976). p. 12-26. See 25.

73   Leff, G. "Heresy and the decline of the medieval church." *Past and present*, 20 (1961), 36-51.

74   ——. "Hérésie savante et hérésie populaire dans le bas moyen âge." With discussion. *Hérésies et sociétés* (1968). p. 219-227. See 65.

75   ——. *Heresy in the later middle ages: the relation of heterodoxy to dissent c.*

1250 – c. 1450. Manchester: Manchester University Press; New York: Barnes and Noble, c1967. 2 v.

Rev. L. E. Boyle, *The Thomist*, 33 (1969), 588-591; J. I. Catto, *JTS*, 20 (1969), 341-343; F. C. Copleston, *RS*, 7 (1971), 79-82; J. Crompton, *MÆ*, 38 (1969), 99-107; D. Douie, *The tablet*, 222 (1968), 11; W. Faix, *AER*, 161 (1969), 355-356; J. Garcia, *Antonianum*, 43 (1968), 327-329; H. Grundmann, *DAEM*, 24 (1968), 284-286; R. Harrington, *Journal of the history of philosophy*, 8 (1970), 205-211; S. Hoyer, *DLZ*, 91 (1970), 630-632; J. Jolivet, *RHR*, 175 (1969), 71-74; M. D. Lambert, *History*, 55 (1970), 75-79; J.-P. Massaut, *MA*, 76 (1970), 582-589; M.-R. Mayeux, *RHEF*, 55 (1969), 329-331; R. Mols, *NRT*, 91 (1969), 105; H. A. Oberman, *JEH*, 20 (1969), 342-344; H. S. Offler, *EHR*, 84 (1969), 572-576; F. Rapp, *RHPR*, 51 (1971), 95-96; E. G. Rupp, *New Blackfriars*, 50 (1968), 107-108; anon., *TLS*, 25 Jan. 1968, p. 84; P. de Vooght, *RHE*, 63 (1968), 989-995; E. I. Watkin, *The Downside review*, 86 (1968), 190-196; J. Wicks, *TR*, 65 (1969), 308-309; D. E. Flood, *WW*, 34 (1971), 42-47; A. T. Hart, *The modern churchman*, 11 (1968), 180; A. Molnár, *CV*, 11 (1968), 162-168, *TPKR*, 35 (1968), 115-118, and *TLZ*, 94 (1969), 280-281; J. R. Meyer, *TS*, 30 (1969), 707-710; A. C. Shannon, *CHR*, 56 (1970), 356-358; P. C. Boeren, *TG*, 82 (1969), 410; A. J. Visser, *Nederlands theologisch tijdschrift*, 23 (1969), 300-303; G. E. Duffield, *The churchman*, 82 (1968), 34-35.

76   Lerner, R. E. "The uses of heterodoxy: the French monarchy and unbelief in the thirteenth century." *French historical studies*, 4 (1965), 189-202.

77   Lietzmann, H. "Bibliographie Herbert Grundmann." *DAEM*, 26 (1970), 354-367. Rpt. (of p. 354-365) in H. Grundmann, *Ausgewählte Aufsätze*, I (Stuttgart: Hiersemann, 1976), 26-37.

78   Lindeboom, J. *Stiefkinderen van het Christendom*. The Hague, 1929. Rpt. Arnhem: Gijsbers and Van Loon, 1973. xi, 392 p.

79   Macek, J. "Villes et campagnes dans le hussitisme." With discussion. *Hérésies et sociétés* (1968). p. 243-258. See 65.

80   McCrillis, L. N. "The demonization of minority groups in Christian society during the central middle ages." Diss. Univ. of California, Riverside. *DAI*, 38A (1977), 411.

81   Mackiewicz, S. *Herezje i prawdy*. Warsaw: Instytut Wydawniczy "Pax," 1962. 269 p. [Heresies and truths]

82   McLaughlin, E. "Les femmes et l'hérésie médiévale: un problème dans l'histoire de la spiritualité." *Concilium*, 111 (1976), 73-90. —

83   Manselli, R. "La 'christianitas' medioevale di fronte all'eresia." *Concetto, storia, miti e immagini del medio evo*. Ed. V. Branca. Florence: Sansoni, c1973. p. 91-133.

84   ——. "Cristo nell' alto medio evo e nei movimenti ereticali." *La figura di Gesù Cristo*. Ulisse, 81. Florence: Sansoni, 1976. p. 67-75.

85 ——. *La religione popolare nel medioevo (sec. VI-XIII)*. Corsi universitari. Turin: Giappichelli, 1974. 128 p.
Rev. J. C. Schmitt, *ASSR*, 40 (1975), 251; B. Badia, *Studia monastica*, 19 (1977), 416-417.

86 ——. "La religione popolare nel medio evo: prime considerazioni metodologiche." *Nuova rivista storica*, 58 (1974), 29-43.

87 ——. *La religion populaire au moyen âge: problèmes de méthode et d'histoire*. Conférence Albert-le-Grand 1973. Montréal: Institut d'études médiévales Albert-le-Grand; Paris: Vrin, 1975. 234 p.
Rev. D. Gagnan, *CF*, 48 (1978), 173-175; J. Paul, *RHEF*, 63 (1977), 82-84.

88 ——. "San Bernardo e la religiosità popolare." *Studi su S. Bernardo di Chiaravalle nell'ottavo centenario della canonizzazione*. Biblioteca cisterciensis, 6. Rome: Editiones cistercienses, 1975. p. 245-260. —

89 Marrou, H.-I. "L'héritage de la chrétienté." With discussion. *Hérésies et sociétés* (1968). p. 51-57. See 65.

90 Maselli, D. *Breve storia dell' altra chiesa in Italia: tendenze ereticali ed evangeliche nell'Italia medioevale e moderna*. Naples: Centro Biblico [1972]. 47 p.

91 Mencucci, V. "I moti popolari di ispirazione religiosa nel medioevo." *Humanitas* (Brescia), 28 (1973), 286-300.

92 Merlo, G. G. "Qualche spunto su eresia e società in Italia tra XIII e XIV secolo." *BSSV*, 144 (1978), 15-19.

93 Mikulka, J. "Heretická hnutí v polských zemích v době před evropskou reformací." *Slovanský přehled*, 56 (1970), 392-400. [Heretical movements in Poland in the pre-reformation period]

94 Mitre Fernández, E. *Sociedad y herejía en el occidente medieval*. Pueblo de Dios, ser. D, 6. [Algorta: Zero, 1972.] 115 p.

95 Molnár, A. "Elementi ecclesiologici della prima riforma." *Protestantesimo*, 19 (1964), 65-77.

96 ——. "Das Ketzertum des späten Mittelalters." Trans. V. D. Schneeberger. *CV*, 11 (1968), 162-168. See 75.

97 Moore, R. I. "Heresy as disease." *The concept of heresy in the middle ages* (1976). p. 1-11. See 25.

98 Morghen, R. "Storia della chiesa e storia dell'eresia in tre opere recenti." *BISIM*, 81 (1969), 297-316. See 190, 346, 627.

99 Mudroch, V. "Medieval heresy: gleanings and reflections." *Essays on the reconstruction of medieval history*. Ed. V. Mudroch and G. S. Couse. Montreal and London: McGill-Queen's University Press, 1974. p. 146-170.

100 Nelli, R. *Dictionnaire des hérésies méridionales et des mouvements hétérodoxes ou indépendants apparus dans le midi de la France depuis l'établissement du Christianisme*. Toulouse: Privat, c1968. 304 p., ill.

Rev. H. Desroche, *RHEF*, 55 (1969), 365; A. C. Shannon, *CHR*, 57 (1971), 326.

101 ——, comp. *Paroles d'hérétiques*. Toulouse: Privat, c1968. 93 p.

102 Nickson, M. A. E. "A critical edition of the treatise on heresy ascribed to pseudo-Reinerius, with an historical introduction." Diss. Queen Mary College, Univ. of London, 1962. —

103 ——. "The 'Pseudo-Reinerius' treatise, the final stage of a thirteenth century work on heresy from the diocese of Passau." *Archives d'histoire doctrinale et littéraire du moyen âge*, 34 (1967), 255-314.

104 Nigg, W. *Das Buch der Ketzer*. 3d ed. Zürich: Artemis, 1962. 525 p. Orig. publ. 1949.

105 ——. *The heretics*. Ed. and trans. R. & C. Winston. New York: Knopf, 1962. 412, xi p. Abridged trans. of *Das Buch der Ketzer* (Zürich, 1949). See 104.

106 Olagüe, I. "L'hérésie dans le domaine pyrénéen." *Mémoires de l'Académie des sciences, inscriptions et belles-lettres de Toulouse*, 128 (1966), 85-98.

107 Oliver, A. "Heterodoxia en la Mallorca de los siglos XIII-XV." *Boletin de la Sociedad arqueològica luliana*, 32 (1961-67), 157-176. —

108 Paraskevopoulou, V. "Some aspects of the phenomenon of heresy in the Byzantine empire and in the west, during the 11th and 12th centuries." Diss. New York Univ. *DAI*, 37A (1977), 5986-5987.

109 Patschovsky, A. *Der Passauer Anonymus: ein Sammelwerk über Ketzer, Juden, Antichrist aus der Mitte des 13. Jahrhunderts*. Monumenta Germaniae historica, Schriften, 22. Stuttgart: Hiersemann, 1968. xi, 208 p.
Rev. P. Ladner, *ZSKG*, 65 (1971), 416; P. Courcelle, *BEC*, 127 (1969), 497-498; H. S. Offler, *JTS*, 20 (1969), 338-340; K.-V. Selge, *ZKG*, 82 (1971), 118-119.

110 ——. "Probleme ketzergeschichtlicher Quellenforschung." *Mittelalterliche Text-überlieferungen und ihre kritische Aufarbeitung*. Beiträge der Monumenta Germaniae Historica zum 31. Deutschen Historikertag, Mannheim 1976. Munich: MGH, 1976. p. 86-91, ill.

111 Paul, J. "La religion populaire au moyen âge (à propos d'ouvrages récents)." *RHEF*, 63 (1977), 78-86.

112 Pfleger, L. "Les hérétiques strasbourgeois aux XIIIe et XIVe siècles." *CEC*, 29, no. 79 (1978), 57-60.

113 Pluquet, F. A. A. *Dictionnaire des hérésies, des erreurs et des schismes*. Paris, 1847-53. Rpt. Amsterdam: Associated publishers, 1969. 2 v.

114 Pozo, C. "La noción de 'herejía' en el derecho canónico medieval." *Miscelanea Antonio Perez Goyena*. Estudios eclesiasticos, 35. Madrid: Fax, 1960. p. 235-251.

115 Preus, J. S. "Theological legitimation for innovation in the middle ages." *Viator*, 3 (1972), 1-26.

116 Runciman, S. *The medieval Manichee: a study in Christian dualist heresy.* Cambridge, 1947. Rpt. Cambridge: Cambridge university press, 1960; New York: Viking, 1961. x, 212 p. Trans. S. Pétrement and J. Marty, *Le manichéisme médiéval: l'hérésie dualiste dans le christianisme* (Paris, 1949; rpt. Paris: Payot, 1972), 206 p.
Rev. (French rpt.) F. Masai, *RBPH*, 52 (1974), 108-111.

117 Russell, J. B. "Courtly love as religious dissent." *CHR*, 51 (1965), 31-44.

118 ———. "Interpretations of the origins of medieval heresy." *MS*, 25 (1963), 26-53.

119 ———, ed. *Religious dissent in the middle ages.* New York, etc.: John Wiley, c1971. xi, 161 p.
Rev. G. Filoramo, *RSLR*, 9 (1973), 172-173; J.-P. Massaut, *MA*, 81 (1975), 562-563; I. Montgomery, *Kyrkohistorisk årsskrift* (1974), p. 262-263; L. B. Pascoe, *TS*, 32 (1971), 734; A. C. Shannon, *CHR*, 60 (1974), 132-133; C. Thouzellier, *CCM*, 17 (1974), 182-183.

120 *Schism, heresy and religious protest.* Ed. D. Baker. Studies in church history, 9. Cambridge: Cambridge University Press, 1972. xv, 404 p.
Rev. R. H. Bainton, *CH*, 42 (1973), 275-276; P. Collinson, *JRH*, 8 (1974), 110-111; J. B. Russell, *CHR*, 61 (1975), 606-609; J. Séguy, *ASSR*, 18 (1973), 173-174; F. H. Shriver, *ATR*, 55 (1973), 246-248; M. Simon, *JEH*, 25 (1974), 89-90; S. H. Hendrix, *JAAR*, 41 (1973), 636-637; B. Hamilton, *Eastern churches review*, 5 (1973), 200-201; D. Walker, *The modern churchman*, 16 (1973), 216-217; X. Pérouse de Montclos, *Cahiers d'histoire*, 19 (1974), 390-392; J. M. González del Valle, *Ius canonicum*, 14 (1974), 439-442.

121 Schwital, J. *Großkirche und Sekte: eine Studie zum Selbstverständnis der Sekte.* Hamburg: Saatkorn-Verlag, 1962. 191 p.

122 Selge, K. V. "Die Ketzerpolitik Friedrichs II." *Probleme um Friedrich II.* Ed. J. Fleckenstein. Vorträge und Forschungen, 16. Sigmaringen: Thorbecke, c1974. p. 309-343.

123 Šimeček, Z. "Heretická hnutí v severovýchodní Evropě (před reformací)." In L. E. Havlík, *Lidová hnutí na staré Rusi* = Práce z dějin východní Evropy, 2: Heretická hnutí ve východní Evropě. Prague: Československá Akademia Věd, 1969. p. 111-153.

124 Tabacco, G. "Chiesa ed eresia nell'orizzonte giuridico e politico della monarchia papale." *BSSV*, 144 (1978), 9-13.

125 *Testi per il seminario su Le eresie popolari dei secoli XI-XIV.* Ed. Comitato studentesco del seminario di storia medievale, Università degli studi di Firenze, Facoltà di lettere e filosofia, 1967-1968. [Florence, 1968.] 95 p.

126 Thouzellier, C. *Hérésie et hérétiques: vaudois, cathares, patarins, albigeois.* Storia e letteratura, 116. Rome: Storia e Letteratura, 1969. viii, 275 p. maps.
Rev. M. d'Alatri, *CF*, 40 (1970), 192-193; R. Cegna, *RSLR*, 6 (1970), 642-644; J. A. Corbett, *CHR*, 57 (1971), 485-487; Y. Dossat, *AM*, 84 (1972), 326-328, and *RHE*, 67 (1972), 499-501; M. Fois, *La civiltà cattolica*, 122, v. 4

(1971), 403-404; J. Jolivet, *RHR*, 178 (1970), 197-199; A. S. Muñoz, *Archivo teológico granadino*, 33 (1970), 396; E. Pásztor, *SM*, 3rd ser., 12 (1971), 1138-1139; J. B. Russell, *Speculum*, 45 (1970), 692-694; M. Villard, *BEC*, 128 (1970), 262-264.

127 ——. "Hérésie et pauvreté à la fin du xiie et au début du xiiie siècle." *Études sur l'histoire de la pauvreté*. Ed. M. Mollat. Paris: Publications de la Sorbonne, 1974. I, 371-388.

128 ——. "Histoire des sectes dans l'occident médiéval." *École pratique des hautes études, v^e section, sciences religieuses: annuaire*, 75 (1967-68), 202-208. [Continued annually thereafter]

129 Trawkowski, S. "Entre l'orthodoxie et l'hérésie: *vita apostolica* et le problème de la désobéissance." *The concept of heresy in the middle ages* (1976). p. 157-166. See 25.

130 Urrutia, F. J. "Pertinacia y mala fe en la noción canónica de herejía." *Estudios de Deusto*, 26 (1978), 253-271.

131 Ventura [Subirats], J. *Els heretges catalans*. With pref. letter by M. Batllori. Biblioteca Selecta, 348; assaigs, 22. Barcelona: Selecta, [1963]. 248 p. 2d, rvsd., ed., 1976 (258 p.).

132 Verbeke, G. "Philosophy and heresy: some conflicts between reason and faith." *The concept of heresy in the middle ages* (1976). p. 172-197. See 25.

133 Verbesselt, J. "De oudst gekende pastoor van Neder-Heembeek was een ketter." *Eigen Schoon en de Brabander*, 44 (1961), 185-188. —

134 Vergani, M. L. "San Bernardo e Pietro il Venerabile di fronte agli eretici ed agli infedeli." Diss. Università Cattolica del Sacro Cuore, Milan, 1960. —

135 Vlăduţescu, G. *Ereziile evului mediu creştin*. Bucharest: Editura enciclopedică română, 1974. 160 p. ill.

136 Volpe, G. *Movimenti religiosi e sette ereticali nella società medievale italiana, secoli XI-XIV*. Florence: Sansoni, 1961 [etc.]. xvi, 281 p. Orig. publ. Florence 1922.

137 Wakefield, W. L., and A. P. Evans. *Heresies of the high middle ages: selected sources translated and annotated*. Records of civilization, Sources and studies, 81. New York and London: Columbia University Press, 1969. xiv, 865 p.

Rev. M. d'Alatri, *CF*, 41 (1971), 189-190; A. W. Godfrey, *Liturgical arts*, 39 (1971), 78-80; G. Leff, *JEH*, 22 (1971), 139-140; A. Patschovsky, *DAEM*, 26 (1970), 268-269; M. Reeves, *MÆ*, 39 (1970), 232-235; A. Riising, *Historisk tidsskrift*, ser. 12, v. 5 (1971), 218-219; J. B. Russell, *Speculum*, 45 (1970), 333-335; A. C. Shannon, *CHR*, 58 (1973), 609-610.

138 Werner, E. "Messianische Bewegungen im Mittelalter." *ZG*, 10 (1962), 371-396, 598-622. Abstract, "Les mouvements messianiques au moyen âge," in *ASR*, 16 (1963), 73-75.

139   Werner, K. *Geschichte der apologetischen und polemischen Literatur der christ-lichen Theologie*. Regensburg, 1861-1867. Rpt. Osnabrück: Zeller, 1966. 5 v.

140   Wos, J. W. "Le eresie nel commento di Jacopo della Lana al canto IX dell'Inferno dantesco." *Bollettino storico pisano*, 36-38 (1967-69), 71-80.

141   Wyndham, M. W. "The concept of the gnostic heretic in patristic literature." Diss. Univ. of California, Riverside. *DAI*, 37A (1977), 6673-6674.

142   Zazo, A. "Appunti di *haeretica pravitas* in Benevento." *Samnium*, 50 (1977), 1-11.

143   Zilverberg, S. B. J. *Ketters in de middeleeuwen*. Fibulareeks, 38. Bussum: Fibu-la – Van Dishoeck, 1968. 112 p. ill.
      Rev. A. H. Bredero, *CCM*, 12 (1969), 98; H. van Rij, *TG*, 83 (1970), 88-89.

144   Zumkeller, A., ed. *Hermanni de Scildis O.S.A. Tractatus contra haereticos negantes immunitatem et iurisdictionem sanctae ecclesiae et Tractatus de concep-tione gloriosae virginis Mariae*. Cassiciacum, suppl. 4. Würzburg: Augustinus-Verlag, 1970. xxi, 182 p.
      Rev. J. Auer, *TR*, 69 (1973), 289-291; C. Dumont, *NRT*, 95 (1973), 99; R. Haacke, *ZKG*, 84 (1973), 363-366; L. Hödl, *Münchener theologische Zeitschrift*, 23 (1972), 389-391; W. Kölmel, *Historisches Jahrbuch*, 93 (1973), 155-156; E. Zlabinger, *Zeitschrift für katholische Theologie*, 95 (1973), 115-116; J. M. Alonso, *Ephemerides mariologicae*, 22 (1972), 453.

Part Two

Heresy and Reform 700-1140

ENTRIES 145 TO 212

145 Ambrosioni, A. "Il più antico elenco di chierici della diocesi ambrosiana ed altre aggiunte al *Decretum* di Burcardo in un codice della Biblioteca Ambrosiana (E 144 sup.). Una voce della polemica antipatarinica?" *Aevum*, 50 (1976), 274-320, ill.

146 Basler, Đ, "Porijeklo naziva 'pataren': prilog istraživanja naziva za heretika u srednjem vijeku." *Pregled*, 64 (1974), 1203-1206. [Origins of the term "patarene": contribution to a study of the terminology for heretics in the middle ages]

147 Bautier, R.-H. "L'hérésie d'Orléans et le mouvement intellectuel au début du XIᵉ siècle: documents et hypothèses." *Actes du 95ᵉ congrès national des sociétés savantes, Reims, 1970*, p. 63-88; summary in *Bulletin de la Société nationale des antiquaires de France*, 1970, p. 366-368.

148 Bolton, B. "Sources for the early history of the humiliati." *The materials, sources and methods of ecclesiastical history.* Ed. D. Baker. Studies in church history, 11. Oxford: Blackwell, 1975. p. 125-133.

149 Borst, A. "Mittelalterliche Sekten und Massenwahn." *Massenwahn in Geschichte und Gegenwart.* Ed. W. Bitter. Stuttgart: Klett, c1965. p. 173-184.

150 Broëns, M. "Les gnostiques d'Orléans de 1022 et le dualisme en France au moyen âge." *Bulletin trimestriel de la Société archéologique et historique de l'Orléanais*, n.s. 4 (1965), 42-43.

151 Châtillon, J. "Pierre le Vénérable et les Pétrobrusiens." With discussion. *Pierre Abélard, Pierre le Vénérable.* Colloques internationaux du Centre de la recherche scientifique, 546 (Cluny, 2 au 9 juillet 1972). Paris: C.N.R.S., 1975. p. 165-179.

152 Colish, M. L. "Peter of Bruys, Henry of Lausanne, and the façade of St.-Gilles." *Traditio*, 28 (1972), 451-460, ill.

153 Cowdrey, H. E. J. "The papacy, the patarenes and the church of Milan." *Transactions of the Royal historical society*, 18 (1968), 25-48.

154 Cracco, G. "Pataria: *opus* e *nomen* (tra verità e autorità)." *RSCI*, 28 (1974), 357-387. Abridged version in *The concept of heresy in the middle ages* (1976), p. 167-171. See 25.

155 ———. *Realtà e carisma nell'Europa del mille*. Turin: Giappichelli, 1971. 146 p.

156 ———. "Riforma ed eresia in momenti della cultura europea tra X e XI secolo." *RSLR*, 7 (1971), 411-477.

157 Dando, M. "Petite histoire des hérésies pré-cathares en occident." *CEC*, 28, no. 76 (1977), 3-37; 29, no. 78 (1978), 3-31.

158 De Sandre Gasparini, G. "Le eresie in Europa nella prima metà del sec. XI." Colloquio Paolo Lamma, Università di Padova, 16-18 aprile 1970. *RSCI*, 24 (1970), 610-617.

159 Dunn, J. R. "An index and analysis of major themes in Ælfric's homilies: the Trinity, the sacraments, eschatology, heresy." Diss. Univ. of Colorado. *DAI*, 37A (1977), 5106-5107.

160 Edelsbrunner, G. "Arnold von Brescia: Untersuchungen über die weltliche Herrschaft der Kurie und die häretische Bewegung in Rom um die Mitte des 12. Jahrhunderts." Diss. Graz, 1965. xiv, 159 p. map and charts.

161 Fearns, J. "Peter von Bruis und die religiöse Bewegung des 12. Jahrhunderts." *AKG*, 48 (1966), 311-335.

162 ———, ed. *Petri Venerabilis Contra Petrobrusianos hereticos*. Corpus Christianorum, continuatio mediaevalis, 10. Turnhout: Brepols, 1968. xviii, 179 p. Rev. J. Kritzeck, *Speculum*, 45 (1970), 296-297; D. Luscombe, *MÆ*, 41 (1972), 141-143; H. Maisonneuve, *RHE*, 66 (1971), 168-175; E. von Severus, *ZKG*, 82 (1971), 116-117.

163 Ferrari, M. "Note su Claudio di Torino 'episcopus ab ecclesia damnatus'." *Italia medioevale e umanistica*, 16 (1973), 291-308.

164 Formenti, A. L. "Landolfo Seniore cronista della pataria." Diss. Università del Sacro Cuore, Milan, 1970. —

165 Fossier, R. "Remarques sur l'étude des 'commotions' sociales aux XIe et XIIe siècles." *CCM*, 16 (1973), 45-50.

166 French, J. M. "The innovative imagery of the Beaulieu portal program: sources and significance." *Studies in medieval culture*, 8-9 (1976), 19-30, ill.

167 Frugoni, A. "Le eresie medievali dei secoli XI-XII." *Cultura e scuola*, 1, no. 3 (1962), 84-89.

168 Gritsch, H. "Die Pataria von Mailand 1057-1075." Diss. Universität Innsbruck, 1972. —

169 Gurevich, A. I. "Iz istorii narodnoĭ kultury i eresi." *Srednie veka*, 38 (1975), 159-185. [Incl. summary, "From the history of folk culture and heresy: pseudo-prophets and the church in the Frankish kingdom"]

170 Hauser, R. "Zur Spiritualität der Mailänder Pataria (1045-1065)." Diss. Universität Freiburg im Breisgau, 1974. —

171   Keller, H. "Pataria und Stadtverfassung, Stadtgemeinde und Reform: Mailand im
      'Investiturstreit'." *Investiturstreit und Reichsverfassung*. Ed. J. Flecken-
      stein. Vorträge und Forschungen, 17. Sigmaringen: Thorbecke, c1973.
      p. 321-350.

172   Magnou, E. "Note critique sur les sources de l'histoire de Henri l'hérétique jusqu'à
      son départ du Mans." *BPH*, 1962 (1965), p. 539-547.

173   Manselli, R. "Grundzüge der religiösen Geschichte Italiens im 12. Jahrhundert."
      Trans. K.-V. Selge. *Beiträge zur Geschichte Italiens im 12. Jahrhundert*.
      Vorträge und Forschungen, Sonderband 9. Sigmaringen: Jan Thorbecke,
      c1971. p. 5-35.

174   ——. "Motivi spirituali dei nuovi ordini e dei movimenti religiosi popolari nel
      secolo XI." *Chiesa e riforma nella spiritualità del sec. XI*. Convegni del
      Centro di studi sulla spiritualità medievale, 6. Todi: Accademia Tudertina,
      1968. p. 117-135.

175   Manteuffel, T. "Naissance d'une hérésie." With discussion. *Hérésies et sociétés*
      (1968). p. 97-103. See 65.

176   Marchand, J. W. "On the origin of the term *Popelican(t)*." *MS*, 38 (1976), 496-498.
      See 205.

177   Miccoli, G. "Per la storia della pataria milanese." *Chiesa gregoriana: ricerche sulla
      riforma del secolo XI*. Florence: La Nuova Italia, c1966. p. 101-160. Orig.
      publ. *BISIM*, 70 (1958), 43-123.

178   Moore, R. I., ed. *The birth of popular heresy*. Documents of medieval history, 1.
      London: Edward Arnold, c1975. viii, 166 p.
      Rev. C. Morris, *History*, 61 (1976), 442-443; M. E. Reeves, *MÆ*, 46 (1977),
      158-160; B. M. Bolton, *JEH*, 28 (1977), 412-413; F. L. Cheyette, *History:
      reviews of new books*, 4 (1976), 202; C. Thouzellier, *CCM*, 20 (1977), 283-
      284; D. W. van der Merwe, *Kleio*, 8 (1976), 77.

179   ——. *The origins of European dissent*. London: Allen Lane, 1977. xiii, 322 p.
      Rev. R. E. Lerner, *AHR*, 83 (1978), 698-699; J. B. Russell, *Speculum*, 53
      (1978), 831-833; B. Smalley, *EHR*, 93 (1978), 853-856; M. B. Becker,
      History: reviews of new books, 7 (1978), 2-3; A. Black, *The tablet*, 232
      (1978), 57; A. Murray, *Durham university journal*, 71 (1978); 100-101; M.
      Aston, *History*, 64 (1979), 81-82; C. Morris, *JEH*, 30 (1979), 283-284; G.
      Leff, *TLS*, 26 May 1978, p. 588; J. Bossy, *Encounter*, 49, no. 5 (1977), 73-
      75; M. Pacaut, *RH*, 261 (1979), 216-218; W. L. Wakefield, *The historian*,
      41 (1979), 765-766.

180   ——. "The origins of medieval heresy." *History*, 55 (1970), 21-36.

181   ——. "St. Bernard's mission to the Languedoc in 1145." *BIHR*, 47 (1974), 1-10.

182   ——. "Some heretical attitudes to the renewal of the church." *Renaissance and
      renewal in Christian history*. Ed. D. Baker. Studies in church history, 14.
      Oxford: Blackwell, 1977. p. 87-93.

183 Morghen, R. "Problèmes sur l'origine de l'hérésie au moyen âge." *RH*, 236 (1966), 1-16. Rvsd. rpt. in *Hérésies et sociétés* (1968). p. 121-138, with discussion. Ital. trans., "Aspetti ereticali dei movimenti religiosi popolari," in *I laici nella "societas christiana" dei secoli XI e XII*, Atti della terza Settimana internazionale di studio (Milan: Vita e pensiero, c1968), p. 582-596. See 65.

184 Morrison, S. St. Clair. "St. Bernard, Abelard and Arnald of Brescia." *IER*, 97 (1962), 304-312.

185 Musy, J. "Mouvements populaires et hérésies au XIᵉ siècle en France." *RH*, 253 (1975), 33-76.

186 Nelson, J. L. "Society, theodicy and the origins of heresy: towards a reassessment of the medieval evidence." *Schism, heresy and religious protest* (1972). p. 65-77. See 120.

187 Pisani, V. "Eretici." *Paideia* (Brescia), 30 (1975), 195-196.

188 Poerck, G. de. "Un préréformateur liégeois au milieu du XIIᵉ siècle, Pierre, auteur de l'*Antigraphum*." *Mélanges offerts à Rita Lejeune*, I. Gembloux: Duculot, c1969. p. 581-600.

189 Russell, J. B. "À propos du synode d'Arras en 1025." *RHE*, 57 (1962), 66-87.

190 ———. *Dissent and reform in the early middle ages*. Publications of the Center for medieval and renaissance studies, 1. Berkeley and Los Angeles: University of California Press, 1965. 323 p.
Rev. C. N. L. Brooke, *JTS*, 18 (1967), 256-258; H. E. J. Cowdrey, *History*, 52 (1967), 67-68; M. Deanesly, *CQR*, 167 (1966), 536-537; R. Folz, *RHEF*, 52 (1966), 154-156; D. Knowles, *The tablet*, 220 (1966), 729-730; G. Leff, *MÆ*, 36 (1967), 100-101; R. Luman, *JR*, 47 (1967), 260-263; L. G. McAllister, *Encounter*, 27 (1966), 368-369; R. Morghen, *CCM*, 12 (1969), 197-201, and *BISIM*, 81 (1969), 297-316; J. W. O'Malley, *TS*, 27 (1966), 682-683; S. Runciman, *JEH*, 18 (1967), 89-90; R. E. Sullivan, *Speculum*, 42 (1967), 187-189; P. D. Thomas, *JCS*, 9 (1967), 415-416; G. S. M. Walker, *Scottish journal of theology*, 20 (1967), 246-248; E. I. Watkin, *The Downside review*, [84] (1966), 436-439; H. Grundmann, *DAEM*, 24 (1968), 283-284; E. A. Payne, *The Baptist quarterly*, 22 (1968), 377.

191 ———. "Heresy in the diocese of Liège before 1160." Diss. Emory Univ. *DAI*, 22A (1962), 3623.

192 ———. "Saint Boniface and the eccentrics." *CH*, 33 (1964), 235-247.

193 Siegwart, J. "Die Pataria des 11. Jahrhunderts und der heilige Nikolaus von Patara." *ZSKG*, 71 (1977), 30-92.

194 Skazkin, S. D., and V. V. Samarkin. "Dolchino i bibliia." *Srednie veka*, 38 (1975), 84-99. [Incl. summary, "Fra' Dolcino e la Bibbia (sulla questione dell'esegesi della Sacra scrittura come mezzo della propaganda rivoluzionaria nel medioevo)"]

195   Smet, J.-M. de. "De monnik Tanchelm en de Utrechtse bisschopszetel in 1112-1114." *Scrinium lovaniense: mélanges historiques / historische opstellen Etienne van Cauwenbergh*. Gembloux: Duculot; Louvain: Bibliothèque de l'Université, 1961. p. 207-234.

196   Taviani, H. "Le mariage dans l'hérésie de l'an mil." *Annales*, 32 (1977), 1074-1089.

197   ——. "Naissance d'une hérésie en Italie du nord au xiᵉ siècle." *Annales*, 29 (1974), 1224-1252.

198   Teruzzi, P. G. "Il *Contra petrobrusianos* di Pietro il Venerabile." Diss. Università Cattolica del Sacro Cuore, Milan, 1969. —

199   Teunis, H. "The failure of the patarine movement." *The journal of medieval history*, 5 (1979), 177-184.

200   Thouzellier, C. "Polémique sur l'origine de l'hérésie à Bergame aux xiiᵉ-xiiiᵉ s." *RHE*, 62 (1967), 421-428.

201   ——. "Tradition et résurgence dans l'hérésie médiévale: considérations." With discussion. *Hérésies et sociétés* (1968). p. 105-120. Rvsd. rpt. in her *Hérésie et hérétiques* (Rome: Storia e Letteratura, 1969), p. 1-15. See 65.

202   Toubert, P. "Hérésies et réforme ecclésiastique en Italie au xiᵉ et au xiiᵉ siècles: à propos de deux études récentes." *Revue des études italiennes*, n.s. 8 (1961), 58-71. Rpt. in his *Études sur l'Italie médiévale (ixᵉ-xivᵉ s.)* (London: Variorum, 1976), sect. 8.

203   Trawkowski, S. *Między herezją a ortodoksją: rola społeczna premonstratensów w xii wieku*. Warsaw: Państwowe Wydawnictwo Naukowe, 1964. 214 p. [Incl. summary, p. 205-210, "Entre l'hérésie et l'orthodoxie: le rôle social des prémontrés au xiiᵉ siècle"]

204   Turreni, A. "La condizione giuridica degli eretici patarini in Orvieto." Diss. Università di Perugia, 1967 —

204a Vego, M. "Patarenstvo u Hercegovini u svjetlu arheoloških spomenika." *Glasnik Zemaljskog Muzeja*, n.s. 18 (1963), 196-215. —

205   Vesce, T. E. "On identifying the *popelican(t)*." *ms*, 32 (1970), 352-353. See 176.

206   Violante, C. "Hérésies urbaines et hérésies rurales en Italie du 11ᵉ au 13ᵉ siècle." With discussion. *Hérésies et sociétés* (1968). p. 171-198. Ital. trans. in *Studi sulla cristianità medioevale* (c1972), p. 349-379, and in O. Capitani, ed., *L'eresia medievale* (c1971), p. 157-184. See 17, 65.

207   ——. "I laici nel movimento patarino." With discussion. *I laici nella "societas christiana" dei secoli xi e xii*. Atti della terza Settimana internazionale di studio (Mendola, 21-27 agosto 1965). Milan: Vita e pensiero, c1968. p. 597-697. Rpt. in *Studi sulla cristianità medioevale* (c1972), p. 145-246.

208   ——. "La povertà nelle eresie del secolo xi in occidente." *Studi sulla cristianità medioevale*. Comp. P. Zerbi. Milan: Vita e pensiero, c1972. p. 69-107. Rpt. in *La concezione della povertà nel medioevo*, ed. O. Capitani (Bologna: Pàtron, c1974), p. 194-255. Rvsd., abridged trans., "La pauvreté dans les

hérésies du xɪᵉ siècle en occident," in *Études sur l'histoire de la pauvreté*, ed. M. Mollat (Paris: Sorbonne, 1974), I, 347-369.

209 Voosen, E. "L'hérésie de Tanchelin." *Revue diocésaine de Namur*, 15 (1961), 144-151.

210 Werner, E. *Häresie und Gesellschaft im 11. Jahrhundert*. Sitzungsberichte der Sächsischen Akademie der Wissenschaften zu Leipzig, Philol.-hist. Klasse, 117, no. 5. Berlin: Akademie-Verlag, 1975. 83 p.

    Rev. B. Töpfer, *zg*, 23 (1975), 1086-1087; W. Kirsch, *daem*, 32 (1976), 291; G. Mühlpfordt, *dlz*, 97 (1976), 989-992.

211 ——. "Spiritualismus und heterodoxe Dialektik im 11. Jahrhundert." *Jahrbuch für Geschichte*, 13 (1975), 7-30.

212 Zanoni, L. *Gli umiliati nei loro rapporti con l'eresia, l'industria della lana ed i comuni nel secoli xii e xiii sulla scorta di documenti inediti*. Biblioteca di storia economica, 3. Milan, 1911. Rpt. Rome; Multigrafica, 1970. xvi, 381 p.

Part Three

Bogomils

ENTRIES 213 TO 289

213 Angelov, D. "Aperçu sur la nature et l'histoire du bogomilisme en Bulgarie."
Hérésies et sociétés (1968). p. 75-81. See 65.

214 ———. *Les Balkans au moyen âge: la Bulgarie des Bogomils aux Turcs*. London:
Variorum, 1978. 320 p. [Collected essays]

215 ———. *Bogomili*. Biblioteka Geroichna letopis, II, 1. Sofia: Izd-vo na Natsionalniia
suvet na Otechestvennia front, 1961. 75 p.

216 ———. *Bogomilstvoto v Bŭlgariia*. 2nd ed. Sofia: Nauka i Izkustvo, 1961. 318 p.
[Orig. publ. Moscow, 1954.] Trans. L. Pétrova-Boinay, *Le bogomilisme en
Bulgarie* (Sofia: Nauka i Izkustvo, 1969), 562 p.; abridged trans., with
intro. by J. Duvernoy (Toulouse: Privat, 1972), 128 p. Trans. V. Spasova,
Il bogomilismo: un'eresia medievale bulgara (Rome: Bulzoni, 1979),
547 p.
Rev. A. Constantinescu, *Studii: revista de istorie*, 17 (1964), 198-199; P.
Tivčev, *Izvestiia na Instituta za istoriia* (Sofia), 12 (1963), 219-227; A.
Každan, *Vizantiĭskiĭ vremennik*, 23 (1963), 299-300.
Rev. (Fr. trans.) P. Tivčev, *Byzantinobulgarica*, 4 (1973), 333-344.

217 ———, B. Primov, and G. Batakliev. *Bogomilstvoto v Bŭlgariia, Vizantiia i Zapadna
Evropa v izvori*. Sofia: Nauka i Izkustvo, 1967. 234 p.

218 ———. "Bogomilstvoto v istoriiata na slavianskite narodi i vliianieto mu v zapadna
Evropa." *Slavjanska filologiia*, 5 (1963), 167-178. [Bogomilism in the
history of the Slavic peoples and its influence in Western Europe]

219 ———. "Eine Ketzerlehre, die zum rationalistischen Denken anregte." *Bulgarische
Beiträge zur europäischen Kultur*. Ed. E. Georgiev et al. Sofia: Sofia-Press,
1968. p. 51-84, ill.

220 ———. "Le mouvement bogomile dans les pays balkaniques et son influence en
Europe occidentale." *Actes du Colloque international de civilisations
balkaniques ... Sinaïa, 8-14 juillet 1962*. [Bucarest: UNESCO, 1963] p. 173-
182.

221 ——. "Le mouvement bogomile dans les pays slaves balkaniques et dans Byzance." *L'oriente cristiano nella storia della civiltà.* Accademia nazionale dei Lincei, Problemi attuali di scienza e di cultura, Quaderno 62 (Rome, 1964). p. 607-618. [Incl. discussion]

222 ——. "Ursprung und Wesen des Bogomilentums." *The concept of heresy in the middle ages* (1976). p. 144-156. See 25.

223 Babić, A. *Bosanski heretici.* Sarajevo: Svjetlost, 1963. 177 p. [The heretics of Bosnia] Rpt. in his *Iz istorije srednjovjekovne Bosne* (Sarajevo: Svjetlost, 1972), p. 195-304.

224 Backvis, C. "Un témoignage bulgare du xe siècle sur les bogomiles: le *Slovo* de Cosmas le prêtre." *Annuaire de l'Institut de philologie et d'histoire orientales et slaves,* 16 (1961-62), 75-100.

225 Balotă, A. "Bogomilismul şi cultura maselor populare din Bulgaria şi ţările romîne." *Romanoslavica,* 10 (1964), 19-71. [Incl. summary, "Le bogomilisme et la culture des masses populaires de Bulgarie et des pays roumains"]

226 Begunov, I. K. "K izucheniiu istorii teksta *Becedy na novoiavivshuiusia eres' bogomilu* bolgarskogo pisatelia x v. Kozmy Presvitera." *Vizantiiskii vremennik,* 30 (1969), 166-189. [Study of the history of the text *Sermon on the newly-arisen heresy of the Bogomils* by the 10th-century Bulgarian writer Cosmas Presbyter]

227 ——. *Kozma presviter v slavianskikh literaturakh.* Sofia: Izdatel'stvo Bolgarskoĭ Akademii Nauk, 1973. 559 p. ill.
Rev. A. Danti, *Aevum,* 51 (1977), 384-385.

228 ——. "Serbskaia kompiliatsiia xiii v. iz *Besiedy* Kozmy Presvitera." *Slovo,* 18-19 (1969), 91-108. [Incl. summary, "Srpska kompilacija xiii stoljeca iz *Besjede* Kozme Prezvitera" (13th-century Serbian compilation of the *Sermon against the bogomils* of Cosmas)]

229 Bešlagić, Š. "Naknadna zapazhanie na nekropoli stećaka u Boljunima." *Starinar,* 22 (1971 [1974]), 177-178, ill. [Further remarks on the bogomil funerary *stèles* at Boljunima]

230 ——. *Stećci centralne Bosne.* Srednjovjekovni nadgrobni spomenici Bosne i Hercegovine, 9. Sarajevo: Zavod za zaštitu spomenika kulture Bosne i Hercegovine, 1967. 116 p. ill. [Incl. summary, "Stèles médiévales de la Bosnie centrale"]

231 ——. *Stećci: kataloško-topografski pregled.* [Sarajevo: Veselin Masleša, 1971] 495 p. ill. [Incl. summary, "Catalogue des *stećak*"]

232 ——. "Les 'stećci' médiévaux: recherches et études." *Archaeologia iugoslavica,* 5 (1964), 113-126, ill.

233 ——. "Stećci u Brotnjicama." *Anali historijskog instituta Jugoslavenske akademie znanosti i umjetnosti u Dubrovniku,* 8-9 (1962), 65-83, ill. [Incl. summary, "Les stećci (monuments funéraires bogomiles) à Brotnjice"]

234   Bihalji-Merin, O., and A. Benac. *Stećci*. With photographs by T. Dabac. Belgrade,
        1962. xxxv p. + 80 plates. map. Trans., *Bogomil sculpture* (Belgrade, 1962;
        New York: Harcourt, Brace, and World [1963]); *The Bogomils* (London:
        Thames and Hudson [1962]). Trans., *L'art des bogomiles* (Paris: Arthaud
        [1963]). Trans., *Steine der Bogomilen* (Vienna and Munich: Schroll [1964]).
235   Cankova-Petkova, G. "Apparition et diffusion du bogomilisme et les rapports des
        Bulgares avec l'Europe occidentale au moyen âge." *Études historiques*
        (Sofia), 7 (1975), 69-87.
236   Ćirković, S. M. "Die bosnische Kirche." *L'oriente cristiano nella storia della
        civiltà*. Accademia nazionale dei Lincei, Problemi attuali di scienza e di
        cultura, Quaderno 62 (Roma, 1964). p. 547-577. [Incl. discussion]
237   Davidov, A. *Rechnik-indeks na Prezviter Kozma*. Sofia: Bulgarska akademiia na
        naukite, 1976. 375 p. [Cosmas concordance]
238   Dragojlović, D. "Bogomilisme et mouvements hérétiques dualistes du moyen
        âge." *Balcanica*, 4 (1973), 121-143.
239   ———. "Marginalne glose srpskih rukopisnih krmčija o neomanihejima." *Jugoslo-
        venski istorijski časopis*, 11, no. 1-2 (1972), 5-15. [Incl. summary,
        "Marginalglossen serbischer handschriftlicher Nomokanons"]
240   ———. "Poreklo i geneza babunske jeresi u Srbiji." *Jugoslovenski istorijski časopis*,
        7, no. 3-4 (1968), 103-111. [Origin and genesis of the babun heresy in
        Serbia]
241   Dujčev, I. "I bogomili nei paesi slavi e la loro storia." *L'oriente cristiano nella
        storia della civiltà*. Accademia nazionale dei Lincei, Problemi attuali di
        scienza e di cultura, Quaderno 62 (Rome, 1964). p. 619-641.
242   ———. "Aux origines des courants dualistes à Byzance et chez les Slaves méridio-
        naux." RESEE, 7 (1969), 51-62.
243   Fine, J. V. A., jr. *The Bosnian church: a new interpretation. A study of the Bosnian
        church and its place in state and society from the 13th to the 15th centuries*.
        East European monographs, 10. New York and London: Columbia
        University Press for East European Quarterly, 1975. ix, 447 p.
        Rev. P. Mojzes, CH, 45 (1976), 251-252; J. L. Wieczynski, CHR, 64 (1978),
        306-307.
244   Hamilton, B. "The origins of the dualist church of Drugunthia." *Eastern churches
        review*, 5 (1973), 115-124.
245   Hamm, J. "Apokalipsa bosanskih krstjana." *Slovo*, 9-10 (1960), 43-104. [Incl.
        summary, "L'apocalypse des 'chrétiens' bosniaques"]
246   Ivanov, I. *Livres et légendes bogomiles (aux sources du catharisme)*. Trans. of
        Bogomilski knigi i legendi (Sofia, 1925) by M. Ribeyrol, with preface by
        R. Nelli. Les littératures populaires de toutes les nations, n.s. 22. Paris:
        Maisonneuve et Larose, 1976. 398 p.
        Rev. J. Séguy, ASSR, 44 (1976), 251.
247   Knievald, D. "Hierarchie und Kultus Bosnischer Christen." *L'oriente cristiano*

nella storia della civiltà. Accademia nazionale dei Lincei, Problemi attuali di scienza e di cultura, Quaderno 62 (Rome, 1964). p. 579-605.

248   Krleza, M. "The funerary art of the bogomiles: the stones with the raised hands." *The UNESCO courier,* 24 (May 1971), 17-22, ill. [Published simultaneously in 12 other languages]

249   Kutzli, R. *Die Bogumilen: Geschichte, Kunst, Kultur.* Stuttgart: Urachhaus, 1977. 261 p. ill.

250   Loos, M. "Certains aspects du bogomilisme byzantin des 11e et 12e siècles." *Byzantinoslavica,* 28 (1967), 39-53.

251   ——. "Où en est la question du mouvement paulicien?" *Izvestiia na Instituta za istoriia* (Sofia), 14-15 (1964), 357-371.

252   ——. "La question de l'origine du bogomilisme (Bulgarie ou Byzance?)." *Actes du premier Congrès international des études balkaniques et sud-est européennes,* 3. Sofia: Académie bulgare des sciences, 1969. p. 265-270. [Brief replies by P. Năsturel and D. Angelov, p. 272-273]

253   ——. "Satan als Erstgeborener Gottes (ein Beitrag zur Analyse des bogomilischen Mythus)." *Byzantinobulgarica,* 3 (1969), 23-35.

254   Mandić, D. *Bosna i Hercegovina: povjesno-kritička istraživanja, II. Bogomilska crkva bosanskih krstjana.* Chicago: Croatian Historical Institute, 1962. 509 p. ill. [Bogomil church of the Bosnian Christians]
Rev. S. Sakač, *Orientalia christiana periodica,* 29 (1963), 281-282; E. Werner, *SM,* 3rd ser., 5 (1964), 675-683.

255   ——. "Bosanski krstjani u turskim izvorima." *Rasprave i prilozi iz stare hrvatske porijesti.* Rome, 1963. p. 568-575. — [The Bosnian Christians according to Turkish sources]

256   ——. "Vlaška teza o bosansko-hercegovačkim stećcina." *Revue croate,* 2-4 (1966), 237-246. —

257   Manselli, R. "Les 'chrétiens' de Bosnie: le catharisme en Europe orientale." *RHE,* 72 (1977), 600-614.

258   Moore, R. I. "Nicétas, émissaire de Dragovitch, a-t-il traversé les Alpes?" *AM,* 85 (1975), 85-90.

259   Obolensky, D. *The Bogomils: a study in Balkan neo-manichaeism.* Cambridge, 1948. Rpt. Twickenham, Eng.: A. C. Hall, 1972; New York: AMS, 1978. xiv, 317 p.

260   Okiç, M. T. "Les Kristians (bogomiles parfaits) de Bosnie d'après des documents turcs inédits." *Südost-Forschungen,* 19 (1960), 108-133.

261   Primov, B. "Bogomilskiiat dualizum: proizkhod, sushtnost i obshtestveno-politichesko znachenie." *Izvestiia na Instituta za istoriia* (Sofia), 8 (1960), 73-151. [Incl. summary, "Le dualisme des bogomiles: son origine, sa nature et sa portée sociale et politique"]

262   ——. *Bugrite: kniga za pop Bogomili negovite posledovateli.* Biblioteka belezhiti bŭlgari, 7. Sofia: Izdatelstvo na Otechestveniia Front, 1970. 388 p. ill.

Trans. M. Ribeyrol, *Les bougres: histoire du pope Bogomile et de ses adeptes* (Paris: Payot, 1975), 325 p.
Rev. G. Părvev and H. Kolarov, *Études historiques*, 6 (1973), 365-370.
Rev. (French trans.) R. Berlo, *Revue théologique de Louvain*, 7 (1976), 246; J. C. Schmitt, *ASSR*, 40 (1975), 265.

263 ——. "Svedeniia iz anonimen izvor za bliianieto na bulgarskoto bogomilstvo v zapadna Evropa." *Izvestiia na Instituta za istoriia* (Sofia), 14-15 (1964), 299-313. [Incl. summary, "Renseignements d'une source anonyme sur l'influence du mouvement bogomile bulgare en Europe occidentale"]

264 Radoičič, Dž. "Odlomak bogomilskog jevanđelja bosanskog tepačije Batala iz 1393 godine." *Izvestiia na Instituta za istoriia* (Sofia), 14-15 (1964), 495-509, ill. [Fragment of a bogomil gospel of 1393 once owned by the Bosnian sovereign Batalo Santić]

265 Ratsin, K. "The Dragovitian bogomils." *Macedonian review*, 6, no. 1 (1976), 9-27.

266 Šanjek, F. *Bosansko-humski krstjani i katarsko-dualistički pokret u srednjem vijeku.* Analecta croatica christiana, 6. Zagreb: Kršćanska Sadašnjost, 1975. 216 p. ill. Trans., *Les chrétiens bosniaques et le mouvement cathare, XIIe-XVe siècles*, Publications de la Sorbonne, n.s. recherches 20 (Louvain: Nauwelaerts; Paris: Vander-Oyez, c1976), 260 p., ill.
Rev. (French trans.) R. Granier, *CEC*, 28, no. 74 (1977), 78-81; J. V. A. Fine, *Speculum*, 53 (1978), 414-416; P. Gautier, *Revue des études byzantines*, 35 (1977), 306; J. Jolivet, *RHR*, 193 (1978), 249-250; S. Runciman, *EHR*, 93 (1978), 159-160; G. G. Merlo, *RSI*, 90 (1978), 415-421; M. D. Lambert, *JEH*, 29 (1978), 244; A. Patschovsky, *DAEM*, 34 (1978), 639-640; M. Pacaut, *RH*, 261 (1979), 253-254.

267 Šidak, J. "O autentičnosti i značenju jedne isprave bosanskog 'djeda' (1427)." *Slovo*, 15-16 (1965), 282-297. [Incl. summary, "Über die Echtheit und die Bedeutung einer Urkunde des bosnischen 'djed' (1427)"]

268 ——. "O nekim posljednjim prilozima B. Primova problemu bogumilstva." *Slovo*, 14 (1964), 160-163. [Comments on recent studies by B. Primov and others]

269 ——. "Problem popa Bogumila u suvremenoj nauci." *Slovo*, 9-10 (1960), 193-197. [The problem of the Bogomil priest in current scholarship]

270 ——. *Studije o "Crkvi bosanskoj" i bogumilstvu.* Zagreb: Sveučilišna Naklada Liber, 1975. 401 p. ill. [Collected essays on the Bosnian church and bogomilism, with Ger. summaries]
Rev. A. Nazor, *Slovo*, 25-26 (1976), 440-445.

271 Škobalj, A. *Obredne gomile.* Sveti Križ na Čiovu, 1970. viii, 17-683 p. ill. [Incl. summary, "Tumuli rituales"]

272 Snegarov, I. "Bogomilstvoto prez pogleda na grutski istorik." *Izvestiia na Instituta za istoriia* (Sofia), 8 (1960), 369-381. [The bogomil movement from the point of view of a Greek historian]

273 Svane, G., trans. and comm. *Kozma Presbyterens Traktat mod de bulgarske kættere (Bogomilerne)*. Copenhagen: Munksgaard, 1971. 143 p. ill.

274 Tashkovski, D. *Bogomilism in Macedonia*. Macedonian heritage collection. Skopje: Macedonian review, 1975. 128 p.

275 Vaillant, A. "Un apocryphe pseudo-bogomile: la Vision d'Isaïe." *Revue des études slaves*, 42 (1963), 109-121.

276 Vasilescu, D. "Der Bogomilismus." *Studii teologice*, 2nd ser., 15 (1963), 444-460. —

277 Verlinden, C. "Patarins ou bogomiles réduits en esclavage." *Studi in onore di Alberto Pincherle*. Studi e materiali di storia delle religioni, 38. Rome: Ateneo, 1967. II, 683-700.

278 Vitray-Meyerovitch, E. de, and D. Bogdanovic. "Les monuments funéraires de Bosnie Herzégovine sont-ils bogomiles?" *Archeologia*, 76 (nov. 1974), 21-33, ill.

279 Wenzel, M. "Bosnian and Herzegovinian tombstones – who made them and why." *Südost-Forschungen*, 21 (1962), 102-143, ill.

280 Werner, E. "Die Bogomilen in Bulgarien: Forschungen und Fortschritte." *SM*, 3rd ser., 3 (1962), 249-278.

281 ——. "Gnosisforschung und Balkandualismus." *Studia z dziejów kultury i ideologii ofiarowane Ewie Maleczyńskiej w 50 rocznicę pracy dydaktycznej i naukowej*. Wrocław, Warsaw, and Kraków: Zakład Narodowy im. Ossolińskich, 1968. p. 43-62.

282 ——. *Ketzer und Weltverbesserer: zwei Beiträge zur Geschichte Südosteuropas im 13. und 15. Jahrhundert*. Sitzungsberichte der Sächsischen Akademie der Wissenschaften zu Leipzig, Philol.-hist. Klasse, 116, no. 5. Berlin: Akademie-Verlag, 1974. 57 p.

283 ——. "Spätbogomilisch-adamitische Spekulationen und Praktiken im religions-historischer Sicht." *Byzantine studies*, 1 (1974), 40-53.

284 ——. "Theophilos – Bogumil." *Balkan studies*, 7 (1966), 49-60.

285 Wild, G. "'Bogu mili' als Ausdruck des Selbstverständnisses der mittelalterlichen Sektenkirche." *Kirche im Osten*, 6 (1963), 16-33.

286 ——. "Die bogumilische Häresie in einigen südslavischen Volksliedern." *WS*, 9 (1964-65), 258-276.

287 ——. "Die Darstellung des bogumilischen 'Perfectus' auf den mittelalterlichen Grabdenkmälern (stećci) Bosniens und der Herzegowina." *Balcanica*, 4 (1973), 111-120, ill.

288 ——. "Symbol und Dogma im Bogumilentum: das Problem der Darstellungen auf den mittelalterlichen Grabsteinen Bosniens und der Herzegowina." *Saeculum*, 21 (1970), 383-392, ill.

289 Zaitsev, V. K. "K voprosu o vzaimootnoshenii bogomil'stva i nekotorykh zapadnykh ereticheskikh dvizheniĭ." *Vestnik Leningradskogo universiteta*, 1976, no. 14, p. 109-116. [On the connection between bogomilism and some heretical concepts in Western Europe]

Part Four

Cathars

ENTRIES 290 TO 709

A. *General (Entries 290 to 382)*

290 Azaïs, G. "L'histoire de l'Albigeois à travers le drame cathare aux xie, xiie, xiiie siècles." *Revue du Tarn*, 31 (1963), 339-356; 32 (1963), 454-466.

291 Bachelier, E. "Les cathares en Velay." *Bulletin historique, scientifique, littéraire, artistique et agricole illustré, publié par la Société académique du Puy et de la Haute-Loire*, 44 (1966), 207-210. —

292 Barber, M. C. "Women and catharism." *Reading medieval studies*, 3 (1977), 45-62.

293 Barbera, S. Merelo de. "Les Barbera dans l'histoire du catharisme et de l'Occitanie." *Annales de l'Institut d'études occitanes*, 1962-63, p. 23-28. —

294 Barbero, A. "I catari di Chieri." *Testi i problemi di storia del cristianesimo.* Esercitazioni del Seminario di storia del cristianesimo diretto da F. Bolgiani. Ed. D. Devoti. Turin, 1967. p. 94-111. —

295 Bayrou, Dr. "Les albigeois." *Les amis du vieux Saint-Étienne*, 60 (1965), 98-102. —

296 Bécamel, M. "À propos de Sainte-Juliane, note." *Cathares en Languedoc*, p. 253-258. See 305.

297 ——. "Le catharisme dans le diocèse d'Albi." *Cathares en Languedoc*, p. 237-252. See 305.

298 Belloc, H. *The great heresies.* New York, 1938. Rpt. Freeport, N.Y.: Books for libraries, [1968]. 277 p.

299 Besson, S. "Les cathares." *Les amis de Solliès-Ville*, 10 (1966), 10-17. —

300 Biehler, P. "L'hérésie de la pureté." *Atlantis*, 43, no. 254 (1969), 69-80. —

301 Blanc, P. "Le tympan de Perse et les cathares." *Revue du Rouergue*, 21 (1967), 341-343.

302 Blaquière, H., and Y. Dossat. "Les cathares au jour le jour: confessions inédites de cathares quercynois." *Cathares en Languedoc.* p. 259-298. ill. See 305.

303 Blasco, R. "Roquemartine, château cathare de Provence?" *CEC*, 29, no. 78 (1978), 65-70, ill.

304 Cassé, P. *Mes ancêtres, les cathares*. Paris: Cascade, 1968. 301 p. ill.

305 *Cathares en Languedoc*. Cahiers de Fanjeaux, 3. Toulouse: Privat, c1968. 332 p. ill.
    Rev. R. Mols, *NRT*, 92 (1970), 995; H. Maisonneuve, *RHE*, 65 (1970), 670-672; B. Guillemain, *AM*, 83 (1971), 108-113; R. Cegna, *RSLR*, 5 (1969), 496; D. Roché, *CEC*, 20, no. 42 (1969), 3-17; A. Molnár, *Protestantesimo*, 25 (1970), 256-258; M. Reynaud, *Cahiers d'histoire*, 15 (1970), 70-71.

306 Cauvin, A. *Découvrir la France cathare*. Guide Marabout, 4. Verviers: Marabout, 1974. 191 p. ill.
    Rev. J. Paul, *RHEF*, 61 (1975), 296.

307 Cèbe, O. "Le catharisme vu depuis les Monts de Lacaune." *Atlantis*, 44, no. 255 (1970), 146-152. —

308 Charles-Géniaux, C. "Albigéisme ou catharisme?" *Revue du Tarn*, 44 (1966), 435-440.

309 Conterno, G. "Catari a Monforte." *Bollettino della Società per gli studi storici, archeologici ed artistici nella provincia di Cuneo*, 60 (1969), 25-33.

310 Cristiani, L. "Le catharisme, hier et aujourd'hui." *L'ami du clergé*, 77 (1967), 230-231.

311 Delaruelle, E. "L'état actuel des études sur le catharisme." *Cathares en Languedoc*. p. 19-41. See 305.

312 Delattre, L. *Les cathares*. Mont-de-Marsan: Jean-Lacoste, 1966. 24 p.

313 Dossat, Y. "L'hérésie en Champagne aux xiie et xiiie siècles." *Mémoires de la Société d'agriculture, commerce, science et arts du département de la Marne*, 84 (1969), 57-73.

314 Dubuc, J.-P. *Histoire du christianisme cathare du i^er au xxe siècle*. Narbonne: Croix de Vie, c1970. 199 p.

315 Duchaussoy, J. "Miscellanées préliminaires à l'étude du catharisme." *Atlantis*, 43, no. 254 (1969), 11-18. —

316 Dupré-Theseider, E. "Le catharisme languedocien et l'Italie." *Cathares en Languedoc*. p. 299-316. See 305.

317 Ennesch, C. *Les cathares dans la cité*. Paris: Picard; Esch-sur-Alzette, Lux.: Journal d'Esch, 1969. 145 p. ill.

318 ——. *L'épopée albigeoise*. 2nd ed. Esch-sur-Alzette, Lux.: Éditions du Journal d'Esch, 1962. 111 p. ill. Orig. publ. 1961.
    Rev. [M. Broëns], *Chthonia*, 4 (1964), 62.

319 Falbel, N. "As heresias dos séculos xii e xiii." *Revista de história* (São Paulo), 38, no. 78 (1969), 325-352; 41, no. 82 (1970), 271-287; 42, no. 86 (1971), 335-350.

320 Frugoni, A. "L'eresia catara." *Cultura e scuola*, 9 (1964), 94-98.

321 ——. *L'eresia catara nell'occidente medievale*. [Rome]: Ateneo, 1966. 155 p.

322 Goïty, B. "Les Basques en pays cathare." *Gure Herria*, 1975, p. 65-76.

323 Grisart, M. "Les cathares dans le nord de la France." *CEC*, 22, no. 50 (1971), 12-31.

324 ——. "Les cathares dans le nord de la France." *Revue du nord* (Lille), 49 (1967), 509-519.

325 Guillemain, B. "L'histoire religieuse du Languedoc à la fin du XIIe siècle et au début du XIIIe." *AM*, 83 (1971), 101-117.

326 Guillot, R.-P. *Le défi cathare*. Paris: Laffont, c1975. 251 p. ill.

327 Guirdham, A. *Catharism: the medieval resurgence of primitive Christianity*. Tenth Maurice Elliot memorial lecture, 1969. London: Churches' Fellowship for Psychical and Spiritual Studies, [1969]. 23 p.

328 ——. *The great heresy*. Jersey, Channel Islands: Neville Spearman, 1977. 183 p.

329 Häring, N. M. "Die Rolle der Hl. Schrift in der Auseinandersetzung des Alanus de Insulis mit dem Neu-Manichäismus." *Die Mächte des Guten und Bösen*. Ed. A. Zimmermann. Miscellanea mediaevalia, 11. Berlin and New York: de Gruyter, 1977. p. 315-343.

330 Hannedouche, S. "XIVme Congrès de la Société du souvenir et des études cathares." *CEC*, 12, no. 9 (1961), 25-35.

331 ——. *Manichéisme et catharisme*. Arque (Aude): Cahiers d'études cathares, [1967]. 93 p. [Contains one new essay, "Catharisme et église romaine au XIIe siècle," and seven essays orig. publ. in *CEC*, 1952 to 1954]

332 Honoré, G. C. "La déviation cathare." *Atlantis*, 43, no. 254 (1969), 95-97. ——

333 Jentet, J. "Le catharisme en Champagne." *Atlantis*, 44, no. 255 (1970), 159-166. ——

334 Kühner, H. "Die Katharer." *Die Wahrheit der Ketzer*. Ed. H. J. Schultz. Stuttgart and Berlin: Kreuz-Verlag, c1968. p. 50-59, 242-250.

335 Lambert, M. "The motives of the Cathars: some reflections." *Religious*, no. 989 (1978), 49-59.

336 Lataillade, J. B. "Catharisme en Comminges, Couserans et Armagnac." *Revue de Comminges*, 86 (1973), 212-216.

337 Le Cour, P. "Les cathares." *Atlantis*, 43, no. 254 (1969), 87-94. ——

338 Lévis Mirepoix, Duke of. "La tragédie cathare." *Historia*, 168 (1960), 590-598.

339 Lindeboom, J. "Nieuwe studiën over de katharen." *Nederlands archief voor kerk-geschiedenis*, 43 (1959-60), 87-118.

340 Loos, M. *Dualist heresy in the middle ages*. Trans. I. Lewitová. Prague: Academia, for the Czechoslovak academy of sciences, 1974. 397 p.
      Rev. M. Erbstößer, *DLZ*, 97 (1976), 45-47; J.-C. Schmitt, *ASSR*, 43 (1977), 273-274; A. Davids, *Byzantinische Zeitschrift*, 71 (1978), 112-113; M. de Waha, *Byzantion*, 47 (1977), 553-554; G. Filoramo, *RSLR*, 14 (1978), 303-304; J. Gouillard, *RHR*, 194 (1978), 97-98.

341 ——. "L''église bosnienne' dans le contexte du mouvement hérétique européen." *Balcanica*, 4 (1973), 145-161.

342   Luitse, N. "Les cathares aux Pays-Bas." *CEC*, 20, no. 43 (1969), 17-22; 21, no. 45 (1970), 36-40.

343   Madaule, J. *Le drame albigeois et le destin français*. Paris: Grasset, 1961. 262 p. 2nd ed. (245 p.), *Le drame albigeois et l'unité française* (Paris: Gallimard, 1973). Trans. A. and H. Henze, *Das Drama von Albi: der Kreuzzug gegen die Albigenser und das Schicksal Frankreichs*, with afterword by K. Rinderknecht (Olten and Freiburg im Breisgau: Walter-Verlag, c1964), 261 p., ill. Trans. B. Wall, *The Albigensian crusade: an historical essay* (London: Burns and Oates; New York: Fordham University Press, 1967), xiii, 177 p.

Rev. (1st French ed.) J. Séguy, *ASR*, 13 (1962), 181-182; L. Julien and D. Roché, *CEC*, 13, no. 14 (1962), 50-56; G. F. Klenk, *Stimmen der Zeit*, 176 (1965), 634.

Rev. (Eng. trans.) R. I. Burns, *Speculum*, 44 (1969), 311-312; D. Knowles, *The tablet*, 221 (1967), 1094; C. H. Lawrence, *The clergy review*, 53 (1968), 239-240; E. I. Watkin, *The Downside review*, 85 (1967), 441-445; D. Nolan, *Studies* (Dublin), 58 (1969), 223-224.

344   Maillard, B. de. "Le catharisme." *L'initiation*, 40 (1966), 97-109. —

345   [Manier, C.] "Cathares en Champagne: Montwimer." *CEC*, 27, no. 70 (1976), 45-56.

346   Manselli, R. *L'eresia del male*. Collana di storia, 1. [Naples]: Morano, c1963. 351 p.

Rev. B. Smalley, *RSI*, 80 (1968), 380-384; R. Morghen, *BISIM*, 81 (1969), 297-316; P. Brezzi, *Studium*, 60 (1964), 554-555.

347   ——, ed. *Testi per lo studio della eresia catara*. Turin: Lauri, 1964. 83 p. —

348   Meadows, I. "The cathars of Languedoc." *The spectator*, no. 7569 (21 July 1973), 73-74.

349   Nataf, A. *Le miracle cathare*. Paris: Laffont, c1968. 254 p. ill.

350   Nelli, R. *Les cathares, ou l'éternel combat*. Histoire des personnages mystérieux et des sociétés secrètes. Paris: Grasset, 1972. 286 p. ill.

Rev. R. Manselli, *CCM*, 17 (1974), 72-74; J. Paul, *RHEF*, 60 (1974), 143.

351   ——, ed. and trans. *Écrivains anticonformistes du moyen-âge occitan, II: hérétiques et politiques*. Paris: Phébus, 1977. 415 p.

352   ——. "'Exempla' et mythes cathares." *Folklore* (Carcassonne), 23, no. 3 (1970), 2-13.

353   ——, F. Niel, D. Roché, and J. Duvernoy, eds. *Les cathares: documents et articles*. Paris: Delphes, 1964. 455 p. —

354   Niel, F. *Albigeois et cathares*. Que sais-je? no. 689. 5th ed. Paris: Presses Universitaires de France, 1967. 127 p.

355   Palau-Martí, M. "Le catharisme et ses conséquences sur le statut politique actuel de l'Andorre." *Pirineos*, 98 (1970), 91-101.

356   ——. "Le catharisme et ses conséquences sur le statut politique d'Andorre." *BPH*,
       1969 (1972), p. 437-449.

357   Perret, F. "Catharisme et psychanalyse." *CEC*, 28, no. 76 (1977), 38-42. [To be
       continued]

358   Prince, J. L. de. "La Chanson de Roland et les cathares." *CEC*, 29, no. 79 (1978),
       27-30.

359   Radcliff-Umstead, D. "The catharists and the failure of the community."
       Mediaevalia, 1, no. 2 (1975), 63-87.

360   Ricau, O. "U drin d'istoère ... a perpaus dous albigès." *Reclams de Biarn e
       Gascougne*, 66, nos. 1-2 (1962), 12-14. —

361   Roché, D. *L'église romaine et les cathares albigeois.* 3d ed. Narbonne: Cahiers
       d'Études Cathares [1969]. 327 p. [Orig. publ. 1957]
       Rev. A. Sarg, *RHPR*, 52 (1972), 121-122.

362   ——. "Exposé et commentaire des Cahiers de Fanjeaux: *Cathares du Langue-
       doc.*" *CEC*, 20, no. 42 (1969), 3-17. See 305.

363   Rousseau, H. "Problèmes cathares." *Critique* (Paris), 25 (1969), 915-934. [Survey-
       review of recent publications]

364   Šanjek, F. "Raynerius Sacconi O.P., Summa de catharis." *AFP*, 44 (1974), 31-60.

365   Sarrand, J. "Alix de Montmorency et Marguerite de Marly." *Bulletin de la
       Commission archéologique de Narbonne*, 32 (1970), 173-175. —

366   Sède, G. de. *Le secret des cathares.* L'aventure mystérieuse, 316. Paris: J'ai lu,
       1974. 304 p.

367   Shriver, G. H. "Images of catharism and the historian's task." *Contemporary
       reflections on the medieval Christian tradition: essays in honor of Ray C.
       Petry.* Ed. G. H. Shriver. Durham, N.C.: Duke University Press, 1974.
       p. 67-80. See 368.

368   ——. "A summary of 'Images of catharism and the historian's task." *CH̄*, 40
       (1971), 48-54. See 367.

369   Spire, O. "Horizons du catharisme." *Revue du Tarn*, 49 (1968), 87-98.

370   Swoboda, W. "Początki herezji na ziemiach polskich." *Europa – Słowiańs-
       zczyzna – Polska: studia ku uczczeniu profesora Kazimierza Tymieniec-
       kiego.* Prace Wydziału filozoficzno-historycznego, seria historia, 36.
       Poznań: Uniwersytet im Adama Mickiewicza, 1970. p. 385-396. [The
       beginnings of heresy in Poland]

371   [Syndicat d'Initiative de Mazamet.] *Exposition d'histoire locale: horizons cathares.*
       [Mazamet: Syndicat d'Initiative, 1966] 47 [+ 6] p.

372   Talbot, L. "Au-delà des cathares." *Atlantis*, 44, no. 256 (1970), 224-228. [Biblio-
       graphy, p. 229-231] —

373   Talmage, F. "An Hebrew polemical treatise, anti-cathar and anti-orthodox." *The
       Harvard theological review*, 60 (1967), 323-348.

374   Thouzellier, C. *Catharisme et valdéisme en Languedoc à la fin du XIIe et au début
       du XIIIe siècle.* Publications de la Faculté des lettres et sciences humaines de

Paris, Recherches, 27. Paris: Presses Universitaires de France, 1966.
2nd ed. Louvain: Nauwelaerts; Paris: Béatrice-Nauwelaerts, 1969.
525 p.

Rev. (1st ed.) A. Borst, *HZ*, 206 (1968), 737-739; J. A. Corbett, *CHR*, 54
(1969), 685-686; E. Delaruelle, *RHE*, 62 (1967), 482-489; J. Jolivet, *RHR*,
171 (1967), 87-90; M. D. Knowles, *EHR*, 83 (1968), 155-156; E. Magnou,
AM, 79 (1967), 233-238; E. Pásztor, *SM*, 3rd ser., 8 (1967), 233-239; J. Paul,
RHEF, 54 (1968), 93-95; F. Pirot, *MA*, 74 (1968), 123-126; K.-V. Selge, *TLZ*,
93 (1968), 116-118; T. Venckeleer, *RBPH*, 47 (1969), 993-997; W. L. Wakefield, *Speculum*, 41 (1966), 775-777.

Rev. (2nd ed.) H. Bernard-Maitre, *RSyn*, 90 (1969), 137-138; R. Cegna,
RSLR, 6 (1970), 406-409; J.-M. D'Heur, *RBPH*, 53 (1975), 564-565; M.
Erbstösser, *DLZ*, 91 (1970), 152-154; E. Griffe, *BLE*, 70 (1969), 138-140; G.
Leff, *MÆ*, 39 (1970), 364-366; R. Manselli, *CCM*, 12 (1969), 203-205; G.
Michiels, *RTAM*, 35 (1968), 327-329; R. Mols, *NRT*, 92 (1970), 1113-1114; C.
Morris, *JTS*, 21 (1970), 210-212; K.-V. Selge, *TLZ*, 94 (1969), 842; F. Simoni
Balis-Crema, *RSCI*, 26 (1972), 531-534; B. Smalley, *JEH*, 21 (1970), 184-186;
M. Villard, *BEC*, 128 (1970), 259-264; J. Vives, *AST*, 40 (1967), 386-387; E.
I. Watkin, *The Downside review*, 87 (1969), 309-314.

375 ——, ed. *Une somme anti-cathare: le* Liber contra manicheos *de Durand de
Huesca.* Spicilegium sacrum lovaniense, Études et documents, 32. Louvain: Spicilegium Sacrum Lovaniense, 1964. 376 p.

Rev. C. N. L. Brooke, *JTS*, 16 (1965), 530-531; J. Jolivet, *RHR*, 169 (1966),
77-80; G. Koch, *DLZ*, 87 (1966), 1094-1097; E. Pásztor, *SM*, 3d ser., 6
(1965), 309-312; S. Runciman, *JEH*, 16 (1965), 231-232; A. C. Shannon,
Speculum, 41 (1966), 182-183; B. Töpfer, *TLZ*, 92 (1967), 118-120; T.
Venckeleer, *RHE*, 62 (1967), 489-493.

376 ——. "Les versions bibliques utilisées par Durand de Huesca au début du XIIIe
siècle." *Mélanges Eugène Tisserant*, 1. Studi e testi, 231. Vatican: Biblioteca Apostolica Vaticana, 1964. p. 419-435.

377 Ventura Subirats, J. "El catarismo en Cataluña." *Boletín de la Real academia de
buenas letras de Barcelona*, 28 (1959-60), 75-168.

378 ——. "Le catharisme en Catalogne." Trans. L. Julien. *CEC*, 14, no. 19 (1963),
3-25.

379 Vicaire, M.-H. "Les cathares albigeois vus par les polémistes." *Cathares en
Languedoc*. p. 105-128. See 305.

380 ——. "L'élargissement universel de la prédication de saint Dominique en
Languedoc (1206-1217)." *Saint Dominique en Languedoc*. Cahiers de Fanjeaux, 1. Toulouse: Privat, c1966. p. 133-158.

381 Walther, D. "A survey of recent research on the Albigensian cathari." *CH*, 34
(1965), 146-177.

382 Warner, H. J. *The Albigensian heresy*. London, 1922-1928. Rpt. New York:
Russell and Russell [1967]. 2 v. in 1.

B. *Origins to 1200 (Entries 383 to 413)*

383   Angebert, J. *Catharisme et mystique solaire.* [Paris: Institut d'Herméneutique, 1973.] 27 p.

384   Angelov, D. "L'influence du bogomilisme sur les cathares d'Italie et de France." *Études historiques* (Sofia), 4 (1968), 175-190.

385   Bedin, J. "Les origines du catharisme languedocien." *Atlantis,* 43, no. 254 (1969), 6-10. —

386   Bonenfant, P. "Un clerc cathare en Lotharingie au milieu du xıı^e siècle." *MA,* 69 (1963), 271-280.

387   Crema, G. "I catari nel territorio veronese e il loro rifugio di Sirmione (secolo xıı)." Diss. Università Cattolica del Sacro Cuore, Milan (sede di Brescia), 1973. —

388   Dando, M. *Les origines du catharisme.* Cahiers du Cercle Ernest-Renan, 56. Paris: Cercle Ernest-Renan, 1967; Paris: Pavillon, [1968]. 46 p.

389   Delaruelle, E. "La ville de Toulouse vers 1200 d'après quelques travaux récents." *Saint Dominique en Languedoc.* Cahiers de Fanjeaux, 1. Toulouse: Privat, c1966. p. 107-122.

390   Dossat, Y. "À propos du concile cathare de Saint-Félix: les Milingues." *Cathares en Languedoc.* p. 201-214. ill. See 305.

391   Dupuy-Pacheraud, F. "De Zoroastre et Mani aux doctrines cathares." *Atlantis,* 43, no. 254 (1969), 19-37. —

392   Duvernoy, J. "Les 'Actes de Saint-Félix' sont-ils des faux?" *CEC,* 19, no. 40 (1968-69), 16-20.

393   Fau, G. *De Priscillien aux cathares: survivances gnostiques en occident.* Cahiers du Cercle Ernest-Renan, 84. Paris: Cercle Ernest-Renan, 1974. 24 p.

394   Gérard, A. "Qui a instruit les cathares?" *Atlantis,* 43, no. 254 (1969), 55-59. —

395   Griffe, E. "Le catharisme dans le diocèse de Carcassonne et le Lauragais au xıı^e siècle." *Cathares en Languedoc.* p. 215-236. See 305.

396   ——. *Les débuts de l'aventure cathare en Languedoc (1140-1190).* Paris: Letouzey et Ané, 1969. 218 p., map.
      Rev. J. Lecler, *Études,* 331 (1969), 764-765; J. Jolivet, *RHR,* 179 (1971), 98-99; R. Mols, *NRT,* 97 (1975), 764-765; O. de Saint-Blanquat, *BEC,* 130 (1972), 635-637; J. Séguy, *ASSR,* 31 (1971), 205-206; K.-V. Selge, *ZKG,* 82 (1971), 393-396; Y. Dossat, *AM,* 84 (1972), 328-329.

397   ——. "Les débuts de l'implantation cathare en Toulousain et en Albigeois." *BLE,* 68 (1967), 107-127.

398   Hamilton, B. "The cathar council of Saint-Félix reconsidered." *AFP,* 48 (1978), 23-53.

399   Manselli, R. "C'è davvero una risposta dell'occidente a Zaratustra nel medioevo?" With discussion. *Atti del Convegno internazionale sul tema: La Persia nel medioevo (Roma, 31 marzo – 5 aprile 1970).* Rome: Accademia Nazionale dei Lincei, 1971. p. 69-86.

400   ——. "Ecberto di Schönau e l'eresia catara in Germania all metà del secolo XII." *Arte e storia: studi in onore di Leonello Vincenti*. Turin: Giappichelli, 1965. p. 309-338.

401   Marc-Manoël, A. "Introduction du catharisme dans le pays castrais par les vallées de l'Agout et du Gijou." *CEC*, 22, no. 52 (1971), 44-51.

402   Picasso, G. "Note sul contributo di alcune collezioni canoniche alla storia religiosa milanese del sec. XII." *Problemi di storia religiosa lombarda*. Como: Cairoli, c1972. p. 65-73.

403   Primov, B. "Medieval Bulgaria and the dualistic heresies in Western Europe." *Études historiques à l'occasion du XIe Congrès international des sciences historiques – Stockholm, août 1960* [= *Études historiques*, 1]. Sofia: Académie des sciences de Bulgarie, 1960. p. 79-106. Incl. summaries.

404   Roché, D. "De Platon aux chrétiens cathares par les origènistes et les manichéens." *CEC*, 16, no. 26 (1965), 26-52.

405   ——. "Le moyen-âge chrétien, selon le Professeur R. Morghen." *CEC*, 14, no. 18 (1963), 13-25.

406   Russell, J. "Les cathares de 1048-1054 à Liège." *Bulletin de la Société d'art et d'histoire du diocèse de Liège*, 42 (1961), 1-8.

407   Šanjek, F. "Le rassemblement hérétique de Saint-Félix-de-Caraman (1167) et les églises cathares au XIIe siècle." *RHE*, 67 (1972), 767-799.

408   Topentcharov, V. *Boulgres et cathares: deux brasiers une même flamme*. Paris: Seghers, c1971. 205 p.

409   Vicaire, M.-H. "Saint Dominique à Prouille, Montréal et Fanjeaux." *Saint Dominique en Languedoc*. Cahiers de Fanjeaux, 1. Toulouse: Privat, c1966. p. 15-33, ill.

410   ——. "Sources méridionales de l'histoire de saint Dominique." *Saint Dominique en Languedoc*. Cahiers de Fanjeaux, 1. Toulouse: Privat, c1966. p. 34-40.

411   Vitray Meyerovitch, E. de, and D. Bogdanovic. "Aux origines du mouvement cathare? Les Bogomiles." *Archeologia*, 75 (oct. 1974), 62-69, ill.

412   Walther, D. "Studies in catharism (Albigenses of southern France, *ca.* twelfth century)." *American philosophical society, Year book 1964*, p. 629-632. [Summary of funded research project]

413   Werner, E. "Geschichte des mittelalterlichen Dualismus: neue Fakten und alte Konzeptionen." *ZG*, 23 (1975), 538-551.

C. *Albigensian Crusade (Entries 414 to 503)*

414   Alimena, P. "La crociata contro gli albigesi nelle lettere di Innocenzo III." Diss. Università di Roma, 1968. —

415   Bagley, C. P. "*Paratge* in the anonymous *Chanson de la croisade albigeoise*." *French studies*, 21 (1967), 195-204.

416   Belperron, P. *La croisade contre les albigeois et l'union du Languedoc à la France (1209-1249)*. Paris, 1942. Rvsd. rpt. Paris: Perrin, c1967. 477 p. ill.

417   Berge-Lefranc, P. *Le catharisme et la croisade des albigeois*. Rouen: Cour d'Appel, [1971]. 21 p.

418   Blaquière, H. "Les hospitaliers en Albigeois à l'époque de la croisade: la commanderie de Rayssac." *Paix de Dieu et guerre sainte en Languedoc au XIIIe siècle*. Cahiers de Fanjeaux, 4. Toulouse: Privat, c1969. p. 335-351.

419   Bonnaud-Delamare, R. "La convention régionale de paix d'Albi de 1191." *Paix de Dieu et guerre sainte en Languedoc au XIIIe siècle*. Cahiers de Fanjeaux, 4. Toulouse: Privat, c1969. p. 91-101.

420   Bouysson, P., and S. Bouysson. "Le combat de Montgey." *Revue du Tarn*, 86 (1977), 177-196. —

421   Boyer, C. "Pèlerinage d'un Occitan à Lévis-Saint-Nom: à la recherche de souvenirs sur le second chef de la croisade albigeoise Guy de Lévis." *Bulletin de la Société d'études scientifiques de l'Aude*, 71, no. 65 (1964-65), 287-294.

422   Briad, R. "Les châteaux forts du Languedoc cathare." *Les monuments historiques de la France*, 1977, no. 2, p. 50-60, ill.

423   Camboulives, R. "La bataille de Muret de 1213." *Bulletin de la Société de géographie de Toulouse*, 244 (1964), 3-9.

424   Capul, M. "Notes sur le catharisme et la croisade des albigeois en Agenais." *Revue de l'Agenais*, 90 (1964), 1-15, ill.

425   Cartier, J.-P. *Histoire de la croisade contre les Albigeois*. Paris: Grasset, c1968. 373 p.

426   Coincy-Saint-Palais, S. *Donjons et castels au pays des cathares: splendeurs défuntes des gloires occitanes*. 2nd ed. [Paris: by the author, 1964.] 430 p. ill.

427   ———. *La ville sainte des cathares*. [Paris: by the author, 1960.] 264 [+ 19] p. ill.

428   Curie-Seimbres, L. "La grande pitié de Minerve." *Revue du Tarn*, 53 (1969), 33-40.

429   ———. "Les 6.000 croisés d'Auvesine." *Revue du Tarn*, 55 (1969), 333-334.

430   Dalmau i Ferreres, R. *L'heretgia albigesa i la batalla de Muret*. Barcelona: Dalmau, c1960. 58 p.

431   Delaruelle, E. "La critique de la guerre-sainte dans la littérature méridionale." *Paix de Dieu et guerre sainte en Languedoc au XIIIe siècle*. Cahiers de Fanjeaux, 4. Toulouse: Privat, c1969. p. 128-139.

432   ———. "L'idée de croisade dans la *Chanson* de Guillaume de Tudèle." *Annales de l'Institut d'études occitanes*, 1962-63, p. 49-63. —

433   ———. "Paix de Dieu et croisade dans la Chrétienté du XIIe siècle." *Paix de Dieu et guerre sainte en Languedoc au XIIIe siècle*. Cahiers de Fanjeaux, 4. Toulouse: Privat, c1969. p. 51-71.

434   ———. "Les saints militaires de la région de Toulouse." *Paix de Dieu et guerre sainte en Languedoc au XIIIe siècle*. Cahiers de Fanjeaux, 4. Toulouse: Privat, c1969. p. 174-183.

435   ——. "Templiers et hospitaliers en Languedoc pendant la croisade des Albi-
       geois." *Paix de Dieu et guerre sainte en Languedoc au xiii*ᵉ *siècle*. Cahiers
       de Fanjeaux, 4. Toulouse: Privat, c1969. p. 315-334.

436   Delor, J. "La Réole et la croisade des Albigeois." *Les cahiers du Réolais*, 18, no. 66
       (1966), 2-4.

437   Delpoux, C. "Les comtes de Toulouse et le catharisme." cec, 22, no. 49 (1971), 42-
       55; 22, no. 52 (1971), 28-40; 23, no. 53 (1972), 30-45; 24, no. 60 (1973),
       28-37; 25, no. 61 (1974), 18-23; 25, no. 62 (1974), 46-52; 25, no. 64
       (1974), 22-44; 26, no. 67 (1975), 38-48.

438   Dossat, Y. "À propos du chroniqueur Guillaume de Puylaurens." *Gens et choses
       de Bigorre*. Fédération des sociétés académiques et savantes de Languedoc-
       Pyrénées-Gascogne, Fédération Gascogne-Adour, Actes de leur xxiiᵉ Con-
       grès d'études régionales. [Paris]: c.n.r.s., 1967. p. 47-52.

439   ——. "La croisade vue par les chroniqueurs." *Paix de Dieu et guerre sainte en
       Languedoc au xiii*ᵉ *siècle*. Cahiers de Fanjeaux, 4. Toulouse: Privat, c1969.
       p. 221-259.

440   ——. "Simon de Montfort." *Paix de Dieu et guerre sainte en Languedoc au
       xiii*ᵉ *siècle*. Cahiers de Fanjeaux, 4. Toulouse: Privat, c1969. p. 281-302.

441   Drutel, M. "Un Mount Segur de Champagne: Lou Mont Aimé (Marno)." *Gai
       saber*, 59, no. 385 (1977), 12-18.

442   Ducam, P. "Un drin d'istori: la crousade albigèse." *Reclams de Biarn e Gascou-
       gne*, 65, nos. 9-10 (1961), 138-142. —

443   Dupré, J. "Le catharisme et la croisade en Périgord." cec, 17, no. 32 (1966-67),
       27-37.

444   Dupront, A. "Guerre sainte et Chrétienté." *Paix de Dieu et guerre sainte en
       Languedoc au xiii*ᵉ *siècle*. Cahiers de Fanjeaux, 4. Toulouse: Privat, c1969.
       p. 17-50.

445   Durban, P. *Itinéraires en pays cathares*. [Finhan]: Cap e Cap, 1976. 127 p. ill.
       Rev. C. Delpoux, cec, 29, no. 79 (1978), 62-63.

446   Duvernoy, J., ed. and trans. *Guillaume de Puylaurens, Chronique; Chronica
       magistri Guillelmi de Podio Laurentii*. Paris: c.n.r.s., 1976. 230 p.
       Rev. J.-L. Lemaitre, rhef, 64 (1978), 135-136; A. Patschovsky, daem, 34
       (1978), 603-604; B. Töpfer, zg, 25 (1977), 1118-1119.

447   Evans, A. P. "The Albigensian crusade." *A history of the crusades, II: The later
       crusades, 1189-1311*. Ed. R. L. Wolff and H. W. Hazard. Philadelphia:
       University of Pennsylvania Press, c1962. p. 277-324.

448   Eydoux, H. P. "Châteaux sauvages de France." *Aesculape*, 55, no. 5 (1972),
       3-68, ill.

449   Foreville, R. "Arnaud Almaric, archevêque de Narbonne (1196-1225)." *Nar-
       bonne: archéologie et histoire*. Montpellier: [Fédération historique du
       Languedoc méditerranéen et du Roussillon], 1973. II, 129-146.

450   ——. "Innocent iii et la croisade des Albigeois." *Paix de Dieu et guerre sainte en*

Languedoc au XIIIe siècle. Cahiers de Fanjeaux, 4. Toulouse: Privat, c1969. p. 184-217.

451   Galibert, R. "Ancienneté du catharisme: importance de la croisade des albigeois en Agenais." *Annales de l'Institut d'études occitanes*, 1962-63, p. 80-86. —

452   Garrigue, G. "Conséquences de la croisade albigeoise en Bigorre." *CEC*, 23, no. 55 (1972), 55-57.

452A   Gastand, A. "Chronologie schématique de la croisade." *CEC*, 30, no. 83 (1979), 54-57.

453   Gibert, U. "Notes concernant la croisade contre les albigeois dans les Corbières occidentales." *Bulletin de la Société d'études scientifiques de l'Aude*, 72 (1972), 193-205. Rpt. in *CEC*, 25, no. 62 (1974), 27-45, ill.

454   Griffe, E. *Le Languedoc cathare au temps de la croisade (1209-1229).* Paris: Letouzey et Ané, 1973. 253 p.
       Rev. R. Mols, *NRT*, 97 (1975), 764-765; J. Paul, *RHEF*, 61 (1975), 266-269.

455   ———. *Le Languedoc cathare de 1190 à 1210.* Paris: Letouzey et Ané, 1971. 320 p.
       Rev. Y. Dossat, *CCM*, 16 (1973), 172-173; R. Mols, *NRT*, 97 (1975), 764-765; J. Paul, *RHEF*, 61 (1975), 266-269; O. de Saint-Blanquat, *BEC*, 130 (1972), 635-639.

456   *Guerre contre les albigeois par un anonyme occitan-français*, 1-. Croisade contre les albigeois, 2 – . [Carcassonne: Cercle artistique et littéraire occitan, 1971 – .] 229 p.

457   Guida, S. "L'attività poetica di Gui de Cavaillon durante la crociata albigese." *Cultura neolatina*, 33 (1973), 235-271.

458   [Guizot, F., trans.] *Chronique de Guillaume de Puylaurens, XIIIe s.* Croisade contre les Albigeois, 1. [Carcassonne: Centre littéraire occitan; Toulouse: Midi, 1970.] 148 p. ill.

459   Hamilton, B. *The Albigensian crusade.* Historical Association pamphlets, G.85. London: Historical Association, 1974. 40 p.

460   Julien, L. "Archéologie et histoire." *CEC*, 17, no. 31 (1966), 33-38.

461   Kovarik, R. J. "The Albigensian crusade: a new view." *Studies in medieval culture*, 3 (1970), 81-91.

462   ———. "Simon de Montfort (1165-1218), his life and work: a critical study and evaluation based on the sources." Diss. St. Louis Univ. *DAI*, 25A (1964), 422-423.

463   Kuttner, S., and A. García y García. "A new eyewitness account of the Fourth Lateran Council." *Traditio*, 20 (1964), 115-178.

464   Lacger, L. de. *Histoire religieuse de l'Albigeois.* Albi: Sud-Ouest, 1962. 375 p.

465   Lafont, R. "Composition et rythme épiques dans la seconde partie de la *Chanson de la croisade albigeoise.*" *Revue de langue et littérature provençales*, 9 (1962), 42-56.

466 ——. "Las ideologias dins la part anomima de la *Cançon de la crosada.*" *Annales de l'Institut d'études occitanes,* 1962-63, p. 87-94. —

467 Lejeune, R. "L'esprit de croisade dans l'épopée occitane." *Paix de Dieu et guerre sainte en Languedoc au xiiie siècle.* Cahiers de Fanjeaux, 4. Toulouse: Privat, c1969. p. 143-173.

468 Lignières, M. *L'hérésie albigeoise et la croisade.* Paris: Scorpion, 1964. 192 p.
    Rev. Y. Dossat, *ccm,* 8 (1965), 446.

469 Luchaire, A. *Innocent iii, 2: La croisade des albigeois.* 2nd ed. Paris, 1906. Rpt. Farnborough, Hants.: Gregg, 1969. 262 p.

470 Madaule, J., R. Nelli, and M. Roquebert. *Albigeois et cathares.* Réalmont: Taurines, 1976. 146 p. ill. [Catalogue of 1972 exhibit at Réalmont]
    Rev. Y. Roqueta, *Revue du Tarn,* 85 (1977), 144-145. —

471 Martin-Chabot, E., ed. and trans. *La chanson de la croisade albigeoise.* 3 v. Les classiques de l'histoire de France au moyen âge, 13, 24, 25. Paris: Belles Lettres (v. 1: Champion), 1931-1961. Reissued 1972.
    Rev. Y. Dossat, *am,* 74 (1962), 336-337.

472 Marvejols. Hôtel de ville. *Catalogue de l'exposition Marvejols et la croisade albigeoise, Bernard Sicart de Marvejols, organisée à l'Hôtel de ville de Marvejols, 14 juillet – 1er septembre 1964.* Marvejols: Hôtel de ville, 1964. 18 p. ill. —

473 Montégut, O. de. *Le drame albigeois: dénouement tragique de l'histoire secrète du moyen âge.* Paris: Nouvelles éditions latines, 1962. 190 p.

474 Mouzat, J. "Une croisade oubliée: l'expédition Auvergnate, Limousin et Aquitaine contre les cathares de Quercy et de l'Agenais, mai-juin 1209." *Bulletin de la Société scientifique, historique et archéologique de la Corrèze,* 96 (1974), 79-86. —

475 Mundy, J. H. "La croisade contre les albigeois et l'interdiction de l'usure à Toulouse." *Archeologia,* 19 (nov.-déc. 1967), 28-33, ill.

476 Nelli, R. "Le vicomte de Béziers (1185-1209) vu par les troubadours." *Paix de Dieu et guerre sainte en Languedoc au xiiie siècle.* Cahiers de Fanjeaux, 4. Toulouse: Privat, c1969. p. 303-314.

477 Niel, F. "La dernière nuit de Montségur." *Cahiers du sud,* 61 (1966), 221-226.

478 Ormières, P. "Identification de l'anonyme de la *Chanson de la croisade.*" *Bulletin de la Commission archéologique de Narbonne,* 34 (1972), 153-160. —

479 *Paix de Dieu et guerre sainte en Languedoc au xiiie siècle.* Cahiers de Fanjeaux, 4. Toulouse: Privat, c1969. 366 p., ill.
    Rev. F. Simoni, *sm,* 3rd ser., 12 (1971), 1127-1131; H. Maisonneuve, *rhe,* 66 (1971), 598-605; R. Mols, *nrt,* 94 (1972), 876-877; B. Guillemain, *am,* 83 (1971), 113-117.

480 Paladilhe, D. *Les grandes heures cathares.* Paris: Perrin, c1969. 281 p. ill.

481 Piquemal, M. "Fanjeaux, berceau d'hommes illustres." *cec,* 29, no. 79 (1978), 40-42.

482   Pitangue, F. "Aspects historiques de la guerre contre les Albigeois: fut-elle une croisade? une guerre de religion? ou une expédition politique?" *Bulletin de l'Académie des sciences et lettres de Montpellier*, n.s. 1 (1970), 53-67.

483   "La prise de Pujol: signification de cet épisode à la veille de Muret." *Annales de l'Institut d'études occitanes*, 1962-63, p. 124-132. —

484   Read, J. "The 'Catholic' and the 'believers': Pedro II of Aragon and the Albigenses." *History today*, 25 (1975), 826-833, ill.

485   Renouard, Y. "La famille féodale la plus marquante de l'occident au XIIIe siècle: les Montfort." *Études d'histoire médiévale*. Paris: SEVPEN, 1968. II, 959-976. Rpt. from *L'information historique*, 9 (1947), 85-94.

486   Roquebert, M. "Citadelles du vertige." *Plaisir de France*, 371 (1969), 50-59, ill.

487   ——. "La crise albigeoise et la fin de l'autonomie occitane." *Annales de l'Institut d'études occitanes*, 4th ser., 2, no. 6 (1972), 119-171.

488   ——. *L'épopée cathare, 1198-1212: l'invasion.* Toulouse: Privat, c1970. 595 p. ill.
      Rev. R. L. de Lavigne, *TLS*, 13 October 1978, p. 1176; P. Wolff, *AM*, 91 (1979), 107-109.

489   ——. *L'épopée cathare, 1213-1216: Muret ou la dépossession.* Toulouse: Privat, c1977. 487 p. ill.
      Rev. P. Rousset, *SZG*, 28 (1978), 184-185; R. Mols, *NRT*, 100 (1978), 613; R. L. de Lavigne, *TLS*, 13 October 1978, p. 1176; N. Coulet, *ETR*, 53 (1978), 587-589; P. Wolff, *AM*, 91 (1979), 107-109.

490   ——, and C. Soula. *Citadelles du vertige.* Toulouse: Imprimerie régionale, 1966. 188 p. ill.

491   Rousseau, H. "L'interprétation du catharisme." *Annales*, 24 (1969), 138-141.

492   Sénesse, P. D. *Languedoc, ici fut brûlée l'âme de Jésus.* Paris: Scorpion, c1964. 189 p.

493   Sicard, G. "Paix et guerre dans le droit canon du XIIe siècle." *Paix de Dieu et guerre sainte en Languedoc au XIIIe siècle.* Cahiers de Fanjeaux, 4. Toulouse: Privat, c1969. p. 72-90.

494   Simonde de Sismondi, J. C. L. *History of the crusades against the Albigenses in the thirteenth century.* London, 1826; rpt. New York: AMS, 1973. xl, 266 p. Trans., with introductory essay by anon. translator, from his *Histoire des Français*, v. 6 and 7 (1823 and 1826).

495   Strayer, J. R. *The Albigensian crusades.* New York: Dial Press, 1971. [xi], 201 p.
      Rev. F. L. Cheyette, *Speculum*, 48 (1973), 411-415; J. B. Russell, *AHR*, 77 (1972), 1433; W. L. Wakefield, *CHR*, 60 (1974), 134-136; H. L. Stansell, *Review for religious*, 31 (1972), 152.

496   Sumption, J. *The Albigensian crusade.* London: Faber and Faber, 1978. 269 p.
      Rev. D. H. Williams, *Cîteaux*, 28 (1978), 146-147; J. Read, *History today*, 28 (1978), 271; M. Lambert, *TLS*, 27 October 1978, p. 1254; R. Cobb, *New statesman*, 7 July 1978, p. 23-24; T. Zeldin, *The listener*, 99 (1978), 341;

A. K. McHardy, *The expository times*, 89 (1978), 376-377; E. E. Y. Hales, *The tablet*, 232 (1978), 351-353; B. Hamilton, *History*, 64 (1979), 443-445.

497　Valcernet, L. *Occitanie: la tragédie cathare, survivance du catharisme.* Paris: Pensée universelle, c1977. 192 p.

498　Veltman, W. F. *Sänger und Ketzer.* Trans. E. Julius. Zeist: Vrij Geestesleven, 1967. 84 p. Orig. publ. in *Vrije opvoedkunst*, 26 (1962).

499　Ventura, J. *Pere el Catòlic i Simó de Montfort.* Biblioteca biogràfica catalana, 24. Barcelona: Aedos [1960]. 341 p. ill.

500　Vicaire, M.-H. "'L'affaire de paix et de foi' du midi de la France (1203-1215)." *Paix de Dieu et guerre sainte en Languedoc au xiiie siècle.* Cahiers de Fanjeaux, 4. Toulouse: Privat, c1969. p. 102-127.

501　———. "Les clercs de la croisade." *Paix de Dieu et guerre sainte en Languedoc au xiiie siècle.* Cahiers de Fanjeaux, 4. Toulouse: Privat, c1969. p. 260-280.

502　Wakefield, W. L. "The family of Niort in the Albigensian crusade and before the inquisition." *Names*, 18 (1970), 97-117, 286-303.

503　———. *Heresy, crusade and inquisition in southern France, 1100-1250.* Berkeley and Los Angeles: University of California Press; London: George Allen and Unwin, 1974. 288 p.

Rev. F. T. Allmand, *The month*, 235 (1974), 780-781; M. Barber, *JEH*, 26 (1975), 181-182; C. N. L. Brooke, *MÆ*, 44 (1975), 333-334; C. H. Lawrence, *HJ*, 16 (1975), 325-326; G. Leff, *EHR*, 90 (1975), 883; J. N. Hillgarth, *AHR*, 81 (1976), 113-114; C. Morris, *History*, 61 (1976), 99; J. Mundy, *CHR*, 62 (1976), 78-79; B. H. Rosenwein, *CH*, 44 (1975), 247; J. O. Ward, *JRH*, 8 (1975), 424-426; A. White, *New Blackfriars*, 56 (1975), 286-287; anon., *TLS*, 9 Aug. 1974, p. 862; R. M. Golden, *JCS*, 18 (1976), 548-550; J. B. Russell, *Speculum*, 52 (1977), 448-449; M. Turnell, *The tablet*, 228 (1974), 747; Y. Dossat, *AM*, 87 (1975), 370-372.

Ọ. *After 1200 (Entries 504 to 564)*

504　Angebert, J. M. "Une hérésie cathare en Corse au xive siècle: les Giovannali." *Folklore*, 23, no. 140 (1971), 8-13.

505　Blasco, R. "Les 'Judas' de Montségur." *CEC*, 28, no. 75 (1977), 54-59.

506　Bonnal, A. H. *Guide de Montségur, la Peyregade, Morenci, Roquefixade, les monts d'Olmes.* Paris: Éditions du Temps, c1969. 128 p. ill.

507　———. "Montségur, château-temple." *Connaissance du monde*, n.s. 4 (1962), 20-30.

508　Cazenave, A. "Les cathares en Catalogne et Sabarthès, d'après les registres d'inquisition: la hiérarchie cathare en Sabarthès après Montségur." *BPH*, 1969 (1972), p. 387-436, ill.

509　———. "L'entraide cathare et la chasse à l'hérétique en Languedoc au xiiie siècle." *Actes du 96e congrès national des sociétés savantes, Toulouse, 1971,*

section de philologie et d'histoire jusqu'à 1610. Paris: Bibliothèque Nationale, 1978. II, 97-125. —

510 Davis, N. Zemon. "Les conteurs de Montaillou." *Annales*, 34 (1979), 61-73.

511 Delaruelle, E. "Les avatars du catharisme du xive au xxe siècle." *Archeologia*, 19
     (nov.-déc. 1967), 34-41, ill.

512 ——. "Saint Louis devant les cathares." *Septième centenaire de la mort de saint
     Louis. Actes des colloques de Royaumont et de Paris (21-27 mai 1970).*
     Paris: Belles Lettres, 1976. p. 273-280.

513 Delcor, M. "L'*Ascension d'Isaïe* à travers la prédication d'un évêque cathare en
     Catalogne au quatorzième siècle." *RHR*, 185 (1974), 157-178.

514 Delpoux, C. "Alphonse de Poitiers et l'inquisition." *CEC*, 27, no. 69 (1976), 47-55;
     no. 70 (1976), 27-44.

515 ——. "Le catharisme en Armagnac." *CEC*, 21, no. 48 (1970-71), 28-34.

516 Dengerma, J. *Les cinq cents cathares emmurés de Lombrives.* Foix: Gadrat-
     Doumenc, 1967. 48 p.

517 ——. *Montségur, symbòle d'amour?* [Suc-et-Sentenac: by the author], 1968.
     88 p. ill.

518 Deschamps, A., and D. Roché. "Découvertes à Montségur." *CEC*, 15, no. 24 (1964-
     65), 30-35, ill.

519 Dossat, Y. "À propos du prieur des Pauvres catholiques: Durand de Huesca ou
     de Losque en Rouergue?" *BPH*, 1967 = *Actes du 92e Congrès national des
     Sociétés savantes tenu à Strasbourg et Colmar.* Paris: Bibliothèque Natio-
     nale, 1969. II, 673-685.

520 ——. "Un évêque cathare originaire de l'Agenais, Vigouroux de la Bacone." *BPH*,
     1965 = *Actes du 90e Congrès national des Sociétés savantes tenu à Nice.*
     Paris: Bibliothèque Nationale, 1968. p. 623-639.

521 Durban, J. *Montségur: citadelle occitane, haut-lieu cathare.* [Finhan]: Cap e Cap,
     [1976]. 47 p. ill.
     Rev. C. Delpoux, *CEC*, 29, no. 79 (1978), 63-64.

522 Duvernoy, J. "Albigeois et vaudois en Quercy, d'après le registre des pénitences de
     Pierre Sellan." *Moissac et sa région.* Fédération des sociétés académiques
     et savantes de Languedoc-Pyrénées-Gascogne, Actes du xixe Congrès
     d'études régionales. [Paris]: C.N.R.S., 1964. p. 110-121.

523 ——. "Bertrand Marty." *CEC*, 19, no. 39 (1968), 19-35.

524 ——. "Guilhabert de Castres." *CEC*, 18, no. 34 (1967), 32-42.

525 ——. "Pierre Autier." *CEC*, 21, no. 47 (1970), 9-49.

526 Eydoux, H. P. "Un grand récit historique: la fin du château de Montségur."
     Pensée française, 19, nos. 7-8 (1960), 48-60.

527 Ferlus, J. *Autour de Montségur: de l'histoire ou des histoires?* [Perpignan: Impri-
     merie du Midi, 1960.] 147 p.

528 Ilarino da Milano. "Il dualismo cataro in Umbria al tempo di S. Francesco."
     Filosofia e cultura in Umbria tra medioevo e rinascimento: atti del IV

convegno di studi umbri. Perugia: Università degli studi, Facoltà di lettere e filosofia, 1967. p. 175-216. —

529   Julien, L. "Montségur pendant le siège de 1243-44." *CEC*, 27, no. 71 (1976), 65-71.

530   Kercorb, E. "Les chevaliers d'Usson." *CEC*, 27, no. 72 (1976), 47-48.

531   Lapoudge, C. "Montségur oublié." *Le cerf-volant*, 40 (1962), 30-33. —

532   Le Roy Ladurie, E. *Montaillou, village occitan de 1294 à 1324*. Paris: Gallimard, 1975. 642 p. Trans. B. Bray, *Montaillou: cathars and Catholics in a French village, 1294-1324* (London: Scolar Press, 1978); *Montaillou: the promised land of error* (New York: Braziller, 1978), xvii, 383 p.

       Rev. J. Dariège, *CEC*, 27, no. 71 (1976), 91-96; [P. Quennell], *History today*, 27 (1977), 405-406; P. F. Moreau, *La nouvelle revue française*, no. 279 (March 1976), 93-95; J. Paul, *RHEF*, 63 (1977), 85-86; R. Fossier, *BEC*, 135 (1977), 196-200; M. Doni Garfagnini, *ASI*, 135 (1977), 281-282; R. Wernick, *Smithsonian*, 8, no. 12 (March 1978), 114-130, ill.; R. Cobb, *New statesman*, 95 (1978), 779-781; E. Benson, *The French review*, 51 (1978), 931-932; M. J. Walsh, *HJ*, 20 (1979), 101-102; N. Zemon Davis, *Annales*, 34 (1979), 61-73; R. S. Lopez, *The chronicle of higher education*, 11 December 1978, p. R-12; J. Bossy, *Encounter*, 49, no. 5 (1977), 73-75; G. H. Shriver, *Religious studies review*, 5 (1979), 133; C. Morris, *History*, 64 (1979), 85-86; D. Vidović, *Pregled*, 67 (1977), 1504-1508; H. Cooper, *MÆ*, 48 (1979), 151-152.

533   Lévis-Mirepoix, A., duc de. "Montségur: le catharisme et l'unité nationale." *Archeologia*, 10 (nov.-déc. 1967), 8-15, ill.

534   Manning, W. F. "Three curious miniatures of Saint Dominic." *AFP*, 38 (1968), 43-46, ill.

535   Manselli, R. "Les hérétiques dans la société italienne du 13ᵉ siècle." *Hérésies et sociétés* (1968). p. 199-202. See 65.

536   Merklen, P. "Les brûlés de Beoulaygues: un épisode agenais du drame cathare (1249)." *CEC*, 21, no. 45 (1970), 20-35.

537   "Montségur: naissance d'un mythe au xxᵉ siècle." Contributions by R. Pernoud, A. P. M. Lévis-Mirepoix, S. Stym-Popper, E. Delaruelle, and J. H. Mundy. *Archeologia*, 19 (nov.-déc. 1967), 7-43, ill. See 544, 533, 555, 511, 475.

538   Moulis, A. *Montségur et le drame cathare, avant, pendant, après la tragédie*. Verniolle: by the author, 1968. 154 p. ill. 2nd ed., c1972 (171 p., ill.).

539   Nelli, R., trans. "Le folklore de Montségur vu par Otto Rahn (*Luzifers Hofgesind*: la cour de Lucifer, 1937)." *Folklore* (Carcassonne), 26, no. 1 (1973), 14-17.

540   Niel, F. *Les cathares de Montségur*. Paris: Seghers, c1973. 329 p. ill.

541   ——. *Montségur, le site, son histoire*. Grenoble: Allier, 1962. 309 p. ill. —

542   ——. *Montségur, temple et forteresse des cathares d'Occitanie*. Grenoble: Allier, 1967. 402 p. ill.

543   Oldenbourg, Z. *Le bûcher de Montségur, 16 mars 1244*. Trente journées qui ont fait la France, 6. Paris: Gallimard, 1967. 454 p. ill. Orig. publ. 1959. Trans.

P. Green, *Massacre at Montségur: a history of the Albigensian crusade* (London: Weidenfeld and Nicolson; New York: Pantheon, c1961), [xii] 420 p., ill.

Rev. (Eng. trans.) C. T. Wood, *Speculum*, 37 (1962), 645-647.

544 Pernoud, R. "Montségur: naissance d'un mythe au xxᵉ siècle." *Archeologia*, 19 (nov.-déc. 1967), 7.

545 Rihs, W. *Le manuscrit de Montségur*. Geneva: Éditions C3, Bettex, 1976. 188 p. —

Rev. A. del Moral, CEC, 28, no. 73 (1977), 98-101; H. Valeix, CEC, 27, no. 70 (1976), 77.

546 Roché, D. "À Montségur." *L'initiation*, 41 (1967), 55-58. —

547 ——. "Dominicains et cathares." CEC, 18, no. 34 (1967), 3-8.

548 ——. "Inauguration d'une stèle du souvenir aux martyrs cathares de Montségur." CEC, 11, no. 7 (1960), 3-5.

549 ——. "Un traité cathare inédit du début du xiiiᵉ siècle d'après le *Liber contra manicheos* de Durand de Huesca." CEC, 12, no. 10 (1961), 3-17.

550 *Saint Dominique en Languedoc*. Cahiers de Fanjeaux, 1. [Toulouse]: Privat, c1966. 178 p. ill. map.

Rev. R. W. Emery, *Speculum*, 43 (1968), 190-191; B. Guillemain, AM, 83 (1971), 101-103; W. A. Hinnebusch, CHR, 54 (1969), 686-687; J. Lecler, *Études*, 326 (1967), 131-132; R. Mols, NRT, 90 (1968), 435.

551 Šanjek, F. "Albigeois et 'chrétiens' bosniaques." RHEF, 59 (1973), 251-267.

552 ——. "Les 'chrétiens bosniaques' et le mouvement cathare au moyen âge." RHR, 182 (1972), 131-181, ill.

553 ——. *Les chrétiens bosniaques et le mouvement cathare, xiiᵉ-xvᵉ siècles*. Publications de la Sorbonne, N.S. recherches, 20. Louvain: Nauwelaerts, [1976]. 260 p. ill. maps.

Rev. R. Granier, CEC, 28, no. 74 (1977), 78-81.

554 Sarrand, J. "Qui était Bouchart de Marly, prisonnier du seigneur de Cabaret?" *Mémoires de la Société des arts et des sciences de Carcassonne*, 6 (1968-70), 121-122. —

555 Stym-Popper, S. "Fouilles à Montségur (une interview)." *Archeologia*, 19 (nov.-déc. 1967), 16-19, ill.

556 Thouzellier, C. "Le 'Liber antiheresis' de Durand de Huesca et le 'Contra hereticos' d'Ermengaud de Béziers: autour de la polémique anti-cathare." RHE, 55 (1960), 130-141. Rvsd. rpt. in her *Hérésie et hérétiques* (Rome: Storia e Letteratura, 1969), p. 39-52.

557 ——. *Un traité cathare inédit du début du xiiiᵉ siècle d'après le* Liber contra Manicheos *de Durand de Huesca*. Bibliothèque de la Revue d'histoire ecclésiastique, 37. Louvain: Bibliothèque de l'Université, 1961. 119 p.

Rev. E. Delaruelle, RHE, 60 (1965), 524-528; M. Reeves, JEH, 14 (1963),

95-96; W. L. Wakefield, *Speculum*, 36 (1961), 689-690; E. Werner, DLZ, 83 (1962), 669-672.

558 Ventura Subirats, J. "Catharisme et valdisme en pays catalan." CEC, 25, no. 63 (1974), 30-39.

559 ——. "Les derniers contacts entre le catharisme et la Catalogne." Trans. L. Julien. CEC, 16, no. 26 (1965), 8-19; 16, no. 28 (1965-66), 26-37.

560 ——. "Hérétiques du Roussillon et de Cerdagne au temps de Jaime Ier." Trans. L. Julien. CEC, 15, no. 21 (1964), 49-56; 15, no. 23 (1964), 3-12; 15, no. 24 (1964-65), 4-12; 16, no. 25 (1965), 3-10.

561 Wakefield, W. L. "Some unorthodox popular ideas of the thirteenth century." MH, n.s. 4 (1973), 25-35.

562 Waltenberg, H. "Méditations sur le château de Montségur." CEC, 27, no. 72 (1976), 37-42, ill.

563 ——. "Montségur." CEC, 27, no. 72 (1976), 43-46.

564 ——. "Les secrets de Montségur." CEC, 26, no. 65 (1975), 3-7, ill.

E. *Doctrine and Society (Entries 565 to 709)*

565 Abel, A. "Aspects sociologiques des religions 'manichéennes'." *Mélanges offerts à René Crozet*. Éd. P. Gallais and Y.-J. Riou. Poitiers: Société d'études médiévales, 1966. I, 33-46.

565A Abels, R., and E. Harrison, "The participation of women in Languedocian catharism." MS, 41 (1979), 215-251.

566 Adhémar de Panat, L. d'. "Note sur la croix dite 'de Toulouse' et les croix discoïdales de l'Aveyron." *Revue du Rouergue*, 16, no. 61 (1962), 54-62. —

567 Alatri, M. da. "'Eresie' perseguite dall'inquisizione in Italia nel corso del duecento." *The concept of heresy in the middle ages* (1976). p. 211-224. See 25.

568 Ambelain, R. "Le dualisme dans la religion cathare." *L'initiation*, 40 (1966), 143-146. —

569 Anatole, C. "Sur une stèle discoïdale de la Couvertoirade." CEC, 11, no. 5 (1960), 3-6.

570 Arès, J. d'. *Cathares et Albigeois, hérésie ou retour aux sources?* Paris: Institut d'herméneutique, 1972. 22 p. —

571 Berger, D. "Christian heresy and Jewish polemic in the twelfth and thirteenth centuries." *Harvard theological review*, 68 (1975 [c1977]), 287-303.

572 Bordenave, J., and M. Vialelle. *Aux racines du mouvement cathare: la mentalité religieuse des paysans de l'Albigeois médiéval*. Toulouse: Privat, c1973. 350 p., ill.
Rev. J. Paul, RHEF, 60 (1974), 367-369; H. Taviani, *Annales*, 31 (1976), 525-527; R. Mols, NRT, 97 (1975), 153-154; J.-C. Schmitt, ASSR, 40 (1975), 198-199.

573 Bordenave, J., and M. Vialelle. "Aux racines du mouvement cathare albigeois: les monuments funéraires chthoniens." *Document Archeologia*, 2 (1973), 92-99, ill. —

574 Borghi, L. "La lingua della Bibbia di Lione (ms. Palais des arts 36): vocalismo." *Cultura neolatina*, 30 (1970), 5-58.

575 Borst, A. *Les cathares*. Trans. of *Die Katharer* (Stuttgart, 1953) with afterword by C. Roy. Bibliothèque historique. Paris: Payot, 1974. 290 p.
Rev. J. Paul, *RHEF*, 61 (1975), 78-81; R. Mols, *NRT*, 97 (1975), 764.

576 Briad, R. "Pèlerinage aux lieux saints du catharisme." *Plaisir de France*, 268 (1961), 4-15.

577 [Broëns, M.] "Les 'texerants' pseudo-cathares et leurs hypogées." *Chthonia*, 3 (1964), 1-16.

578 Canal, H. L. "La double voie cathare." *L'initiation*, 42 (1968), 15-36. —

579 Cazenave, A. "Bien et mal dans un mythe cathare languedocien." *Die Mächte des Guten und Bösen*. Ed. A. Zimmermann. Miscellanea mediaevalia, 11. Berlin and New York: de Gruyter, 1977. p. 344-387.

580 Cegna, R. "*Oportet et haereses esse*: Guido Terreni su Catari e Valdesi." *RSLR*, 3 (1967), 28-64.

581 Chabert, Peire [collective pseudonym]. *Actualité du catharisme*. Toulouse: Crux de Lux, 1961. 58 p.

582 Chapeau, G. "Sur une stèle discoïdale et un signe lapidaire de la Couvertoirade." *CEC*, 11, no. 7 (1960), 6-9.

583 Clédat, L., ed. *Le Nouveau Testament traduit au XIIIe siècle en langue provençale suivi d'un rituel cathare: reproduction photolithographique du manuscrit de Lyon, publiée avec une nouvelle édition du rituel*. Paris, 1887; rpt. Geneva: Slatkine, 1968. xxvii, 482 p.

584 Curie-Seimbres, L. "À propos des croix cathares du Lauragais." *Revue du Tarn*, 65 (1972), 85-86.

585 Dando, M. "L'adaptation provençale de l'*Elucidarium* d'Honoré d'Autun et le catharisme." *CEC*, 28, no. 74 (1977), 3-34.

586 Delaruelle, E. "L'art cathare." *Archeologia*, 19 (nov.-déc. 1967), 20-27, ill.

587 ———. "Le catharisme en Languedoc vers 1200: une enquête." *AM*, 72 (1960), 149-167.

588 ———. "Problèmes socio-économiques à Toulouse vers 1200, à propos d'un livre récent [G. Koch, *Frauenfrage und Ketzertum*]." *Saint Dominique en Languedoc*. Cahiers de Fanjeaux, 1. Toulouse: Privat, c1966. p. 123-132, ill.

589 Dionysios, I. "La foi cathare." *Atlantis*, 43, no. 254 (1969), 60-65. —

590 Dorbes, R. "Les citadelles de la lumière: Peyrepertuse." *CEC*, 17, no. 32 (1966-67), 3-11, ill.

591 ———. "La mystérieuse archère du château de Quéribus." *CEC*, 16, no. 28 (1965-66), 3-10, ill.

592 Dossat, Y. "Les cathares d'après les documents de l'inquisition." *Cathares en Languedoc.* p. 71-104. See 305.

593 ——. "Catharisme et Gascogne." *Bulletin de la Société archéologique, historique, littéraire et scientifique du Gers,* 73 (1972), 149-168.

594 Double, L. "La croix de Toulouse et son ésotérisme, ou les secrets de la croix aux douze perles." *Atlantis,* 43, no. 254 (1969), 81-86. ——

595 Durban, P. *Actualité du catharisme.* Toulouse et Bordeaux: P. Durban (Cercle d'études et recherches de psychologie analytique), c1968. 224 p.

596 Duvernoy, J. "Albigéisme ou catharisme?" *Cahiers du sud,* 61 (1966), 196-220.

597 ——. "Les albigeois dans la vie sociale et économique de leur temps." *Annales de l'Institut d'études occitanes,* 1962-63, p. 64-72. ——

598 ——. *Le catharisme: la religion des cathares.* Toulouse: Privat, c1976. 404 p. ill. Rev. H. Jacobs, *NRT,* 99 (1977), 437-438; I. Alban, *CEC,* 28, no. 75 (1977), 77-80; C. Thouzellier, *RHR,* 193 (1978), 218-225; P. Petit, *ETR,* 53 (1978), 111-113.

599 ——. "L'exégèse cathare de Jean ı, 3-4." *CEC,* 19, no. 40 (1968-69), 12-15.

600 ——. "La liturgie et l'église cathares." *CEC,* 18, no. 33 (1967), 3-16; 18, no. 35 (1967), 17-30.

601 ——. "Un traité cathare du début du xıııᵉ siècle." *CEC,* 13, no. 13 (1962), 22-54, ill.

602 ——, and C. Thouzellier. "Une controverse sur l'origine du mot 'cathares'." *AM,* 87 (1975), 341-349.

603 Dykmans, M. "De Jean xxıı au concile de Florence, ou les avatars d'une hérésie gréco-latine." *RHE,* 68 (1973), 29-66.

604 Fano, A. "La dame à la licorne ou 'l'Encaminamen catar'." *Synthèses,* 208 (1963), 219-231, ill.

605 Ferlus, J. "Troubadours et catharisme." *Société ariégeoise, sciences, lettres et arts: bulletin annuel,* 25 (1969), 113-125.

606 Flam, L. "Hétérodoxes, hérétiques, paradoxaux et sceptiques...." *Revue de l'Université de Bruxelles,* 13 (1960-61), 123-136.

607 Fornairon, E. *Le mystère cathare.* Paris: Flammarion, c1964. 234 p. ill. Trans. C. Ceretti, *La tragedia dei catari* (Milan: Sugar, [1969]), 288 p.

608 Fouché, P. "Les Cisterciens du xııᵉ siècle étaient-ils des initiés? Étude sur le symbolisme dans l'abbaye de Thoronet." *CEC,* 22, no. 50 (1971), 40-46.

609 Gadal, A. *Sur le chemin du Saint-Graal: les anciens mystères cathares.* Haarlem: Rozekruis-Pers, 1960. x, 147 p. ill.

610 Gandillac, M. de. "Manichéens et cathares." With discussion. *Entretiens sur l'homme et le diable* (Cerisy-la-Salle, 24 juillet – 3 août 1964). Ed. M. Milner. Paris and The Hague: Mouton, 1965. p. 95-114.

611 ——, et al. "Débat autour du catharisme et de l'amour courtois." *Entretiens sur la renaissance du 12ᵉ siècle* (Cerisy-la-Salle, 21 au 30 juillet 1965). Ed. M.

de Gandillac and E. Jeauneau. Paris and The Hague: Mouton, c1968. p. 437-448.

612 Gibert, U. "Cathares et cagots." *CEC*, 2nd ser., 80 (1978), 50-52.

613 Gobillard, A. "Le comté de Foix et le catharisme, de ses origines à 1325." Diss. École pratique des hautes études, Paris IV, 5th section, 1973. —

614 Gonnet, G. "Les *Glosa Pater* cathares et vaudoises." *Cathares en Languedoc.* p. 59-67. See 305.

615 Gouvernin, M., and A. Gouvernin. "Itinéraire cathare en Languedoc." *Atlantis,* 44, no. 255 (1970), 117-145. —

616 Griffin, R. "*Aucassin et Nicolette* and the Albigensian crusade." *Modern language quarterly,* 26 (1965), 243-256.

617 Guirdham, A. *The cathars and reincarnation.* London: Spearman, c1970. 208 p. ill. Trans. C. Brelet, *Les cathares et la réincarnation* (Paris: Payot, 1971). Rev. S. Tugwell, *The tablet,* 225 (1971), 10.

618 Hannedouche, S. "L'amour cathare." *CEC*, 20, no. 43 (1969), 23-29.

619 ——. "À propos de la gnose [glose] cathare sur le Pater." *CEC*, 21, no. 48 (1970-71), 3-11; 22, no. 49 (1971), 3-11.

620 ——. "L'initiation cathare." *CEC*, 19, no. 38 (1968), 35-40.

621 ——. "Réalité spirituelle du bien et du mal dans le catharisme." *CEC*, 18, no. 33 (1967), 54-62.

622 ——. "Le rituel cathare." *CEC*, 18, no. 35 (1967), 31-46.

623 ——. "Le roman spirituel de Barlaam et Josaphat." With trans. of text by R. Nelli. *CEC*, 18, no. 36 (1967-68), 6-11; 18, no. 37 (1968), 25-55; 18, no. 38 (1968), 13-28; 19, no. 40 (1968-69), 53-55; 20, no. 43 (1969), 30-64.

624 Heisig, K. "Eine gnostische Sekte im abendländischen Mittelalter." *ZRGG*, 16 (1964), 271-274.

625 Hollier, R. "Endura et ascèse mystique." *Atlantis,* 43 (1969), 66-68. —

626 Julien, L. "Le catharisme et la femme." *CEC*, 27, no. 69 (1976), 29-37.

626A ——. "Le catharisme, mouvement initiatique?" *CEC*, 30, no. 83 (1979), 31-38.

627 Koch, G. *Frauenfrage und Ketzertum im Mittelalter: die Frauenbewegung im Rahmen des Katharismus und des Waldensertums und ihre sozialen Wurzeln (12.-14. Jahrhundert).* Forschungen zur mittelalterlichen Geschichte, 9. Berlin: Akademie-Verlag, 1962. 211 p.
     Rev. E. Delaruelle, *AM*, 78 (1966), 130-135, and *RHE*, 60 (1965), 159-161; A. Gerlich, *ZKG*, 74 (1963), 376-377; H. Mohr, *DLZ*, 86 (1965), 233-236; R. Morghen, *CCM*, 9 (1966), 239-243, and *BISIM*, 81 (1969), 297-316; R. Nelli, *Folklore* (Carcassonne), 18, no. 4 (1965), 28-30.

628 ——. "Die Frau im mittelalterlichen Katharismus und Waldensertum." *SM*, 3rd ser., 5 (1964), 741-774.

629 Lamarque, R. "Le catharisme est-il une religion?" *CEC*, 29, no. 78 (1978), 32-42.

630 Lambert, M. D. "The motives of the cathars: some reflections." *Religious moti-*

vation: biographical and sociological problems for the church historian.
Studies in church history, 15. Oxford: Blackwell, 1978. p. 49-59.

631 Lee, S. "The struggle between Cistercian and Cathar, 1145-1220 A.D., and its possible influence on Holy Grail literature." Diss. New York University, 1975. 162 p. Abstract: *DAI*, 36A (1975), 3656.

632 Lévis-Mirepoix, A. P. M. "La doctrine que professaient les cathares au moyen âge: la répression dont ils firent l'objet à cette époque." *Historia*, hors série, no. 36 (July 1974), 2-11. —

633 Lionel, F. "Le bien et le mal et la foi cathare." *CEC*, 25, no. 61 (1974), 51-57.

634 Llobet, G. de. "Variété des croyances populaires au comté de Foix au début du XIVᵉ siècle d'après les enquêtes de Jacques Fournier." *La religion populaire en Languedoc du XIIIᵉ siècle à la moitié du XIVᵉ siècle.* Cahiers de Fanjeaux, 11. Toulouse: Privat, 1976. p. 109-126.

635 Loos, M. "Gnosis und mittelalterlicher Dualismus." *LF*, 90 (1967), 116-127. [Incl. Czech summary]

636 Madec, G. "*Nichil* cathare et *nihil* augustinien." *Revue des études augustiniennes*, 23 (1977), 92-112.

637 Manselli, R. "Amicizia spirituale ed azione pastorale nella Germania del sec. XII: Ildegarde di Bingen, Elisabetta ed Ecberto di Schönau contro l'eresia catara." *Studi in onore di Alberto Pincherle.* Studi e materiali di storia delle religioni, 38. Rome: Ateneo, 1967. I, 302-313.

638 ———. "Dolore e morte nella esperienza religiosa catara." *Il dolore e la morte nella spiritualità dei secoli XII e XIII.* Convegni del Centro di studi sulla spiritualità medievale, 5. Todi: Accademia Tudertina, 1967. p. 233-259.

639 ———. "Églises et théologies cathares." *Cathares en Languedoc.* p. 129-176. See 305.

640 ———. "Il miracolo e i catari." *BSSV*, 140 (1976), 15-19.

641 ———. "Per la storia della fede albigese nel secolo XIV: quattro documenti dell'inquisizione di Carcassona." *Studi sul medioevo cristiano offerti a Raffaello Morghen.* Rome: Istituto Storico Italiano per il Medio Evo, 1974. I, 499-518.

642 Marc-Manoël, A. "Le petit village de Burlats et ses grands seigneurs." *CEC*, 24, no. 60 (1973), 51-60.

643 Marks, C. *Pilgrims, heretics, and lovers: a medieval journey.* New York: MacMillan, c1975. xii, 338 p. ill.

644 Merelo de Barbera, S. "La famille des Barbera dans l'histoire de l'Occitanie et du catharisme." *CEC*, 28, no. 76 (1977), 43-53.

645 Mundy, J. "Noblesse et hérésie. Une famille cathare: les Maurand." *Annales*, 29 (1974), 1211-1223.

646 Nelli, R. "Le catharisme vu à travers les troubadours." *Cathares en Languedoc.* p. 177-197. See 305.

647 ——. "Contribution à l'iconographie du catharisme: la croix cathare." *Folklore* (Carcassonne), 16, no. 3 (1963), 2-11.

648 ——, comp. and trans. *Écritures cathares: La cène secrète, Le livre des deux principes, Traité cathare, Le rituel occitan, Le rituel cathare.* Rvsd. and enlgd. ed. Paris: Planète, c1968. 253 p. Orig. publ. Paris, 1959.

649 ——. *Le musée du catharisme.* [Toulouse]: Privat, c1966. 179 p. ill.
     Rev. E. Dardel, *RHPR*, 47 (1967), 72.

650 ——. *La nature maligne dans le dualisme cathare du XIIIᵉ siècle, de l'inégalité des deux principes.* Toulouse, Université, Travaux du Laboratoire d'ethnographie et de civilisation occitanes, 1. Carcassonne: Éditions de la revue *Folklore*, 1969. 23 p.

651 ——. "Note sur le 'pentagone' bogomile et cathare." *Folklore* (Carcassonne), 24, no. 1 (1971), 31-32.

652 ——. *Le phénomène cathare: perspectives philosophiques, morales et iconographiques.* Nouvelle recherche, 21. Toulouse: Privat; Paris: Presses universitaires de France, c1964. 2nd imp. 1967. 198 p. ill.
     Rev. M. Sendrail, *La table ronde*, no. 204 (1965), 15-21; E. Delaruelle, *CCM*, 11 (1968), 432-433; G. Michiels, *BTAM*, 9 (1964), 522-523; C. Martin, *NRT*, 101 (1979), 430-431; H. Rousseau, *Critique*, 213 (1965), 145-153.

653 ——. *La philosophie du catharisme: le dualisme radical au XIIIᵉ siècle.* Paris: Payot, 1975. 204 p.
     Rev. I. Alban, *CEC*, 27, no. 72 (1976), 77-78; A. Reix, *Revue philosophique de la France et de l'étranger*, 166 (1976), 239-240.

654 ——. "Réflexions sur le dualisme, le principe du mal et l'éternité du monde dans le catharisme médiéval." *Cahiers du sud*, 61 (1966), 181-195.

655 ——. *La vie quotidienne des cathares du Languedoc au XIIIᵉ siècle.* 3d ed. Paris: Hachette, c1969. 299 p.
     Rev. M. Pacaut, *RH*, 243 (1970), 505; J. C. Payen, *MA*, 78 (1972), 153-155; S. Bylina, *PH*, 62 (1971), 324-327; J. M. Mehl, *RHPR*, 50 (1970), 85-86; J. Lecler, *Études*, 331 (1969), 764-765; J. Paul, *RHEF*, 62 (1976), 406-407; U. Gibert, *Folklore* (Carcassonne), 22, no. 3 (1969), 23-24.

656 O'Brien, J. A. "Jews and cathari in medieval France." *Comparative studies in society and history*, 10 (1967-68), 215-220.

657 Pales-Gobillard, A. "Le catharisme dans le comté de Foix des origines au début du XIVᵉ siècle." *RHR*, 189 (1976), 181-200.

658 Pierrefeu, N. de. "Les horizons du catharisme (Conférence faite au Congrès de Montségur, Pentecôte 1961)." *CEC*, 12, no. 10 (1961), 18-31.

659 Primov, B. "Raĭner Sakoni kato izvor za bruzkite mezhdu katari, pavlikiani i bogomili." *Izsledvaniia v csest na Marin S. Drinov.* Sofia: Bulgarska akademiia na naukite, 1960. p. 535-570. [Incl. summary, "Reiner Sacchoni en tant que source historique sur les liens entre cathares, pauliciens et bogomiles"]

660   Qualben, J. D. "The language of exile: an historical typology for medieval and
      early modern dissent." Diss. Northwestern Univ. *DAI*, 33A (1973), 5644-
      5645.

661   Rahn, O. *Kreuzzug gegen den Gral: die Tragödie des Katharismus.* 3rd ed. [Ed. K.
      Rittersbacher.] Stuttgart: Günther, 1974. 305 p. ill. Orig. publ. Freiburg im
      Breisgau, 1933.

662   Riol, J.-L. "Dernières connaissances textuaires et folkloriques sur deux questions
      cathares: le salut spirituel et l'abrègement mystique de la vie (essai de
      critique historique)." *Bulletin de la Société des sciences, arts et belles-
      lettres du Tarn,* n.s. 21 (1961), 193-213.

663   Robin, G. "Les cathares: histoire et numismatique." *Cahiers numismatiques,* 19
      (1969), 659-668. —

664   Roché, D. "À propos du 'Traité cathare' du début du XIIIme siècle." *CEC,* 12, no. 12
      (1961-62), 29-40.

665   ——. "Les cathares, les Templiers et le Graal." *CEC,* 21, no. 47 (1970), 3-8.

666   ——. "Les cathares, précurseurs des temps modernes." *CEC,* 12, no. 12 (1961-62),
      41-47; 13, no. 13 (1962), 3-15.

667   ——. "Le catharisme." *Fédération historique du Languedoc méditerranéen et du
      Roussillon, XXXVIIe et XXXVIIIe congrès (Limoux-Nîmes, 1964-1965).*
      Montpellier: F.H.L.M.R. [1966]. p. 43-50, ill.

668   ——. *Le catharisme,* 1. Rvsd. ed. Narbonne: Cahiers d'études cathares, 1973.
      224 p.
      Rev. A. Sarg, *RHPR,* 54 (1974), 413.

669   ——. "Catharisme et science spirituelle." *CEC,* 24, no. 60 (1973), 3-14; 25, no. 61
      (1974), 3-17.

670   ——. *Contes et légendes du catharisme.* 4th ed. Arques: Cahiers d'études catha-
      res, [1971]. 142 p. ill. Orig. publ. 1951.

671   ——. "Le *Contra haereticos* d'Alain de Lille." *CEC,* 16, no. 28 (1965-66), 38-49;
      17, no. 29 (1966), 13-24.

672   ——. "Deuxième réponse à un pamphlet renouvelé: J.-L. Riol, Dernières con-
      naissances sur des questions cathares." *CEC,* 16, no. 25 (1965), 24-48.
      See 662.

673   ——. "Le Graal pyrénéen: cathares et Templiers." *CEC,* 23, no. 54 (1972), 3-23;
      no. 55, 10-25.

674   ——. "L'initiation cathare." *CEC,* 24, no. 59 (1973), 3-11.

675   ——. "Un recueil cathare: le manuscrit A.6.10 de la 'Collection vaudoise' de
      Dublin." *CEC,* 21, no. 46 (1970), 3-40.

676   ——. "Le rôle des entités sataniques et l'organisation du monde matériel." *CEC,*
      17, no. 31 (1966), 39-46.

677   ——. "La tragédie cathare." *CEC,* 11, no. 8 (1960-61), 23-42.

678   [——.] "XIIIe congrès de la Société du souvenir et des études cathares." *CEC,* 11,
      no. 8 (1960-61), 3-17, ill.

679   Rouanet, G. "Médecine cathare." *Revue du Tarn*, 44 (1966), 441-444.

680   Rougemont, D. de. *L'amour et l'occident*. Paris, 1939. Rpt. Paris: Plon, 1972. 314 p. [Numerous other reprints and translations]

681   Roy, C. "Pensée hindoue, pensée cathare: une même approche de la réalité." *CEC*, 2nd ser., 80 (1978), 24-34.

682   Sarret, J.-P. "Pour une archéologie du catharisme." *CEC*, 27, no. 70 (1976), 15-26.

683   Schmitz-Valckenberg, G. *Grundlehren katharischer Sekten des 13. Jahrhunderts: eine theologische Untersuchung mit besonderer Berücksichtigung von* Adversus catharos et valdenses *des Moneta von Cremona*. Veröffentlichungen des Grabmann-Institutes, n.s. 11. Munich, Paderborn, Vienna: Schöningh, 1971. xx, 351 p.
       Rev. R. E. Lerner, *Speculum*, 48 (1973), 404-406; A. S. Muñoz, *Archivo teologico granadino*, 34 (1971), 315-316; J. Ehlers, *HZ*, 216 (1973), 667-668; J. B. Russell, *CHR*, 58 (1973), 607-609; K. Esser, *FSt*, 54 (1972), 375-376, and 55 (1973), 88-89; F. Merzbacher, *AKK*, 142 (1973), 643-645; C. Vansteenkiste, *Römische Quartalschrift*, 71 (1976), 117-121; O. Schmucki, *CF*, 42 (1972), 422-424; F. Machilek, *Historisches Jahrbuch*, 95 (1977), 246-247; A. G. Matanić, *Antonianum*, 50 (1975), 584.

684   Sède, G. de. *Le trésor cathare*. Paris: Julliard, 1966. 217 p. ill. Republ. as *Le sang des cathares: l'Occitanie rebelle du moyen âge* (Paris: Plon, 1976). Trans. G. Lledo, *El tesoro cataro* (Barcelona: Plaza y Janes, 1968), 269 p.
       Rev. J. Dupré, *CEC*, 20, no. 41 (1969), 56-59.

685   Sendrail, M. "Le phénomène cathare." *La table ronde*, no. 204 (jan. 1965), 15-21. See 652.

686   Shahar, S. "Le catharisme et le début de la cabale." *Annales*, 29 (1974), 1185-1210.

687   ——. "Hakk'ath'arîzm vər'oshîth hakkabbalah bāll'anguedôk." *Tarbiz*, 40 (1971), 483-507. [Summary, p. vii-viii, "Catharism and the beginnings of the Kabbalah in Languedoc: elements common to the catharic scriptures and the book *Bahir*]

688   Smeets, J. R. *Joden en catharen – hun invloed op de Franse Rijmbijbels uit de twaalfde en dertiende eeuw*. Tilliburgis: Publikaties van de katholieke leergangen, 21. 's-Hertogenbosch: Malmberg, 1966. 16 p.

689   Söderberg, H. *La religion des cathares: étude sur le gnosticisme de la basse antiquité et du moyen âge*. Uppsala, 1949. Rpt. New York: AMS, 1978. 300 p.

690   Talbot, L. "Le Verbe et les cathares." *Atlantis*, 44, no. 255 (1970), 167-172. ——

691   Thomov, T. S. "Influences bogomiles bulgares dans le *Rituel cathare* de Lyon." *Actes du Colloque international de civilisation, littératures et langues romanes... Bucarest 1959*. [Bucarest: UNESCO, 1963]. p. 58-78. Publ. also in *Revue de langue et littérature provençales*, 7-8 (1961), 42-67.

692 Thouzellier, C. "La Bible des cathares languedociens et son usage dans la controverse au début du xiiie siècle." *Cathares en Languedoc*. p. 42-58. See 305.

693 ——. "Les cathares languedociens et le 'Nichil' (Jean, 1, 3)." *Annales*, 24 (1969), 128-138.

694 ——. "Controverse médiévale en Languedoc relative au sens du mot 'nichil'." *AM*, 82 (1970), 321-347. [Incl. additional note, "Sur l'égalité des deux dieux dans le catharisme"]

695 ——. "Controverses vaudoises-cathares à la fin du xiie siècle (d'après le livre ii du *Liber antiheresis*, MS. Madrid 1114 et les sections correspondantes du MS. BN Lat. 13446)." *Archives d'histoire doctrinale et littéraire du moyen âge*, 27 (1960), 137-227. Rvsd. rpt. in her *Hérésie et hérétiques* (Rome: Storia e Letteratura, 1969), p. 81-188.

696 ——, ed. *Livre des deux principes*. Sources chrétiennes, 198. Paris: Éditions du Cerf, 1973. 504 p.
Rev. E. Bozóky, *CCM*, 18 (1975), 178-179; C. N. L. Brooke, *JTS*, 25 (1974), 203-204; Y. Dossat, *RHE*, 70 (1975), 520-522; H. Forshaw, *The clergy review*, 59 (1974), 695-696; J. Jolivet, *RHR*, 187 (1975), 237-239; C. Martin, *NRT*, 96 (1974), 200; J. Paul, *RHEF*, 60 (1974), 142-143; W. L. Wakefield, *Speculum*, 50 (1975), 748-751; M. d'Alatri, *RSCI*, 30 (1976), 170-171; P. Courcelle, *Revue des études anciennes*, 76 (1974), 207-209; E. Magnou-Nortier, *AM*, 86 (1974), 109-110; C. Bérubé, *CF*, 44 (1974), 203-204; R. Nelli, *Folklore* (Carcassonne), 26, no. 2 (1973), 13-20, and *CEC*, 25, no. 61 (1974), 24-35; M. Oldoni, *SM*, 3rd ser., 18 (1977), 538-539.

697 ——, ed. and trans. *Rituel cathare*. Sources chrétiennes, 236. Paris: Cerf, 1977. 344 p. ill.
Rev. C. Bérubé, *CF*, 48 (1978), 200; M. T. Laureilhe, *Bulletin des bibliothèques de France*, 23 (1978), *237-238; J. M[onfrin], *Romania*, 99 (1978), 140-141; P. V[erbraken], *RB*, 88 (1978), 330-331; N. Coulet, *ETR*, 53 (1978), 587-589; Y. M. Duval, *Esprit et vie: l'ami du clergé*, 89 (1979), 96; C. N. L. Brooke, *JTS*, 29 (1978), 584-585; J. Jolivet, *RHR*, 194 (1978), 209-210; H. Maisonneuve, *RHE*, 74 (1979), 81-84; E. Magnou-Nortier, *AM*, 91 (1979), 331-333; O. de Saint-Blanquat, *BEC*, 137 (1979), 166-168.

698 ——. "Le vocable 'cathare' et la théorie des deux fils." *Économies et sociétés au moyen âge: mélanges offerts à Édouard Perroy*. Paris: Sorbonne, 1973. p. 650-660.

699 Thut-Weitnauer, M. "Symboles et graffiti de Provence." *CEC*, 13, no. 13 (1962), 16-20.

699A Tripp, D. "Initiation rites of the cathari." *Studia liturgica*, 12 (1977), 184-194.

700 Vachot, C. "Peut-on parler d'orthodoxie cathare?" *Études traditionnelles*, 67, no. 395 (1966), 118-125.

701 Vasoli, C. "Il 'Contra haereticos' di Alano di Lilla." *BISIM*, 75 (1963), 123-172.

702   Venckeleer, T. "Un recueil cathare: le manuscrit A.6.10 de la 'Collection vau-
        doise' de Dublin." *RBPH*, 38 (1960), 815-834; 39 (1961), 759-793.

703   Werner, E. "Die Entstehung der Kabbala und die südfranzösischen Katharer."
        Forschungen und Fortschritte, 37 (1963), 86-89.

704   ——. "Die Stellung der Katharer zur Frau." *SM*, 3d ser., 2 (1961), 295-301.

705   Wessley, S. "The composition of Georgius' *Disputatio inter catholicum et pateri-
        num hereticum*." *AFP*, 48 (1978), 55-61.

706   Wiersma-Verschaffelt, F. "Boeken en geloof der zuidfranse katharen." *Nederlands
        archief voor kerkgeschiedenis*, 46 (1963), 1-13.

707   Wild, G. *Bogumilen und Katharer in ihrer Symbolik, I: Die Symbolik des Katha-
        rertums und das Problem des heterodoxen Symbols im Rahmen der abend-
        ländischen Kultureinheit*. Wiesbaden: Steiner, 1970. xvi, 236 p. ill.
        Rev. M. Erbstößer, *DLZ*, 93 (1972), 759-760; R. Manselli, *SM*, 3rd ser., 13
        (1972), 880-886.

708   ——. "Stèles discoïdales en Allemagne." Trans. S. Hannedouche. *CEC*, 15, no. 23
        (1964), 44-47.

709   Wolff, P. "Villes et campagnes dans l'hérésie cathare." With discussion. *Hérésies
        et sociétés* (1968). p. 203-207. See 65.

Part Five

Valdes and Waldensians

Entries 710 to 855

A. *Valdes (Entries 710 to 723)*

710 Armand-Hugon, A. "Pierre Valdo, précurseur de la Réforme, et les Vaudois." *Bulletin de la société de l'histoire du protestantisme français*, 123 (1977), 300-305. —

711 Fédou, R. "Valdo en son temps." *Unité chrétienne*, 38 (1975), 26-34.

712 Gonnet, G. "La figure et l'œuvre de Vaudès dans la tradition historique et selon les dernières recherches." *Vaudois languedociens et Pauvres catholiques.* Toulouse: Privat, c1967. p. 87-109.

713 ———. "Valdès di Lione e Francesco d'Assisi." *Studi storici in onore di Gabriele Pepe*. [Bari]: Dedalo, 1969. p. 317-329.

714 Malleret, J. *Pierre Valdo et les pauvres de Lyon.* Lyon: Cour d'appel, 1968. 28 p. Summary in *Le tout Lyon et le Moniteur judiciaire réunis*, 1245 (1968), 3, 27-30.

715 Martini, M. *Pierre Valdo, le pauvre de Lyon: l'épopée vaudoise.* Geneva and Paris: Labor et fides, 1961. 172 p.
Rev. A. Molnár, *CV*, 6 (1963), 206; N. Coulet, *Foi et vie*, 62 (1963), 161.

716 Mohr, W. *Waldes von seiner Berufung bis zu seinem Tode.* Horn, Austria: Berger, [1971]. 75 p.
Rev. K.-V. Selge, *ZKG*, 86 (1975), 117-119; V. Vinay, *BSSV*, 134 (1973), 135-136.

717 Molnár, A. "L'initiative de Valdès et des Pauvres Lombards." *CV*, 9 (1966), 155-164, 251-266; 10 (1967), 153-164; 11 (1968), 85-93.

718 Molnar, E. S. "Two ecclesiological betrayals of pre-reformation movements." *ATR*, 47 (1965), 419-426.

719 Porsia, F. "Parallelismi tra Valdo e Francesco." *Studi storici in onore di Gabriele Pepe*. [Bari]: Dedalo, 1969. p. 331-355.

720 Selge, K.-V. "Caractéristiques du premier mouvement vaudois et crises au cours de son expansion." *Vaudois languedociens et Pauvres catholiques*. Toulouse: Privat, c1967. p. 110-142.

721 ———. "La figura e l'opera di Valdez." *BSSV*, 136 (1974), 3-25.

722 Tourn, G. *Valdo e la protesta valdese*. Bollettino della Società di studi valdesi, Supplemento, 134, no. 2. [Torre Pellice: Società di studi valdesi], 1974. 32 p. ill.

723 Verdat, M. "Nouvelles recherches sur l'origine et la vie lyonnaise de Valdo." *BSSV*, 125 (1969), 3-11.

B. *Waldensians (Entries 724 to 855)*

724 Appia, B. "Une famille vaudoise du Piémont du xive au xixe siècle." *BSSV*, 126 (1969), 37-61; 127 (1970), 3-39.

725 Audisio, G. "Les barbes vaudois – xve et xvie siècles." *BSSV*, 139 (1976), 65-75.

726 Baldinger, K. "Die piemontesischen und baden-württembergischen Waldenser. Ernst Hirsch zum 70. Geburtstag." *Zeitschrift für Dialektologie und Linguistik*, 41 (1974), 170-176.

727 Balmas, E. "Note su i lezionari e i sermoni valdesi." *Protestantesimo*, 29 (1974), 149-169.

728 ———. *Pramollo*. Suppl. to *BSSV*, 136. Torre Pellice: Società di studi valdesi, 1975. 49 p. ill.

729 ———, and M. Dal Corso. *I manoscritti valdesi di Ginevra*. Turin: Claudiana, 1977. 101 p. ill.
    Rev. A. Molnár, *CV*, 21 (1978), 161-165.

730 Beaupère, R. "Les 'pauvres de Lyon': un mouvement gauchiste chrétien en plein moyen âge." *Informations catholiques internationales*, no. 452 (15 mars 1974), 23-25, ill.

731 Borghi Cedrini, L. *Appunti per la lettura di un bestiario medievale: il Bestiario valdese*. Turin: Giappichelli, 1976. 145 p.

732 Bouchard, G. *I valdesi, una storia da rileggere*. Attualità protestante, 40. Turin: Claudiana, [1971]. 46 p., ill.

733 Braekman, E. M. "Les vaudois en Wallonie à la fin du moyen âge." *BSSV*, 136 (1974), 85-91.

734 Bredvei, P. A. *Martyrkirken som overlevde*. [Oslo]: Lunde, c1971. 156 p.

735 Cegna, R. "Appunti su valdismo e ussitismo: la teologia sociale di Nicola della Rosa Nera (Cerruc)." *BSSV*, 130 (1971), 3-34; 131 (1971), 3-42.

736 ———. "La dottrina ussita sull'usura nell'innesto valdese: i sermoni sull'usura del MS. 263 (c 5 26) di Dublino." *BSSV*, 140 (1976), 55-70.

737 ———. "Le fonti della teologia del valdismo alpino-occidentale nel '400." *BSSV*, 118 (1965), 17-21.

738 ———. "Il pensiero ussita nella teologia valdese del '400: note per una intro-duzione." *TZ*, 30 (1974), 138-151.

739 ———. "Per uno studio della genesi ideologica della violenza nel valdismo ussita in Piemonte." *BSSV*, 138 (1975), 15-53.

740 ———. "La polemica antivaldese di Samuele di Cassini o.f.m." *BSSV*, 115 (1964), 5-20.

741 ———. "Predestinazione ed escatologismo ussiti nel valdismo medievale." *BSSV*, 128 (1970), 3-28.

742 ———. "Storiografia ed ecclesiologia dei maestri valdesi nel ms. Dd xv 29 di Cambridge: valdesio e la chiesa di Dio." *BSSV*, 135 (1974), 3-25.

743 ———. "I Valdesi di Moravia nell'ultimo medio evo." *RSLR*, 1 (1965), 392-423.

744 ———. "Valdismo e ussitismo: mito e storia tra i fogli dei codici II-3320 della Biblioteca Nazionale di Varsavia e Mil IV 77 della Biblioteca Universitaria di Wroclaw." *BSSV*, 144 (1978), 27-44.

745 Coïsson, F. *Le interpretazioni del valdismo medievale in Italia dopo l'emancipazione*. Turin: Università di Torino, Istituto di paleografia e storia medievale, 1969. ———

746 Comba, Emilio. *History of the Waldenses of Italy, from their origin to the reformation*. Trans. T. E. Comba. London, 1889. Rpt. New York: AMS, 1978. viii, 357 p.

747 Comba, Ernesto. *Breve storia dei valdesi*. 4th ed. Turin: Claudiana, 1961. 199 p. Rev. C. Brütsch, *RHPR*, 42 (1962), 382-383; A. Molnár, *CV*, 5 (1962), 69.

748 Dehlinger, R. "Hérétiques, pénitents ou malades ... qui étaient les vaudois du Pays Messin et du Pays-Haut?" *Bulletin de l'Association des amis de vieux Longwy*, 1972, no. 3, p. 15-23. ———

749 Dossat, Y. "Les vaudois dans le Toulousain pendant la première moitié du XIIIe siècle." *Pierre de Fermat, Toulouse et sa région*. Fédération des sociétés académiques et savantes de Languedoc-Pyrénées-Gascogne, Actes du XXIe Congrès d'études régionales. Toulouse [and Paris]: C.N.R.S., 1966. p. 143-153.

750 ———. "Les Vaudois méridionaux d'après les documents de l'inquisition." *Vaudois languedociens et Pauvres catholiques*; Toulouse: Privat, c1967. p. 207-226.

751 Ducam, P. "La tragédie vaudoise." *Reclams de Biarn e Gascougne*, 66, nos. 11-12 (1962), 175-178. ———

752 Dupré-Theseider, E. "Gli eretici nel mondo comunale italiano." *BSSV*, 114 (1963), 3-23.

753 Duvernoy, J. "L'unité du valdéisme en France à la fin du XIIIe siècle (Bourgogne, Sillon rhodanien, Gascogne)." *BSSV*, 136 (1974), 73-83.

754 Fédou, R. "De Valdo à Luther: les 'pauvres de Lyon' vus par un humaniste lyonnais." *Religion et politique, les deux guerres mondiales, histoire de*

Lyon et du sud-est: mélanges offerts à M. le doyen André Latreille. Lyon: Audin, 1972. p. 417-421.

755 Giampiccoli, F., and C. Papini. *L'eredità del valdismo medievale.* Turin: Claudiana, c1974. 64 p., ill.

Rev. J.-M. Léonard, *ETR*, 49 (1974), 596-597.

756 Gonnet, G. "Casi di sincretismo ereticale in Piemonte nei secoli xiv e xv." *BSSV*, 108 (1960), 3-36.

757 ———. "Le cheminement des vaudois vers le schisme et l'hérésie (1174-1218)." *CCM*, 19 (1976), 309-345.

758 ———. "Le confessioni di fede valdesi prima della riforma." *BSSV*, 117 (1965), 61-95.

759 ———. *Le confessioni di fede valdesi prima della riforma.* Turin: Claudiana, 1967. 196 p.

Rev. R. Cegna, *RSLR*, 5 (1969), 193-194; H. Junghans, *TLZ*, 94 (1969), 224-225; V. Vinay, *ZKG*, 81 (1970), 121-124; F. Wendel, *RHPR*, 49 (1969), 86.

760 ———. "Le développement des doctrines vaudoises de Lyon à Chanforan (1170-1532)." *RHPR*, 52 (1972), 397-406.

761 ———. "La Donazione di Costantino presso gli eretici medioevali." *BSSV*, 132 (1972), 17-29.

762 ———. *Enchiridion fontium valdensium.* Turin: Claudiana, 1958 – . v. 1: 188 p.

763 ———. "Le interpretazioni tipiche del valdismo." *Protestantesimo*, 29 (1974), 65-91.

764 ———. "I primi valdesi erano veramente eretici?" *BSSV*, 123 (1968), 7-17.

765 ———. "La signification religieuse du mouvement vaudois." *BSSV*, 143 (1978), 5-13.

766 ———. "Tavola rotonda su: i manoscritti valdesi medievali." *BSSV*, 144 (1978), 21-25.

767 ———. "I valdesi d'Austria nella seconda metà del sec. 14 (con un'aggiunta sopra il nome, il luogo di nascita, il compagno e la missione di Valdo)." *BSSV*, 111 (1962), 5-41.

768 ———. "Les vaudois et la mystique rhénane." *RHPR*, 59 (1979), 143-159.

769 ———. "Les vaudois languedociens." *CV*, 10 (1967), 92-94.

770 ———. "Waldensia." *RSLR*, 2 (1966), 461-484.

771 ———, and A. Molnár. *Les vaudois au moyen âge.* Turin: Claudiana, [1974]. vii, 510 p.

Rev. J. Séguy, *ASSR*, 39 (1975), 229-230; J. H. Yoder, *The Mennonite quarterly review*, 50 (1976), 136-138; J. [Engels], *Vivarium*, 12 (1974), 173; E. Peschke, *TLZ*, 101 (1976), 859-862; W. L. Wakefield, *CHR*, 64 (1978), 291-292.

772 Groffier, J. *Qui sont les vaudois?* Apt-en-Provence: Reboulin, [1974]. 112 p.

Rev. J. M. Léonard, *ETR*, 50 (1975), 382.

773 Hammann, G. "Mittelalterliche Waldenser in Hessen: Nachrichten und Spuren." *Jahrbuch der hessischen kirchengeschichtlichen Vereinigung*, 27 (1976), 93-128.

774 ———. "Waldenser in Ungarn, Siebenbürgen und der Slowakei." *zof*, 20 (1971), 428-441.

775 Jolliot, A. "Les communautés vaudoises des hautes vallées alpines aux xve et xvie siècles." *Vivarais et Languedoc*. Fédération historique du Languedoc méditerranéen et du Roussillon, xlive congrès, Privas, 1971. Montpellier: Université Paul Valéry, 1972. p. 183-198.

776 Jolliot-Brenon, A. C. "Les livres des vaudois." École nationale des chartes, *Positions des thèses* (1970), p. 99-107.

777 ———. "Les manuscrits littéraires vaudois: présentation d'ensemble." *Cultura neolatina*, 38 (1978), 105-128.

778 Junker, F. *Die Waldenser: ein Volk unter Gottes Wort.* Zürich: evz-Verlag, c1969. 110 p. ill.

779 Kob, K. *Kleines Waldenserbuch: Erlebtes und Erfahrenes.* Berlin: Evangelische Verlagsanstalt [1973]. 191 p. ill.

780 Koch, G. "Waldensertum und Frauenfrage im Mittelalter." *Forschungen und Fortschritte*, 36 (1962), 22-26.

781 Kurze, D. "Märkische Waldenser und Böhmische Brüder: zur brandenburgischen Ketzergeschichte und ihrer Nachwirkung im 15. und 16. Jahrhundert." *Festschrift für Walter Schlesinger.* Ed. H. Beumann. Cologne and Vienna: Böhlau, 1973-74. II, 456-502.

782 ———. "Zur Ketzergeschichte der Mark Brandenburg und Pommerns vornehmlich im 14. Jahrhundert: Luziferianer, Putzkeller und Waldenser." *Jahrbuch für die Geschichte Mittel- und Ostdeutschlands*, 16-17 (1968), 50-94.

783 Leutrat, P. *Les vaudois.* Paris: Éditions Sociales, c1966. 252 p.
     Rev. [M.-R. Mayeux], *rhef*, 53 (1967), 385-386; R. Janin, *Revue des études byzantines*, 26 (1968), 385-386.

784 Lochman, J. M. "Not just one reformation: the Waldensian and Hussite heritage." *The reformed world*, 33 (1975), 218-224.

785 McCulloch, F. "The Waldensian bestiary and the *Libellus de natura animalium*." *mh*, 15 (1963), 15-30.

786 Maselli, D. "Il valdismo e i movimenti spirituali francescani: appunti di una ricerca di équipe." *bssv*, 136 (1974), 93-98.

787 Melia, P., ed. *The origin, persecutions, and doctrines of the Waldenses.* London, 1870. Rpt. New York: ams, 1978. xvi, 138 p. ill.

788 Merlo, G. G. "Distribuzione topografica e composizione sociale delle comunità valdesi in Piemonte nel basso medioevo." *bssv*, 136 (1974), 43-72.

789 ———. *Eretici e inquisitori nella società piemontese del trecento: con l'edizione dei processi tenuti a Giaveno dall'inquisitore Alberto de Castellario (1335) e*

nelle valli di Lanzo dall'inquisitore Tommaso di Casasco (1373). Turin: Claudiana, 1977. 316 p. ill.

Rev. E. Panella, *Memorie domenicane*, n.s. 8-9 (1977-78), 474; P. Péano, *AFH*, 71 (1978), 533-534; J. C. Schmitt, *ASSR*, 46 (1978), 279; H. Kaminsky, *AHR*, 84 (1979), 729-730.

790   Miolo, G. *Historia breve e vera de gl'affari de i valdesi delle valli.* Ed. E. Balmas. Turin: Claudiana, c1971. 156 p. ill.

Rev. G. Cherubini, *ASI*, 129 (1971), 553-554; A. Molnár, *RSLR*, 8 (1972), 388-390; J.-M. Hornus, *RHPR*, 54 (1974), 400-402.

791   Molnár, A. *A challenge to Constantinianism: the Waldensian theology in the middle ages.* Geneva: WSCF, 1976. iv, 74 p. ill.

792   ——. "Deux homélies de Pierre Valdès?" *CV*, 4 (1961), 51-58, ill.

793   ——. "Discreto viro: lettre inédite d'un apostat vaudois du xive siècle." *BSSV*, 119 (1966), 21-24.

794   ——. "Elementi ecclesiologici della prima riforma." *Protestantesimo*, 19 (1964), 65-77.

795   ——. "Fragment de la confession taborite dans un manuscrit vaudois de Cambridge." *MB*, 3 (1971), 253-264.

796   ——. "L'Internationale des taborites et des vaudois." *BSSV*, 122 (1967), 3-13.

797   ——. "La non-violence dans la première réforme (vaudois et hussites)." *Cahiers de la réconciliation*, June 1965, p. 3-31. —

798   ——. "Nuovi studi sui valdesi in Moravia." *Protestantesimo*, 21 (1966), 86-91.

799   ——. "Per un dialogo di contestazione (pagine di storia valdese)." *Protestantesimo*, 23 (1968), 147-156.

800   ——. "La révolte des vaudois préhussites." *RHPR*, 54 (1974), 3-13.

801   ——. "Riforma e rivoluzione nelle convinzioni teologiche dei taboriti." *BSSV*, 133 (1973), 17-28.

802   ——. "Sfida al costantinismo." *Protestantesimo*, 20 (1965), 1-12. —

803   ——. "Les 32 errores Valdensium de la Bohème." *BSSV*, 115 (1964), 3-4.

804   ——. "'Tresor e lume de fe': en marge du traité de dogmatique vaudoise." *CV*, 7 (1964), 285-289.

805   ——. "La Valdensium regula du manuscrit de Prague." *BSSV*, 123 (1968), 3-7.

806   ——. *Valdenští: evropský rozměr jejich vzdoru.* Prague: Kalich, 1973 [1974]. 327 p. [The Waldensians: the European dimension of their defiance] Cf. 771.

Rev. I. Hlaváček, *DAEM*, 30 (1974), 600-601; E. Peschke, *TLZ*, 101 (1976), 859-862; P. de Vooght, *RHE*, 70 (1975), 357-359; M. Vidlák, *CV*, 17 (1974), 241-250, and 18 (1975), 77-88.

807   ——. "I valdesi primitivi: setta religiosa o movimento rivoluzionario?" *Protestantesimo*, 29 (1974), 3-10.

808   ——. "Les vaudois en Bohême avant la révolution hussite." *BSSV*, 116 (1964), 3-17.

809 ——. "Les vaudois et les hussites." *BSSV*, 136 (1974), 27-35.

810 ——. "Les vaudois et l'Unité des frères tchèques." *BSSV*, 118 (1965), 3-16.

811 ——. "Vue nouvelle sur le valdisme médiéval." *BSSV*, 112 (1962), 51-59.

812 ——, and A. Armand-Hugon. *Storia dei valdesi*. Turin: Claudiana, c1974. 2 v. ill. [v. 1: A. Molnár, *Dalle origini all'adesione alla riforma (1176-1532)*]
Rev. M. Miele, *Sapienza*, 29 (1976), 477-480; E. Peschke, *TLZ*, 101 (1976), 859-862; J. Tedeschi, *CHR*, 63 (1977), 82-83; M. Erbstößer, *DLZ*, 97 (1976), 338-340; J. Séguy, *ASSR*, 44 (1976), 274.

813 Montet, E. *Histoire littéraire des vaudois du Piémont, d'après les manuscrits originaux conservés à Cambridge, Dublin, Genève, Grenoble, Munich, Paris, Strasbourg et Zurich*. Paris, 1885. Rpt. Geneva: Slatkine, 1977. xii, 245 p. ill.

814 [Mordant, L.] "Les vaudois et la bible." *BSSV*, 139 (1976), 77-81.

815 Morero, V. *Valdesi*. Turin: Asteria, [1963]. 148 p.
Rev. G. P. Gnudi, *Angelicum*, 43 (1966), 271-275.

816 Patschovsky, A., and K.-V. Selge, eds. *Quellen zur Geschichte der Waldenser*. Texte zur Kirchen- und Theologiegeschichte, 18. Gütersloh: Mohn, c1973. 106 p.
Rev. R. Cegna, *RSLR*, 10 (1974), 172-178; A. Molnár, *CV*, 16 (1973), 217-218; V. Vinay, *TLZ*, 100 (1975), 521-522; E. Potkowski, *Studia źródłoznawcze*, 21 (1976), 209-210.

817 Pezet, M. *L'épopée des vaudois: Dauphiné, Provence, Languedoc, Piémont, Suisse*. Paris: Seghers, c1976. 256 p. ill.
Rev. N. Coulet, *ETR*, 51 (1976), 536.

818 Polastro, M. "Ecclesiologia valdese." *BSSV*, 136 (1974), 117-132.

819 Rol, C. "Valdesi e cattolici in Val Pragelato." *RSCI*, 23 (1969), 135-143.

820 Ronchi de Michelis, L. "Il movimento valdese nella storiografia russa e sovietica." *BSSV*, 144 (1978), 71-76.

821 Santini, L. *De Pierre Valdo à l'église vaudoise*. Trans. J. F. Rebeaud. Geneva: Labor et fides, 1974. 118 p. —
Rev. P. Petit, *ETR*, 50 (1975), 94.

822 ——. *Il valdismo ieri e oggi*. Turin: Claudiana, 1965. 75 p. ill.
Rev. A. Molnár, *CV*, 8 (1965), 271.

823 Sauze, E. "L'installation des vaudois dans le Luberon." *BSSV*, 139 (1976), 57-63.

824 Scuderi, G. "I fondamenti teologici della non violenza nel valdismo anteriore al XVI secolo." *BSSV*, 129 (1971), 3-14.

825 ——. "Il sacramento del battesimo nella fede, nella pietà e nella teologia del valdismo medioevale (dalle origini a Chanforan) 1173-1532." *BSSV*, 124 (1968), 3-16.

826 Selge, K.-V. "L'aile droite du mouvement vaudois et naissance des Pauvres catholiques et des Pauvres réconciliés." *Vaudois languedociens et Pauvres catholiques*. Toulouse: Privat, c1967. p. 227-243.

827   ——. "Discussions sur l'apostolicité entre Vaudois, catholiques et cathares."
       Vaudois languedociens et Pauvres catholiques. Toulouse: Privat, c.1967.
       p. 143-162.
828   ——. "Einige Aspekte des frühen Waldensertums." *TZ*, 30 (1974), 131-137.
829   ——. "Die Erforschung der mittelalterlichen Waldensergeschichte." *Theologi-
       sche Rundschau*, 33 (1968), 281-343.
830   ——. *Die ersten Waldenser, mit Edition des Liber Antiheresis des Durandus von
       Osca* (v. 1: Untersuchung und Darstellung; v. 2: Der Liber Antiheresis
       des Durandus von Osca). Arbeiten zur Kirchengeschichte, 37. Berlin: de
       Gruyter, 1967. xviii, 320; xxvi, 287 p., ill.
       Rev. V. Vinay, *ZKG*, 81 (1970), 260-263; H. Grundmann, *DAEM*, 24 (1968),
       572-573; E. Pásztor, *SM*, 3d ser., 13 (1972), 1132-1135; R. Gerest, *Lumière
       et vie*, 18, no. 94 (1969), 128; F. Rapp, *RHPR*, 51 (1971), 97-98; A. Molnár,
       CV, 12 (1969), 91-92, *MB*, 1 (1969), 157-161, *Protestantesimo*, 24 (1969), 56-
       59, and *TLZ*, 95 (1970), 834-836; G. Mühlpfordt, *DLZ*, 90 (1969), 529-532;
       R. Cegna, *RSLR*, 5 (1969), 655-656; M. d'Alatri, *CF*, 39 (1969), 428-429, and
       Laurentianum, 10 (1969), 473-475; K. Rehberger, *MIÖG*, 79 (1971), 202-
       203; A. H. Thomas, *Tijdschrift voor filosofie*, 31 (1969), 788-790; A.
       Segovia, *Archivo teológico granadino*, 32 (1969), 391-393; L. V. Vaimal,
       BSSV, 125 (1969), 71-75.
831   ——. "Riflessioni sul carattere sociale e sulla religiosità del valdismo francese
       primitivo." *Protestantesimo*, 29 (1974), 11-39.
832   ——. "Il valdismo medievale tra conservazione e rivoluzione." *BSSV*, 133 (1973),
       3-16.
833   Shahar, S. "De quelques aspects de la femme dans la pensée et la communauté
       religieuses aux XIIᵉ et XIIIᵉ siècles." *RHR*, 185 (1974), 29-77.
834   Soggin, J. A. "L'istituto matrimoniale presso i Valdesi pre-riformati nella pro-
       blematica della storia generale del movimento." *Atti della Accademia na-
       zionale dei Lincei*, ser. 8, Rendiconti, 16 (1961), 102-107.
835   Thouzellier, C. "La profession trinitaire du vaudois Durand de Huesca." *RTAM*, 27
       (1960), 267-289. Rvsd. rpt. in her *Hérésie et hérétiques* (Rome: Storia e
       Letteratura, 1969), p. 53-79.
836   ——. "De Waldenzen." *Spiegel historiael*, 4 (1969), 425-430.
837   Tourn, G. *I valdesi: la singolare vicenda di un popolo-chiesa (1170-1976).* Turin:
       Claudiana, 1977. 231 p. ill.
       Rev. C. Cordié, *Paideia*, 32 (1977), 146; T. Aparicio, *Estudio agustiniano*,
       13 (1978), 184.
838   Trout, J. M. "Alan the missionary." *Citeaux*, 26 (1975), 146-154.
839   Valvekens, J. B. "Bernardus Fontis Calidi, abbas o. praem., et errores sui tempo-
       ris." *Analecta praemonstratensia*, 48 (1972), 143-146.
840   Vaucher, A.-F. "The history of conditionalism." *Andrews University seminary
       studies*, 4 (1966), 193-200.

841   Ventura Subirats, J. "La valdesía en Cataluña." *Boletín de la Real academia de buenas letras de Barcelona*, 29 (1961-62), 275-317.

842   Vicaire, M.-H. "Rencontre à Pamiers des courants vaudois et dominicain (1207)." *Vaudois languedociens et Pauvres catholiques*. Toulouse: Privat, c1967. p. 163-194.

843   ——. "Les Vaudois et Pauvres catholiques contre les cathares (1190-1223)." *Vaudois languedociens et Pauvres catholiques*. Toulouse: Privat, c1967. p. 244-272.

844   Villard, M. "Vaudois marseillais au xiiie siècle." *Provincia* (Marseille), 5, no. 281 (1968), 135-136.

845   Vinay, T. "Die Waldenser." *Die Wahrheit der Ketzer*. Ed. H. J. Schultz. Stuttgart and Berlin: Kreuz-Verlag, c1968. p. 60-71, 250-260.

846   ——. "La cosidetta Santa Cena valdese del duomo di Naumburg in Turingia." *BSSV*, 119 (1966), 3-20, ill.

847   ——. "Dottrine e origine dei valdesi, dei poveri di Lione, di Wiclif e Hus." *BSSV*, 143 (1978), 57-61.

848   ——. "Friedrich Reiser e la diaspora valdese di lingua tedesca nel xv secolo." *BSSV*, 109 (1961), 35-56. — Trans., "Friedrich Reiser und die waldensische Diaspora deutscher Sprache im xv. Jahrhundert," *Waldenser: Geschichte und Gegenwart*, ed. W. Erk (Frankfurt am Main: Lembeck, 1971), p. 25-47.

849   ——. "La prima e la seconda riforma nel passato e nel presente della chiesa valdese." *Protestantesimo*, 22 (1967), 129-147.

850   Walther, D. "Were the Albigenses and Waldenses forerunners of the reformation?" *Andrews University seminary studies*, 6 (1968), 178-202.

851   Werner, E. "Ideologische Aspekte des deutsch-österreichischen Waldensertums im 14. Jahrhundert." *SM*, 3rd ser., 4 (1963), 217-237. Trans. V. M. Volodarskiĭ, "Ideologiia nemetsko-avstriĭskogo val'denstva v xiv v.," *Srednie veka*, 25 (1964), 113-127, incl. Ger. summary.

852   ——. "Nachrichten über spätmittelalterliche Ketzer aus tschechoslovakischen Archiven und Bibliotheken." *Wissenschaftliche Zeitschrift der Karl-Marx Universität Leipzig*, Gesellschafts- und Sprachwissenschaftliche Reihe, Beilage, 12, no. 1 (1963), 215-284, ill.

853   Wunderli, P. "Die mittelalterlichen Bibelübersetzungen in Südfrankreich." *ZRGG*, 22 (1970), 97-112.

854   Wyrozumski, J. "Z dziejów waldensów w Polsce sredniowiecznej." *Universitas Iagellonica*. Prace historyczne zeszyt, 56. Kraków: Jagellonian University, 1977. p. 39-51. [Incl. summary, "Sur l'histoire des vaudois en Pologne au moyen âge"]

855   Zezschwitz, G. von. *Die Katechismen der Waldenser und Böhmischen Brüder als Documente ihres wechselseitigen Lehraustausches*. Kritische Textausgabe mit kirchen- und literargeschichtlichen Untersuchungen. Erlangen, 1863. Rpt. Amsterdam: Rodopi, 1967. x, 269 p.

Part Six

Poverty

ENTRIES 856 TO 892

856 Alatri, M. da. "Culto dei santi ed eretici in Italia nei secoli XII e XIII." *CF*, 45 (1975), 85-104.

857 Alessandro, V. d', ed. *Le pergamene degli umiliati di Cremona.* Università degli studi di Palermo, Istituto di storia, Testi e documenti, 2. Palermo: Manfredi, [1964]. 356 p.
Rev. R. Cegna, *RSLR*, 2 (1966), 346-348; M. L. Corsi, *Aevum*, 40 (1966), 200-202.

858 Anagnine, E. *Dolcino e il movimento ereticale all'inizio del trecento.* Biblioteca di cultura, 69. Florence: Nuova Italia, 1964. 285 p.
Rev. M. B. Becker, *Speculum*, 41 (1966), 105-106; S. Hannedouche, *CEC*, 18, no. 34 (1967), 49-51; R. Manselli, *HZ*, 205 (1967), 647-649; B. Nardi, *L'Alighieri*, 5, no. 2 (1964), 45-52; A. F. Grabski, *Kwartalnik historyczny*, 73 (1966), 165-167; G. Santonastaso, *Nuova antologia di lettere, arti e scienze*, 492 (sett.-dic. 1964), 124-125.

859 Bolton, B. "Innocent III's treatment of the *humiliati.*" *Popular belief and practice.* Ed. G. J. Cuming and D. Baker. Studies in church history, 8. Cambridge: Cambridge University Press, 1972. p. 73-82.

860 ———. "*Paupertas Christi:* old wealth and new poverty in the twelfth century." *Renaissance and renewal in Christian history.* Ed. D. Baker. Studies in church history, 14. Oxford: Blackwell, 1977. p. 95-103.

861 Bosl, K. *Das Problem der Armut in der hochmittelalterlichen Gesellschaft.* Österreichische Akademie der Wissenschaften, Phil.-hist. Klasse, Sitzungsberichte, 294, Abh. 5. Vienna: Österreichische Akademie der Wissenschaften, 1974. 29 p.

862 Bossi, A. *Fra Dolcino, gli apostolici e la Valsesia.* Borgosesia: Palmiro Corradini, 1973. 144 p.

863 Bylina, S. "La crise de la société existe-t-elle dans la conscience des groupes hérétiques du XIVe s.?" *MB*, 3 (1970), 163-175.

864 Capitani, O., ed. *La concezione della povertà nel medioevo*. Bologna: Pàtron, 1974. viii, 355 p.

865 Ciotti, A. "Fra Dolcino, Dante e i commentatori trecenteschi della *Commedia*." *Psicoanalisi e strutturalismo di fronte a Dante: dalla lettura profetica medievale agli odierni strumenti critici. Atti dei mesi danteschi 1969-1971*. Florence: Olschki, 1972. I, 429-442.

866 Classen, P. "Eschatologische Ideen und Armutsbewegungen im 11. und 12. Jahrhundert." *Povertà e ricchezza nella spiritualità dei secoli XI e XII*. Convegni del Centro di studi sulla spiritualità medievale, 8. Todi: Accademia Tudertina, 1969. p. 127-162.

867 Davis, N. Zemon. "Poor relief, humanism, and heresy: the case of Lyon." *Nebraska studies in medieval and renaissance history*, 5 (1968), 215-275.

868 Delaruelle, E. "L'idéal de pauvreté à Toulouse au XIIᵉ siècle." *Vaudois languedociens et Pauvres catholiques*. Toulouse: Privat, c1967. p. 64-84.

869 Elm, K. "Ausbreitung, Wirksamkeit und Ende der provençalischen Sackbrüder (Fratres de poenitentia Jesu Christi) in Deutschland und den Niederlanden: ein Beitrag zur kurialen und konziliaren Ordenspolitik des 13. Jahrhunderts." *Francia*, 1 (1973), 257-324.

870 Fanti, M. "Gli inizi del movimento dei disciplinati a Bologna e la Confraternita di Santa Maria della Vita." *Bollettino della Deputazione di storia patria per l'Umbria*, 66 (1969), 181-232.

871 Fumi, L. *Eretici e ribelli nell'Umbria: studio storico di un decennio (1320-1330)*. Città di Castello, 1916. Rpt. Rome; Multigrafica Editrice, 1974 (Biblioteca Umbra, 4). 195 p.

872 La Roncière, C. de. "L'église et la pauvreté à Florence au XIVᵉ siècle." *La pauvreté: des sociétés de pénurie à la société d'abondance*. Recherches et débats du Centre catholique des intellectuels français, n.s. 49. Paris: Fayard, [1964]. p. 47-66.

873 Little, L. K. *Religious poverty and the profit economy in medieval Europe*. Ithaca, N.Y.: Cornell University Press, 1978. xi, 267 p., ill.

874 López Rojo, M. "Los herejes de Durango (s. xv)." *Estudios de Deusto*, 24 (1976), 303-318.

875 Manteuffel, T. "Les mouvements des pauvres au moyen âge, saints et hérétiques." *Acta Poloniae historica*, 13 (1966), 5-13.

876 ——. *Narodziny herezji: wyznawcy dobrowolnego ubóstwa w średniowieczu*. Warsaw: Państwowe Wydawn. Naukowe, 1963. 146 p. Trans. I. Fischer, *Die Geburt der Ketzerei* (Vienna: Europa, [1965]), 124 p. Trans. A. Posner, *Naissance d'une hérésie: les adeptes de la pauvreté volontaire au moyen âge*, Civilisations et sociétés, 6 (Paris and The Hague: Mouton, 1970), 113 p.
Rev. J. Kłoczowski, *RHE*, 61 (1966), 375-376.
Rev. (French trans.) L. K. Little, *Speculum*, 47 (1972), 537-539; J. Jolivet,

RHR, 182 (1972), 105-106; C. M. de La Roncière, *RHEF*, 58 (1972), 95-97;
E. Mitre Fernández, *Hispania*, 120 (1972), 240-241; H. Maisonneuve, *RHE*,
67 (1972), 482-485.
Rev. (German trans.) H. Grundmann, *DAEM*, 21 (1965), 319.

877   Merlo, G. G. "Il problema di fra Dolcino negli ultimi vent'anni." *Bollettino
      storico-bibliografico subalpino*, 72 (1974), 701-708.

878   *Il movimento dei disciplinati nel settimo centenario dal suo inizio (Perugia 1260).*
      Convegno internazionale, Perugia, 25-28 settembre 1960. Deputazione di
      storia patria per l'Umbria, Bollettino, suppl. 9. Perugia, 1962. 652 p.
      Rev. A. Battistoni, *SM*, 3rd ser., 5 (1964), 198-208; R. Manselli, *RSCI*, 18
      (1964), 96-102; G. Sabatelli, *AFH*, 57 (1964), 396-405; E. Werner, *DLZ*, 85
      (1964), 36-40.

879   Nardi, B. "Fra Dolcino e il movimento ereticale all'inizio del trecento." *L'Alighieri*,
      5, no. 2 (1964), 45-52. Rpt. in his *Saggi e note di critica dantesca* (Milan
      and Naples: Ricciardi, 1966), p. 355-366. [Review essay based on 1964
      study by Anagnine. See 858.]

880   Paolini, L., and R. Orioli. *L'eresia a Bologna fra XIII e XIV secolo*. Istituto storico
      italiano per il medio evo, Studi storici, 93-96. Rome: I.S.I.M.E., 1975. 2 v.
      (v. 1, by Paolini, *L'eresia catara alla fine del duecento*; v. 2, by Orioli,
      L'eresia dolciniana).
      Rev. E. Werner, *ZG*, 26 (1978), 468-469.

881   Paul, J. "Mouvements de pauvreté et réflexion théologique au XIIIe siècle." *La
      pauvreté: des sociétés de pénurie à la société d'abondance*. Recherches et
      débats du Centre catholique des intellectuels français, n.s. 49. Paris:
      Fayard, [1964]. p. 38-46.

882   Selge, K.-V. "Die Armut in den nichtrechtgläubigen religiösen Bewegungen des
      12. Jahrhunderts."*La povertà del secolo XII e Francesco d'Assisi*. Atti del II
      Convegno internazionale, Assisi, 17-19 ottobre 1974. Assisi: Società
      Internazionale di Studi Francescani, 1975. p. 179-216.

883   Sogno, E. *La croce e il rogo: storia di fra Dolcino e Margherita*. Storia e docu-
      menti, 16. Milan: Mursia, c1974. 230 p. ill.

884   Töpfer, B. "Die Apostelbrüder und der Aufstand des Dolcino."*Städtische Volks-
      bewegungen des 14. Jahrhunderts*. Ed. E. Engelmann. Berlin: Akademie-
      Verlag, 1960. p. 62-84.

885   Tognetti, G. "Sul moto dei bianchi nel 1399." *BISIM*, 78 (1967), 205-343.

886   Valetti Bonini, I. "Povertà e razionalismo nelle eresie dei secoli XI e XII: riflessioni
      in margine ad uno studio di Cinzio Violante." *Humanitas* (Brescia), 29
      (1974), 532-542. See 208.

887   *Vaudois languedociens et Pauvres catholiques*. Cahiers de Fanjeaux, 2. Toulouse:
      Privat, c1967. 307 p. ill.
      Rev. R. Cegna, *RSLR*, 5 (1969), 192-193; R. W. Emery, *Speculum*, 44
      (1969), 321-322; J. B. Russell, *CCM*, 11 (1968), 434-435; E. Pásztor, *SM*,

3d ser., 9 (1968), 452-456; R. Mols, *NRT*, 90 (1968), 1097-1098; R. Beaupère, *Lumière et vie*, 87 (1968), 117; M. R. Mayeux, *RHEF*, 54 (1968), 344-347; L. Genicot, *RHE*, 63 (1968), 530-533; B. de Gaiffier, *Analecta Bollandiana*, 87 (1969), 312-313; B. Guillemain, *AM*, 83 (1971), 103-108; A. Molnár, *CV*, 13 (1970), 210-213; A. C. Shannon, *AER*, 158 (1968), 411-412; M. Pacaut, *RH*, 241 (1969), 57-68; C. Higounet, *Journal des savants*, 1969, p. 63-64.

888 Werner, E. "Armut und Reichtum in den Vorstellungen ost- und westkirchlicher Haeretiker des 10.-12. Jahrhunderts." *Povertà e ricchezza nella spiritualità dei secoli XI e XII.* Convegni del Centro di studi sulla spiritualità medievale, 8. Todi: Accademia Tudertina, 1969. p. 81-125. Trans., "Povertà e ricchezza nelle concezioni degli eretici della chiesa orientale e occidentale dei secoli X-XII," in *La concezione della povertà nel medioevo*, ed. O. Capitani (Bologna: Pàtron, 1974), p. 301-355.

889 Wessley, S. E. "Enthusiasm and heresy in the year 1300: Guglielma of Milan, Armanno Pungilupo of Ferrara and Gerard Segarelli of Parma." Diss. Columbia Univ. *DAI*, 37A (1976), 3816.

890 ——. "The thirteenth-century Guglielmites: salvation through women." *Medieval women: dedicated and presented to Professor Rosalind M. T. Hill on the occasion of her seventieth birthday.* Ed. D. Baker. Studies in church history, Subsidia, 1. Oxford: Blackwell, 1978. p. 289-303.

891 Whitelaw, J. D. "The idea of poverty as virtue, and its role in the historical development of the church according to some writings of Petrus Ioannis Olivi (1248-1298)." Diss. Univ. of Toronto. *DAI*, 32A (1971), 492.

892 Zumkeller, A. "Die Augustinereremiten in der Auseinandersetzung mit Wyclif und Hus, ihre Beteiligung an den Konzilien von Konstanz und Basel." *Analecta augustiniana*, 28 (1965), 5-56.

Part Seven

Beguines

893   Aerts, J. "Begijnen en begarden te Sint-Truiden rond het midden van de xııı^e eeuw." *Limburg,* 47 (1968), 241-248.

894   Bolton, B. M. "Mulieres sanctae." *Sanctity and secularity: the church and the world.* Ed. D. Baker. Studies in church history, 10. Oxford: Blackwell, 1973. p. 77-95.

895   Bylina, S. "Herezja w xıv-wiecznym Paryżu." *PH,* 59 (1968), 741-748. [Heresy in 14th-century Paris]

896   ——. *Wizje społeczne w herezjach średniowiecznych: humiliaci, begini, begardzi.* Wrocław, etc.: Zakład Narodowy im. Ossolińskich, 1974. 234 p. [Incl. summary, p. 229-234: "Die gesellschaftlichen Vorstellungen in den mittel-alterlichen Häresien: Humiliaten, Beginen und Begharden"]
Rev. I. Hlaváček, *DAEM,* 32 (1976), 291-292.

897   Carozzi, C. "Une béguine joachimite: Douceline, sœur d'Hugues de Digne." *Franciscains d'Oc.* p. 169-201. See 1089.

898   ——. "Douceline et les autres." *La religion populaire en Languedoc du xııı^e siècle à la moitié du xıv^e siècle.* Cahiers de Fanjeaux, 11. Toulouse: Privat, 1976. p. 251-267.

899   ——. "L'estamen de sainte Douceline." *Provence historique,* 23, nos. 93-94 (1973), 270-279.

900   Degler-Spengler, B. "Die Beginen in Basel." *Basler Zeitschrift für Geschichte und Altertumskunde,* 69 (1969), 5-83; 70 (1970), 29-118.
Rev. P. Ladner, *ZSKG,* 66 (1972), 194-195.

901   ——. "Beginen und Begarden am Oberrhein." *ZKG,* 90 (1979), 81-84.

902   Elm, K. "Klarissen und Beginen in Basel: Basler Beiträge zur *Helvetia sacra.*" *Freiburger Diözesan-Archiv,* 90 (1970), 316-332.

903   Gruber, E. "Beginen und Eremiten der Innerschweiz." *ZSKG,* 58 (1964), 79-106. Rpt. in *Festschrift Oskar Vasella* (Freiburg, Switz.: Universitätsverlag, c1964), p. 79-106.

904   Grundmann, H. "Zur Geschichte der Beginen im 13. Jahrhundert." *AKG,* 21

(1931), 296-320. Rpt. in his *Ausgewählte Aufsätze*, I (Stuttgart: Hiersemann, 1976), 201-221.

905 Kauffman, C. J. *Tamers of death, I: The history of the Alexian brothers from 1300 to 1789*. New York: Seabury, 1976. x, 234 p.

906 Kerov, V. L. "Narodnoe ereticheskoe dvizhenie beginov iuga Frantsii i Petr Ioann Olivi." *Frantsuzskiĭ ezhegodnik / Annuaire d'études françaises*, 1968 (Moscow, 1970), p. 5-33. [Incl. summary, "L'hérésie populaire des béguins du midi de la France et Pierre Jean Olivi"]

907 Lapis, D., and B. Lapis. "Beginski w Polsce w xiii-xv wieku." *Kwartalnik historyczny*, 79 (1972), 521-544. [Incl. summary, p. 543-544: "Les béguines en Pologne"]

908 Lerner, R. E. "Vagabonds and little women: the medieval Netherlandish dramatic fragment *De truwanten*." *Modern philology*, 65 (1968), 301-306.

909 ———. "Weltklerus und religiöse Bewegung im 13. Jahrhundert: das Beispiel Philipps des Kanzlers." *AKG*, 51 (1969), 94-108.

910 McDonnell, E. W. *The beguines and beghards in medieval culture, with special emphasis on the Belgian scene*. New Brunswick, 1954. Rpt. New York: Octagon, 1969. xvii, 643 p.

911 Mazur, Z. "Ordinatio beguinarum in mortalitate." *Śląski kwartalnik historyczny, Sobótka*, 23 (1968), 449-451. [In Polish]

912 Mens, A. "De 'Kleine armen van Christus' in de Brabants-Luikse gewesten (einde 12ᵉ, begin 13ᵉ eeuw)." *Ons geestelijk erf*, 36 (1962), 282-331; 37 (1963), 129-169; 38 (1964), 113-144; 39 (1965), 225-271. [Incl. Lat. summary]

913 Neumann, E. G. *Rheinisches Beginen- und Begardenwesen: ein Mainzer Beitrag zur religiösen Bewegung am Rhein*. Mainzer Abhandlungen zur mittleren und neueren Geschichte, 4. Meisenheim am Glan: Hain, 1960. 205 p. map.

Rev. W. H. Struck, *Nassauische Annalen*, 72 (1961), 184-198.

914 Nobluez, Y. "Présence des cathares à Liège? Les béguinages." *CEC*, 23, no. 56 (1972), 42-46.

915 Nübel, O. *Mittelalterliche Beginen- und Sozialsiedlungen in den Nederlanden: ein Beitrag zur Vorgeschichte der Fuggerei*. Studien zur Fuggergeschichte, 23. Tübingen: Mohr (P. Siebeck), 1970. xxi, 335 p. ill.

916 Patschovsky, A. "Strassburger Beginenverfolgungen im 14. Jahrhundert." *DAEM*, 30 (1974), 56-198, ill.

Rev. P. Levresse, *Archives de l'église d'Alsace*, n.s. 22 (1975), 373-374.

917 Péano, P. "Les Béguins du Languedoc ou la crise du t.o.f. dans la France méridionale (xiiiᵉ-xivᵉ s.)." *CF*, 47 (1977), 97-117.

917A Perarnau, J. L'"*Alia Informatio Beguinorum*" d'Arnau de Vilanova. Studia, Textus, Subsidia, 2. Barcelona: Facultat de Teologia de Barcelona, Secciò de Sant Pacià, 1978. 213 p. —

Rev. R. Lerner, *Speculum*, 54 (1979), 842-845.

918   Peters, G. "Norddeutsches Beginen- und Begardenwesen im Mittelalter." *Nieder-sächsisches Jahrbuch*, 41/42 (1969-70), 50-118.

919   Ruh, K. "Beginenmystik: Hadewijch, Mechthild von Magdeburg, Marguerite Porete." *ZDADL*, 106 (1977), 265-277.

920   ———. "'Le miroir des simples âmes' der Marguerite Porete." *Verbum et signum* [Festschrift Friedrich Ohly]. Ed. Hans Fromm, et al. Munich: Fink, 1975. p. 365-387.

921   Schmidt, A., ed. "Tractatus contra hereticos beckardos, lulhardos et swestriones des Wasmud von Homburg." *Archiv für mittelrheinische Kirchenge-schichte*, 14 (1962), 336-386.

922   Schmitt, J. C. "L'église et les clercs face aux béguines et aux béghards du Rhin supérieur du xive au xve siècle." *Positions des thèses* (École nationale des chartes), 1971, p. 171-174.

923   ———. *Mort d'une hérésie: l'église et les clercs face aux béguines et aux béghards du Rhin supérieur du xive au xve siècle.* Civilisations et sociétés, 56. Paris, The Hague, and New York: Mouton; Paris: École des hautes études en sciences sociales, 1978. 264 p.
        Rev. L. Duggan, *AHR*, 84 (1979), 1034-1035; B. Degler-Spengler, *ZKG*, 90 (1979), 81-84; J. Séguy, *ASSR*, 47 (1979), 189-193; E. Maderna, *Nuova rivista storica*, 63 (1979), 213-215; R. Lerner, *Speculum*, 54 (1979), 842-845.

924   ———. "Mort d'un hérétique." 2 v. (v. 1: L'église et les clercs face aux béguines et aux béghards du Rhin supérieur du xive au xve siècle"; v. 2: "Complé-ments et appendice"). Thesis, École pratique des hautes études, Paris, 1973.

925   Tarrant, J. "The Clementine decrees on the beguines: conciliar and papal versions." *AHP*, 12 (1974), 300-308.

926   Thiry, A. *Von sonderbaren und besonderen Heiligen: fromme Geschichten rund um den Beginenhof.* Leipzig: St. Benno, 1961. 123 p. —

927   Thoumyre, C. *Madame Douceline d'Hyères et son frère Hugues de Digne.* Paris: s.o.s., 1977. 174 p. ill.
        Rev. P. Péano, *AFH*, 72 (1979), 213-214.

928   Weiler, A. G. "Begijnen en begarden in de spiegel van een universitair dispuut (Heidelberg 1458)." *Archief voor de geschiedenis van de Katholieke Kerk in Nederland*, 10 (1968), 63-94.

929   Wermter, E. M. "Die Beginen im mittelalterlichen Preussenlande." *Zeitschrift für die Geschichte und Altertumskunde Ermlands*, 33 (1969), 41-52.

Part Eight

Joachim and Millenarianism

Entries 930 to 1037

930 Alatri, M. da. "Predicazione e predicatori nella cronica di fra Salimbene." *CF*, 46 (1976), 63-91.

931 ——. "Presenza di San Francesco nella cronica di Salimbene da Parma." *AFH*, 69 (1976), 321-335.

932 Alcántara Martinez, P. de. "La josefologia de Ubertino de Casale." *San José en los xv primeros siglos de la iglesia*. Rome, 1971. p. 336-359.

933 Baget-Bozzo, G. "Modello trinitario e modello cristologico nella teologia della storia: Gioacchino da Fiore e Tommaso d'Aquino." *Renovatio*, 9 (1974), 39-50.

934 Barrois, G. A. "A note on a manuscript of the pseudo-Joachim." *Studies in medieval culture*, 3 (1970), 117-123.

935 Becker, J. W. *Het eeuwige heimwee: chiliasme en sektarisme, een historisch-sociologische studie*. Alphen aan den Rijn: Samson, 1976. 196 p. Rev. O. J. de Jong, *Nederlands theologisch tijdschrift*, 32 (1978), 167-169.

936 Bett, H. *Joachim of Flora*. London, 1931. Rpt. Richwood, N.Y.: Merrick, 1976. vii, 184 p.

937 Bloomfield, M. W., and H. Lee. "The Pierpont-Morgan manuscript of 'De septem sigillis'." *RTAM*, 38 (1971), 137-148.

938 Bragança, J. de O. "Vestigios de milenarismo em Alcobaça?" *Didaskalia*, 1 (1971), 173-175. —

939 Brown, H. O. J. "Dreams of a third age." *Christianity today*, 15 (1971), 951-953.

940 Camperi, G. "L'*Adversus iudeos* di Gioacchino da Fiore." Diss. Università Cattolica del Sacro Cuore, Milan, 1972. —

941 Cohn, N. "Medieval millenarism: its bearing on the comparative study of millenarian movements." *Millennial dreams in action: studies in revolutionary religious movements*. Ed. S. L. Thrupp. New York: Schocken, [1970]. p. 31-43.

942   Crocco, A. *L'"età dello Spirito Santo" e l'"ecclesia spiritualis" in Gioacchino da Fiore.* 2nd ed. [Naples]: Empireo, 1965. 43 p.

943   ——. *Gioacchino da Fiore, la più singolare ed affascinante figura del medioevo cristiano.* Naples: Empireo, 1960. 203 p. 2nd ed., *Gioacchino da Fiore e il gioachimismo* (Naples: Liguori, 1976), 222 p., ill.
        Rev. (1st ed.) M. Reeves, *JEH*, 13 (1962), 97-98; N. Cilento, *SM*, 3 (1960), 586-590.
        Rev. (2nd ed.) F. A. Prezioso, *Sapienza*, 29 (1976), 235-237.

944   ——. "Simbologia gioachimita e simbologia dantesca." *Sophia*, 29 (1961), 95-102.

945   ——. *Simbologia gioachimita e simbologia dantesca: nuove prospettive d'interpretazione della Divina commedia.* Naples: Empireo, 1961. 3rd ed. 1962. 39 p. ill.

946   Daniel, E. R. "Apocalyptic conversion: the Joachite alternative to the crusades." *Traditio*, 25 (1969), 127-154.

947   ——. "Joachim of Flora and the Joachite tradition of apocalyptic conversion in the later middle ages." Diss. Univ. of Virginia. *DAI*, 28A (1967), 572.

947A   Di Napoli, G. "L'ecclesiologia di Gioacchino da Fiore." *Doctor communis*, 32 (1979), 302-326.

948   Donini, A. "Per una storia del pensiero di Dante in rapporto al movimento gioachimita." *Studi storici in onore di Gabriele Pepe.* [Bari]: Dedalo, 1969. p. 373-390.

949   Falbel, N. "Sao Boaventura e a teologia da história de Joaquim de Fiore: un resumo crítico." *S. Bonaventura, 1274-1974.* Grottaferrata: Collegio S. Bonaventura, [1974]. II, 571-584. [Incl. Lat. summary]

950   Ferrara, V. "Gioacchino da Fiore come esponente della vocazione del popolo di Dio dell'Italia meridionale alla speculazione teologica ed il concilio ecumenico Vaticano secundo." *Monitor ecclesiasticus*, 102 (1977), 116-143.

951   Förschner, F. "Concordia: Urgestalt und Sinnbild in der Geschichtsdeutung des Joachim von Fiore. Eine Studie zum Symbolismus des Mittelalters." Diss. Albert-Ludwigs-Universität, Freiburg im Breisgau, 1970. [vii], 212 p.

952   Fournier, P. *Études sur Joachim de Flore et ses doctrines.* Paris, 1909. Rpt. Frankfurt am Main: Minerva, 1963. vii, 100 p.

953   Gallavotti, M. A. A. "La polemica di Gioacchino da Fiore contro la Curia romana." Diss. Università Cattolica del Sacro Cuore, Milan, 1970. ——

954   Gélinas, Y.-D. "La critique de Thomas d'Aquin sur l'exégèse de Joachim de Flore." *Tommaso d'Aquino nel suo settimo centenario: atti del congresso internazionale, Roma-Napoli, 17-24 aprile 1974.* Naples: Domenicane italiane, 1975. p. 368-376.

955   Gimeno Casalduero, J. "La profecía medieval en la literatura castellana y su relación con las corrientes proféticas europeas." *Nueva revista de filología hispánica*, 20 (1971), 64-89.

956   Graziati, G. "La dottrina trinitaria di Gioacchino da Fiore." Diss. Università Cattolica del Sacro Cuore, Milan, 1975 —

957   Grundmann, H. *Ausgewählte Aufsätze, 2: Joachim von Fiore.* Schriften der Monumenta Germaniae historica, 25, 2. Stuttgart: Hiersemann, 1977. 456 p.
      Rev. C. V. Graves, *AHR*, 83 (1978), 700; H. Fichtenau, *MIÖG*, 86 (1978), 247; W. Ullmann, *JEH*, 29 (1978), 217-219; K. V. Selge, *ZKG*, 90 (1979), 117-120.

958   ———. "Joachim von Fiore." *Die Wahrheit der Ketzer.* Ed. H. J. Schultz. Stuttgart and Berlin: Kreuz-Verlag, c1968. p. 80-88, 264-268.

959   ———. "Kirchenfreiheit und Kaisermacht um 1190 in der Sicht Joachims von Fiore." *DAEM*, 19 (1963), 353-396. Rpt. in his *Ausgewählte Aufsätze*, II, 361-402.

960   ———. "Lex und sacramentum bei Joachim von Fiore." *Lex et sacramentum im Mittelalter.* Ed. P. Wilpert. Miscellanea mediaevalia, 6. Berlin: de Gruyter, 1969. p. 31-48. Rpt. in his *Ausgewählte Aufsätze*, II, 403-420.

961   ———. *Studien über Joachim von Fiore.* Beiträge zur Kulturgeschichte des Mittelalters und der Renaissance, 32. Leipzig and Berlin, 1927. Rpt. with new (1966) preface and corrections. Stuttgart: Teubner, 1975, x, 212 p.

962   ———. "Zur Biographie Joachims von Fiore und Rainers von Ponza." *DAEM*, 16 (1960), 437-546. Rpt. in his *Ausgewählte Aufsätze*, II, 255-360.

963   Guyot, B.-G. "L'*Arbor vitae crucifixae Iesu* d'Ubertin de Casale et ses emprunts au *De articulis fidei* de s. Thomas d'Aquin." *Studies honoring Ignatius Charles Brady.* Ed. R. S. Almagno and C. L. Harkins. Franciscan Institute publications, theology series, 6. St. Bonaventure, N.Y.: Franciscan Institute, 1976. p. 293-307.

964   Hirsch-Reich, B. "Ein bisher unedierter Traktat Joachims von Fiore zur Bekehrung der Juden." *RTAM*, 27 (1960), 141-148.

965   ———. "Joachim von Fiore und das Judentum." *Judentum im Mittelalter.* Ed. P. Wilpert. Miscellanea mediaevalia, 4. Berlin: de Gruyter, 1966. p. 228-263, ill.

966   ———. "The symbolism of musical instruments in the *Psalterium x chordarum* of Joachim of Fiore and its patristic sources." *Studia patristica*, 9, pt. 3. Texte und Untersuchungen, 94. Berlin: Akademie-Verlag, 1966. p. 540-551.

967   Jansen, H. P. H. "Chiliasme in de middeleeuwen." *Spiegel historiael*, 8 (1973), 210-219, 253-254, ill.

968   Joachim of Fiore. *Concordia novi ac veteris testamenti.* Venice, 1519. Rpt. Frankfurt am Main: Minerva, 1964. [iv], 135 f.

969   ———. *Expositio in Apocalypsim.* Venice, 1527. Rpt. Frankfurt am Main: Minerva, 1964. 224 f.

970   ———. *Psalterium decem cordarum.* Venice, 1527. Rpt. Frankfurt am Main: Minerva, 1965. [225]-280 [+ xi] f.

971 Kamlah, W. *Apokalypse und Geschichtstheologie: die mittelalterliche Auslegung der Apokalypse vor Joachim von Fiore.* Historische Studien, 285. Berlin, 1935. Rpt. Vaduz: Kraus, 1965. 131 p.

972 Konrad, R. *De ortu et tempore Antichristi: Antichristvorstellung und Geschichtsbild des Abtes Adso von Montier-en-Der.* Münchener historische Studien, Mittelalterliche Geschichte, 1. Kallmünz: Michael Lassleben, 1964. 151 p.

973 Lee, H. "*Scrutamini scripturas*: Joachimist themes and *figurae* in the early religious writing of Arnold of Vilanova." *Journal of the Warburg and Courtauld Institutes*, 37 (1974), 33-56.

974 Lerner, R. E. "An 'Angel of Philadelphia' in the reign of Philip the Fair: the case of Guiard of Cressonessart." *Order and innovation in the middle ages: essays in honor of Joseph R. Strayer.* Ed. W. C. Jordan, et al. Princeton: Princeton University Press, c1976. p. 343-364, 529-540.

975 ———. "Medieval prophecy and religious dissent." *Past and present*, 72 (1976), 3-24.

976 ———. "Refreshment of the saints: the time after Antichrist as a station for earthly progress in medieval thought." *Traditio*, 32 (1976), 97-144.

977 Lipinsky, A. "Calici per Gioacchino da Fiore: l''argentera' e gli argentieri di Longobucco e le origini di una scuola orafa in Calabria Citeriore." *Dante nel pensiero e nella esegesi dei secoli XIV e XV: Atti del III congresso nazionale di studi danteschi.* Florence: Olschki, 1975. p. 189-209, ill.

978 McGinn, B. "The abbot and the doctors: scholastic reactions to the radical eschatology of Joachim of Fiore." *CH*, 40 (1971), 30-47.

979 ———. "Angel pope and papal antichrist." *CH*, 47 (1978), 155-173.

980 ———. "Apocalypticism in the middle ages: an historiographical sketch." *MS*, 37 (1975), 252-286.

981 ———. "Joachim and the Sibyl: an early work of Joachim of Fiore from ms. 322 of the Biblioteca Antoniana in Padua." *Cîteaux*, 24 (1973), 97-138.

982 ———, comp. and trans. *Visions of the end: apocalyptic traditions of the middle ages.* New York: Columbia University Press, 1979. xv, 377 p.

983 Magalotti, P. P. "Fonti e motivi dell'escatologismo gioachimita e pseudogioachimita nella *Cronica* di Salimbene da Parma." Diss. Università Cattolica del Sacro Cuore, Milan, 1962. —

984 Manselli, R. "L'anno 1260 fu anno gioachimitico?" *Il movimento dei disciplinati nel settimo centenario dal suo inizio (Perugia 1260). Convegno internazionale, Perugia, 25-28 settembre 1960.* Perugia, 1962. p. 99-108.

985 ———. "A proposito del cristianesimo di Dante: Gioacchino da Fiore, gioachimismo, spiritualismo francescano." *Letteratura e critica: studi in onore di Natalino Sapegno.* Rome: Bulzoni, 1974 – . II (1975), 163-192.

986 ———. "L'attesa dell'età nuova ed il gioachimismo." *L'attesa dell'età nuova nella spiritualità della fine del medioevo.* Convegni del Centro di studi sulla spiritualità medievale, 3. Todi: Accademia Tudertina, 1962. p. 145-170.

987 ———. "Joachim de Flore dans la théologie du xiiie siècle." *Septième centenaire de la mort de saint Louis. Actes des colloques de Royaumont et de Paris (21-27 mai 1970).* Paris: Belles Lettres, 1976. p. 291-301.

988 ———. "Il problema del doppio Anticristo in Gioacchino da Fiore." *Geschichtsschreibung und geistiges Leben im Mittelalter: Festschrift für Heinz Löwe.* Ed. K. Hauck and H. Mordek. Cologne and Vienna: Böhlau, 1978. p. 427-449.

989 ———. "La terza età, *Babylon* e l'Anticristo mistico (a proposito di Pietro di Giovanni Olivi)." *BISIM*, 82 (1970), 47-79.

990 ———. "Testimonianze minori sulle eresie: Gioacchino da Fiore di fronte a catari e valdesi." *SM*, 3rd ser., 18, no. 2 (1977), 1-17.

991 ———, et al. "Ricerche sull'influenza della profezia nel basso medioevo." *BISIM*, 82 (1970), 1-157.

992 Manteuffel, T. "W oczekiwaniu ery wolności i pokoju: historiozofia Joachima z Fiore." *PH*, 60 (1969), 233-256. [Incl. summary, "Dans l'attente d'une ère de liberté et de paix: la philosophie de l'histoire de Joachim de Flore"]

993 Márquez, A. "Estado actual de los estudios joaquinitas: obras, doctrina, influencias." *CD*, 183 (1970), 525-535.

994 Meinhold, P. "Thomas von Aquin und Joachim von Fiore und ihre Deutung der Geschichte." *Saeculum*, 27 (1976), 66-76.

995 Mottu, H. *La manifestation de l'Esprit selon Joachim de Fiore: herméneutique et théologie de l'histoire d'après le 'Traité sur les quatre évangiles'.* Neuchâtel and Paris: Delachaux et Niestlé, 1977. 365 p.
Rev. R. Escol, *NRT*, 100 (1978), 598-599; M. Bouttier, *ETR*, 53 (1978), 584-585; B. McGinn, *JR*, 59 (1979), 240-241.

996 Müller, G. "Jugendrevolte und Linksopposition im Hochmittelalter." *ZRGG*, 22 (1970), 113-130.

997 Nardi, B. "Dante e Gioacchino da Fiore." *Almanacco calabrese*, 15 (1965), 59-66.

998 Otto, S. "Bonaventuras christologischer Einwand gegen die Geschichtslehre des Joachim von Fiore." *Die Mächte des Guten und Bösen.* Ed. A. Zimmermann. Miscellanea mediaevalia, 11. Berlin and New York: de Gruyter, 1977. p. 113-130.

999 ———. "Die Denkform des Joachim von Fiore und das *Caput 'Damnamus'* des 4. Laterankonzils." *Münchener theologische Zeitschrift*, 13 (1962), 145-154.

1000 Paoli, C. *Il riformatore Veltro: gioachinismo e francescanesimo nell'allegoria fondamentale della Divina commedia.* Biblioteca dell'Ussero, n.s. 53. Pisa: Guardini, [1969]. 103 p. ill.

1001 Paparatti, S. *Capitoli sull'evangelo eterno: attualità del pensiero gioacchimita.* Cosenza: Pellegrini, c1972. 129 p. ill.

1002 Paul, J. "Le joachisme et les joachimites au milieu du xiiie siècle d'après le témoignage de fra Salimbene." *1274: année charnière.* Colloques internationaux du Centre national de la recherche scientifique, 558. Paris: c.n.r.s., 1977. p. 797-813.

1003 Pásztor, E. "Giovanni xxii e il gioachimismo di Pietro di Giovanni Olivi." *bisim*, 82 (1970), 81-111.

1004 Pickering, F. P. "Irrwege der mittelalterlichen Geschichtsschreibung (Rupert von Deutz, Joachim von Fiore)." *zdadl*, 100 (1971), 270-296.

1005 Piromalli, A. *Gioacchino da Fiore e Dante*. Ravenna: Longo, 1966. 67 p. Publ. also in *Letture classensi*, 1 (1966), 121-170.

1006 Potestà, G. L. "Un secolo di studi sul *Arbor vitae*: chiesa ed escatologia in Ubertino da Casale." *cf*, 47 (1977), 217-267.

1007 ——. "Storia ed escatologia nell'*Arbor vitae crucifixae Jesu* di Ubertino da Casale." Diss. Università Cattolica del Sacro Cuore, Milan, 1974. —

1008 Reeves, M. "The abbot Joachim and the Society of Jesus." *Mediaeval and renaissance studies*, 5 (1961), 163-181.

1009 ——. "History and eschatology: medieval and early Protestant thought in some English and Scottish writings." *mh*, n.s. 4 (1973), 99-123.

1010 ——. "History and prophecy in medieval thought." *mh*, n.s. 5 (1974), 51-75.

1011 ——. *The influence of prophecy in the later middle ages: a study in Joachimism*. Oxford: Clarendon Press; New York: Oxford University Press, 1969. xiv, 574 p.
Rev. I. Brady, *chr*, 58 (1973), 610-613; C. T. Davis, *Speculum*, 50 (1975), 347-349; D. Douie, *jeh*, 21 (1970), 359-360; D. Flood, *cf*, 41 (1971), 131-140; C. Morris, *jts*, 21 (1970), 511-513; R. Pring-Mill, *Estudios lulianos*, 17 (1973), 215-218; B. Tierney, *ahr*, 76 (1971), 140-141; E. I. Watkin, *The Downside review*, 88 (1970), 215-221; F. Wendel, *rhpr*, 51 (1971), 103-105; B. R. White, *The Baptist quarterly*, 23 (1970), 382-383.

1012 ——. "Joachimist influences on the idea of a last world emperor." *Traditio*, 17 (1961), 323-370.

1013 ——. *Joachim of Fiore and the prophetic future*. London: spck, 1976. [vii], 212 p. ill.
Rev. G. Every, *hj*, 19 (1978), 81-83.

1014 ——. "Some popular prophecies from the fourteenth to the seventeenth centuries." *Popular belief and practice*. Ed. G. J. Cuming and D. Baker. Studies in church history, 8. Cambridge: Cambridge University Press, 1972. p. 107-134, ill.

1015 ——, and B. Hirsch-Reich. *The figurae of Joachim of Fiore*. Oxford: Clarendon Press, 1972. xxiii, 350 p. ill.
Rev. G. G. Bischoff, *ch*, 44 (1975), 402-403; M. W. Bloomfield, *Speculum*, 50 (1975), 147-149; D. Douie, *jeh*, 24 (1973), 301-303; J. F. Kelly, *Thought*, 49 (1974), 214-215; G. Leff, *mæ*, 43 (1974), 185-188; R. E. Lerner, *daem*, 29 (1973), 336-337; B. McGinn, *chr*, 62 (1976), 86-88; M.

Thomas, *AKG*, 56 (1974), 228-231; E. I. Watkin, *The Downside review*, 91 (1973), 246-249.

1016   ——, and J. V. Fleming, ed. *Two poems attributed to Joachim of Fiore*. Princeton: Pilgrim, 1978. 45 p.

1017   Rotolo, F. "San Bonaventura e fra Gerardo da Borgo S. Donnino: riflessi del gioachimismo in Sicilia." *O theologos*, 2 (1975), 263-297.

1018   Ruh, K. "Joachitische Spiritualität im Werke Roberts von Boron." *Typologia litterarum: Festschrift für Max Wehrli*. Ed. S. Sonderegger, et al. [Zürich]: Atlantis, c1969. p. 167-196.

1019   Russo, F. "Rassegna bibliografica gioachimita (1958-1967)." *Cîteaux*, 19 (1968), 206-214.

1020   Schachten, W. "*Trinitas et tempora*: Trinitätsdenken und Geschichtslehre Joachims von Fiore." Diss. Universität Freiburg, 1974. —

1020A Schiappa, F. "Joachim of Fiore, predecessor of S. Francis of Assisi." Diss. University of Connecticut. *DAI*, 40A (1979), 890-891.

1021   Schwartz, H. "The end of the beginning: millenarian studies, 1969-1975." *Religious studies review*, 2, no. 3 (July 1976), 1-15.

1022   Schwarz, J. "Chiliasmus als christliche Utopie." *Bohemia sacra: das Christentum in Böhmen 973-1973*. Ed. F. Seibt. Düsseldorf: Schwann, 1974. p. 209-221, 569.

1023   Sendrail, M. "Joachim de Flore, le messager des derniers temps." *Bulletin de l'Association Guillaume Budé*, ser. 4 (1970), 407-424.

1024   Simoni, F. "Il *Super Hieremiam* e il gioachimismo francescano." *BISIM*, 82 (1970), 13-46.

1025   Thomas, M. "Zur kulturgeschichtlichen Einordnung der Armenbibel mit 'Speculum humanae salvationis' unter Berücksichtigung einer Darstellung des 'liber figurarum' in der Joachim de Fiore-Handschrift der Sächsischen Landesbibliothek Dresden (Mscr. Dresden A 121)." *AKG*, 52 (1970), 192-225, ill.

1026   Töpfer, B. "Chiliastische Elemente in der Eschatologie des Matthias von Janov." *Ost und West in der Geschichte des Denkens und der kulturellen Beziehungen: Festschrift für Eduard Winter*. Ed. W. Steinitz, et al. Berlin: Akademie-Verlag, 1966. p. 59-70.

1027   ——. "Eine Handschrift des Evangelium aeternum des Gerardino von Borgo San Donnino." *ZG*, 8 (1960), 156-163.

1028   ——. *Das kommende Reich des Friedens: zur Entwicklung chiliastischer Zukunftshoffnungen im Hochmittelalter*. Forschungen zur mittelalterlichen Geschichte, 11. Berlin: Akademie-Verlag, 1964. 341 p.
        Rev. H. Grundmann, *HZ*, 203 (1966), 388-394; H. Mohr, *DLZ*, 87 (1966), 1097-1100; O. [Schmucki], *CF*, 35 (1965), 435-437; B. Hirsch-Reich, *BTAM*, 9 (1962-65), 512-515; S. Bylina, *PH*, 58 (1967), 542-544.

1029   Tognetti, G. "Note sul profetismo nel rinascimento e la letteratura relativa." *BISIM*, 82 (1970), 129-157.

1030   Ubertino of Casale. *Arbor vitae crucifixae Jesu*. Monumenta politica et philosophica rariora, I, 4. Turin: Bottega d'Erasmo, 1961. viii, 498 p. Rpt. of Venice 1485 ed., with intro. and bibliog. by C. T. Davis.

1031   Vaucher, A.-F. "Les 1260 jours prophétiques dans les cercles joachimites." *Andrews University seminary studies*, 3 (1965), 42-48.

1032   Volpato, A. "La predicazione penitenziale-apocalittica nell'attività di due predicatori del 1473." *BISIM*, 82 (1970), 113-128, ill.

1033   Wendelborn, G. *Gott und Geschichte: Joachim von Fiore und die Hoffnung der Christenheit*. Vienna and Cologne: Böhlau, 1974. 300 p.
       A. Molnár, *TLZ*, 101 (1976), 858-859.

1034   ———. "Die Hermeneutik des kalabresischen Abtes Joachim von Fiore." *CV*, 17 (1974), 63-91.

1035   West, D. C. "Between flesh and spirit: Joachite pattern and meaning in the *Cronica* of Fra Salimbene." *Journal of medieval history*, 3 (1977), 339-352.

1036   ———. "Joachimism and Fra Salimbene." Diss. Univ. of California, Los Angeles. *DAI*, 31A (1971), 3457; *CH*, 40 (1971), 200.

1037   ———, ed. *Joachim of Fiore in Christian thought: essays on the influence of the Calabrian prophet*. New York: Burt Franklin, c1975. 2 v. (xxiv, 631 p.).
       Rev. E. K. Burger, *AHR*, 81 (1976), 1092-1093; J. R. H. Moorman, *JTS*, 28 (1977), 212-213; T. E. Morrissey, *CH*, 46 (1977), 239-240; D. Burr, *CHR*, 63 (1977), 457; M. F. Eller, *The sixteenth century journal*, 8 (1977), 125-126; V. J. Bourke, *The modern schoolman*, 54 (1977), 313; C. L[eonardi], *SM*, 3rd ser., 18 (1977), 542-543; R. Manselli, *Archivio storico per la Calabria e la Lucania*, 43 (1976), 227-231.

Part Nine

Franciscans and Heretics

ENTRIES 1038 TO 1154

1038   Alatri, M. da. "Due aspetti del francescanesimo dugentesco: i fioretti e l'inquisi-zione." *Italia francescana*, 47 (1972), 195-208.

1039   ——. *"Ordo paenitentium* ed eresia in Italia." CF, 43 (1973), 181-197.

1040   Alcántara Martínez, P. de. "La cooperación de María a la obra salvífica de Cristo según el pensamiento de P. J. Olivi." *Studies honoring Ignatius Charles Brady.* Ed. R. S. Almagno and C. L. Harkins. Franciscan Institute publications, theology series 6. St. Bonaventure, N.Y.: Franciscan Institute, 1976. p. 341-355.

1041   Alverny, M.-T. d'. "Un adversaire de Saint Thomas: Petrus Iohannis Olivi." *St. Thomas Aquinas 1274-1974: commemorative studies.* Toronto: Pontifical Institute of Mediaeval Studies, 1974. II, 179-218.

1042   Annibaldi, G. "A proposito del ritrovamento del 'Dialogo contro i fraticelli' (lettere inedite di Gaetano Marini)." *Picenum seraphicum,* 7 (1970), 178-189. —

1043   Auw, L. von. "Angelo Clareno et les spirituels du midi." *Franciscains d'Oc.* p. 243-262. See 1089.

1044   Bąk, F. M. "'If it weren't for Peter Waldo, there would have been no Franciscans'." FS, 25 (1965), 4-16.

1045   Becker, M. B. "Heresy in medieval and renaissance Florence: a comment." With rejoinder by J. N. Stephens. *Past and present,* 62 (1974), 153-161, 162-166. See 1147.

1046   Bedouelle, G. "Chronologie sommaire des événements et des controverses." *Franciscains d'Oc.* p. 21-39. See 1089.

1047   Benvenuti, A. "Il francescanesimo e le sue influenze sulla spiritualità dei laici: i *fratres poenitentiae.*" *Eretici e ribelli del XIII e XIV sec.* Ed. D. Maselli. Pistoia: Tellini, [1974]. p. 157-187.

1048   Benz, E. *Ecclesia spiritualis: Kirchenidee und Geschichtstheologie der franzis-*

kanischen Reformation. Stuttgart, 1934. Rpt. Stuttgart: Kohlhammer [Darmstadt: Wissenschaftliche Buchgesellschaft], 1964. xv, 481 p.

1049   Bérubé, C. "Olivi, critique de Bonaventure et d'Henri de Gand." *Studies honoring Ignatius Charles Brady.* Ed. R. S. Almagno and C. L. Harkins. Franciscan Institute publications, theology series, 6. St. Bonaventure, N.Y.: Franciscan Institute, 1976. p. 57-121.

1050   ———. "Olivi, interprète de saint Anselme." *Analecta Anselmiana,* 4, pt. 1 (1975), 147-158.

1051   Bettoni, E. "La libertà come fondamento dei valori umani nel pensiero di Pier di Giovanni Olivi." *Storia della filosofia antica e medievale.* Atti del XII Congresso internazionale di filosofia (Venezia, 12-18 settembre 1958), 11. Florence: Sansoni, 1960. p. 39-47.

1052   Brooke, R. B. *The coming of the friars.* Historical problems; studies and documents, 24. London: George Allen and Unwin; New York: Barnes and Noble, 1975. 244 p.

1053   Burr, D. "The apocalyptic element in Olivi's critique of Aristotle." *CH,* 40 (1971), 15-29.

1054   ———. "The date of Petrus Johannis Olivi's commentary on Matthew." *CF,* 46 (1976), 131-138.

1055   ———. "Olivi and baptismal grace." *FSt,* 57 (1975), 1-24.

1056   ———. "Olivi and the limits of intellectual freedom." *Contemporary reflections on the medieval Christian tradition: essays in honor of Ray C. Petry.* Ed. G. H. Shriver. Durham, N.C.: Duke University Press, 1974. p. 185-199.

1057   ———. "Olivi on marriage: the conservative as prophet." *The journal of medieval and renaissance studies,* 2 (1972), 183-204.

1058   ———. *The persecution of Peter Olivi.* Transactions of the American Philosophical Society, n.s. 66, pt. 5. Philadelphia: American Philosophical Society, 1976. 98 p.
        Rev. E. R. Daniel, *CH,* 46 (1977), 240-241; M. W. Bloomfield, *Speculum,* 53 (1978), 344-345; G. R. Evans, *JTS,* 29 (1978), 315; C. Schmitt, *AFH,* 71 (1978), 497-498, and *RHE,* 73 (1978), 704-707.

1059   ———. "Petrus Ioannis Olivi and the philosophers." *FS,* 31 (1971), 41-71.

1060   ———. "Quantity and eucharistic presence: the debate from Olivi through Ockham." *CF,* 44 (1974), 5-44.

1061   Camproux, C. "La mentalité 'spirituelle' chez Peire Cardenal." *Franciscains d'Oc.* p. 287-314. See 1089.

1062   ———. "Présence de Peire Cardenal." *Annales de l'Institut d'études occitanes,* 4th ser., 2, no. 5 (1970), 23-47.

1063   Congar, Y. "Les positions ecclésiologiques de Pierre Jean-Olivi, d'après les publications récentes." *Franciscains d'Oc.* p. 155-165, ill. See 1089.

1064   Corsi, D. "Aspetti dell'inquisizione fiorentina nel '200." *Eretici e ribelli del XIII e XIV sec.* Ed. D. Maselli. Pistoia: Tellini, [1974]. p. 65-91.

1065 Daniel, E. R. *The Franciscan concept of mission in the high middle ages.* [Lexington]: University Press of Kentucky, c1975. xvi, 168 p.

1066 ——. "A re-examination of the origins of Franciscan Joachitism." *Speculum,* 43 (1968), 671-676.

1067 ——. "Spirituality and poverty: Angelo da Clareno and Ubertino da Casale." *MH,* n.s. 4 (1973), 89-98.

1068 Davis, C. T. "Le pape Jean XXII et les spirituels, Ubertin de Casale." *Franciscains d'Oc.* p. 263-283. See 1089.

1069 Davis, K. R. "Evangelical Anabaptism and the medieval ascetic tradition: a study in intellectual origins." Diss. Univ. of Michigan. *DAI,* 32A (1971), 1427.

1070 Doino, D. "The grace of justification according to Petrus Johannis Olivi O.F.M., as contained in his *Quaestio de merito Christi.*" Diss. Universität Innsbruck, 1967. —

1071 Dossat, Y. "De Vaudès à saint François à Montauban." *Les mendiants en pays d'Oc au XIIIe siècle.* Cahiers de Fanjeaux, 8. Toulouse: Privat, c1973. p. 403-413.

1072 Douie, D. L. "Olivi's *Postilla super Matthaeum* (MS. New College B. 49)." *FS,* 35 (1975), 66-92.

1073 Dupré Theseider, E. "Sul *Dialogo contro i fraticelli* di S. Giacomo della Marca." *Miscellanea Gilles Gérard Meersseman.* Italia sacra, 15-16. Padua: Antenore, 1970. II, 577-611.

1074 Durieux, F.-R. "Approches de l'histoire franciscaine du Languedoc au XIIIe siècle." *Les mendiants en pays d'Oc au XIIIe siècle.* Cahiers de Fanjeaux, 8. Toulouse: Privat, c1973. p. 79-100.

1075 ——. "Un manuscrit occitan des spirituels de Narbonne au début du XIVe siècle: essai d'interprétation franciscaine." *Franciscains d'Oc.* p. 231-241. See 1089.

1076 Emmen, A. "Doctrina Petri Ioannis Olivi de baptismi parvulorum effectibus: expositio doctrinalis – editio textus." *Antonianum,* 37 (1962), 350-392.

1077 ——. "La dottrina dell'Olivi sul valore religioso dei voti." *SF,* 63 (1966), 88-108.

1078 ——. "Die Eschatologie des Petrus Johannis Olivi." *WW,* 24 (1961), 113-144; 25 (1962), 13-48.

1079 ——. "Verginità e matrimonio nella valutazione dell'Olivi." *SF,* 64, no. 4 (1967), 11-57.

1080 ——, and F. Simoncioli. "La dottrina dell'Olivi sulla contemplazione, la vita attiva e mista." *SF,* 60 (1963), 382-445; 61 (1964), 108-167.
       Rev. V. Heynck, *FSt,* 46 (1964), 384-385.

1081 Erickson, C. "The fourteenth-century Franciscans and their critics." *FS,* 35 (1975), 107-135.

1082 Falbel, N. "Os espirituais do midi da França (fim do século XIII e início do século XIV). Fanjeaux, 8 a 11 de julho de 1974." *Revista de história* (São Paulo), 51, no. 102 (1975), 711-716. See 1089.

1083   Flood, D., ed. *Peter Olivi's rule commentary*. Veröffentlichungen des Instituts für europäische Geschichte Mainz, 67 (Abt. abendländische Religionsgeschichte). Wiesbaden: Steiner, 1972. xvi, 201 p.
        Rev. D. Burr, *CHR*, 62 (1976), 94-95; M. Reeves, *JEH*, 26 (1975), 89-91.

1084   ——. "Petrus Johannis Olivi: ein neues Bild des angeblichen Spiritualenführers." *WW*, 34 (1971), 130-141.

1085   ——. "Pierre Jean-Olivi et la règle franciscaine." *Franciscains d'Oc*. p. 139-154. See 1089.

1086   ——. "Le projet franciscain de Pierre Olivi." *Études franciscaines*, 23 (1973), 367-379.

1087   ——. "Olivi's correspondence." *Studies honoring Ignatius Charles Brady*. Ed. R. S. Almagno and C. L. Harkins. Franciscan Institute publications, theology series, 6. St. Bonaventure, N.Y.: Franciscan Institute, 1976. p. 269-282.

1088   ——. "A statement of P. J. Olivi on gospel life." *Culture* (Québec), 27 (1966), 313-321.

1089   *Franciscains d'Oc: les spirituels ca 1280-1324*. Cahiers de Fanjeaux, 10. Toulouse: Privat, 1975. 398 p. ill.
        Rev. N. Coulet, *ETR*, 51 (1976), 535-536; D. E. Flood, *WW*, 39 (1976), 70-74; B. Schimmelpfennig, *HZ*, 226 (1978), 154-155; J. Séguy, *ASSR*, 41 (1976), 229.

1090   Fraker, C. F., jr. "The 'dejados' and the *Cancionero de Baena*." *Hispanic review*, 33 (1965), 97-117.

1091   Gál, G. "Petrus de Trabibus on the absolute and ordained power of God." *Studies honoring Ignatius Charles Brady*. Ed. R. S. Almagno and C. L. Harkins. Franciscan Institute publications, theology series, 6. St. Bonaventure, N.Y.: Franciscan Institute, 1976. p. 283-292.

1092   Gieben, S. "Bibliographia Oliviana (1885-1967)." *CF*, 38 (1968), 167-195.

1093   Heynck, V. "Studien zu Johannes von Erfurt, II. Sein Verhältnis zur Olivischule." *FSt*, 42 (1960), 153-196.

1094   ——. "Zur Datierung des *Correctorium fratris Thomae* Wilhelms de la Mare: ein unbeachtetes Zeugnis des Petrus Johannis Olivi." *FSt*, 49 (1967), 1-21.

1095   ——. "Zur Datierung einiger Schriften des Petrus Johannis Olivi." *FSt*, 46 (1964), 335-364.

1096   Hoeres, W. "Der Begriff der Intentionalität bei Olivi." *Scholastik*, 36 (1961), 23-48.

1097   ——. "Der Unterschied von Wesenheit und Individuation bei Olivi." *Scholastik*, 38 (1963), 54-61.

1098   Huning, H. A. "*Artes liberales* und Philosophie in der Olivischule." *Arts libéraux et philosophie au moyen âge*. Actes du quatrième Congrès international de philosophie médiévale (Montréal, 27 août – 2 septembre 1967). Montréal: Institut d'études médiévales; Paris: Vrin, 1969. p. 673-682.

1099   ——. "Die Stellung des Petrus de Trabibus zur Philosophie, nach dem zweiten Prolog zum ersten Buch seines Sentenzenkommentars: Ms. 154, Biblioteca Comunale, Assisi." *FSt*, 46 (1964), 193-286; 47 (1965), 1-43.

1100   Ini, A. "Gli spirituali in Toscana." *Eretici e ribelli del xiii e xiv sec.* Ed. D. Maselli. Pistoia: Tellini, [1974]. p. 233-252.

1101   Jeffrey, D. L. *The early English lyric and Franciscan spirituality.* Lincoln: University of Nebraska Press, 1975. xvi, 306 p.

1102   Lambert, M. D. "The Franciscan crisis under John xxii." *FS*, 32 (1972), 123-143.

1103   Lang, J. "Eine Art Geist-Tiere? Überlegungen zur Freiheitslehre des Petrus Johannis Olivi (†1298)." *Mysterium der Gnade: Festschrift für Johann Auer.* Ed. H. Rossman and J. Ratzinger. Regensburg: Pustet, c1975. p. 259-267.

1104   Lasić, D., ed. *S. Iacobus de Marchia, "Dialogus contra fraticellos," addita versione itala saeculi xv.* Falconara M. (Ancona): Biblioteca Francescana, 1975. 341 p.
        Rev. M. Bertagna, *SF*, 72 (1975), 385.

1105   Leff, G. "The making of the myth of a true church in the later middle ages." *The journal of medieval and renaissance studies,* 1 (1971), 1-15.

1106   Lewis, W. "Peter John Olivi, o.f.m., prophet of the year 1200: ecclesiology and eschatology in the *Lectura super Apocalipsim*." Diss. Univ. Tübingen, 1975. viii, 492 p. [Summary in *TLZ*, 102 (1977), 152-153]

1107   Maier, A. "Handschriftliches zu Arnaldus de Villanova und Petrus Johannis Olivi." *Ausgehendes Mittelalter: gesammelte Aufsätze zur Geistesgeschichte des 14. Jahrhunderts.* Rome: Storia e Letteratura, 1964-1967. II, 215-237. Orig. publ. in *AST*, 21 (1948), 53-74.

1108   ——. "Per la storia del processo contro l'Olivi." *Ausgehendes Mittelalter: gesammelte Aufsätze zur Geistesgeschichte des 14. Jahrhunderts.* Rome: Storia e Letteratura, 1964-67. II, 239-253. Orig. publ. in *RSCI*, 5 (1951), 326-339.

1109   ——. "Zur handschriftlichen Überlieferung der Quodlibeta des Petrus Johannis Olivi." *Ausgehendes Mittelalter: gesammelte Aufsätze zur Geistesgeschichte des 14. Jahrhunderts.* Rome: Storia e Letteratura, 1964-67. II, 207-213. Orig. publ. in *RTAM*, 14 (1947), 223-228.

1110   Manselli, R. "L'Antichristo mistico: Pietro di Giovanni Olivi, Ubertino da Casale, e i papi di loro tempo." *CF*, 47 (1977), 5-25.

1111   ——. "Divergences parmi les Mineurs d'Italie et de France méridionale." *Les mendiants en pays d'Oc au xiiie siècle.* Cahiers de Fanjeaux, 8. Toulouse: Privat, c1973. p. 355-373.

1112   ——. "L'idéal du spirituel selon Pierre Jean-Olivi." *Franciscains d'Oc.* p. 99-126. See 1089.

1113   ——. "Pietro di Giovanni Olivi spirituale." *Chi erano gli spirituali?* Assisi, 1976. p. 181-204. ——

1114   ——. "Pietro di Giovanni Olivi ed Ubertino da Casale (a proposito della *Lectura super Apocalipsim* e dell'*Arbor vitae crucifixae Jesu*)." *SM*, 3rd ser., 6, pt. 2 (1965), 95-122.

1115   ——. "Profili del sec. XIII: Pietro di Giovanni Olivi." *Humanitas* (Brescia), 10 (1955), 1121-1133. Trans. Poor Clares of Toulouse, "Une grande figure sérignanaise: Pierre de Jean Olivi," *Études franciscaines*, 22 (1972), 69-83.

1116   ——. "Les opuscules spirituels de Pierre Jean-Olivi et la piété des béguins de langue d'Oc." *La religion populaire en Languedoc du XIIIe siècle à la moitié du XIVe siècle.* Cahiers de Fanjeaux, 11. Toulouse: Privat, 1976. p. 187-201.

1117   ——. "Spirituali e beghini nel mezzogiorno della Francia." *Annales de l'Institut d'études occitanes*, 1965, p. 37-57. —

1118   ——, and M.-H. Vicaire. "Pierre Jean-Olieu, *Lo cavalier armat* (texte provençal édité d'après le ms. 9 de la Bibl. conv. Chiesa Nuova d'Assise)." *La religion populaire en Languedoc du XIIIe siècle à la moitié du XIVe siècle.* Cahiers de Fanjeaux, 11. Toulouse: Privat, 1976. p. 203-216.

1119   Manteuffel, T. "Piotr syn Jana Olivi: swięty czy herezjarcha." *PH*, 55 (1964), 393-404. [Incl. summary, "Pierre fils de Jean Olivi – saint ou hérésiarque?"] Trans., "Pierre-Jean Olivi, saint ou hérésiarque?" *Académie des inscriptions et belles-lettres: comptes rendus des séances*, 1964, p. 61-69.

1120   Maselli, D., ed. *Eretici e ribelli del XIII e XIV sec.: saggi sullo spiritualismo francescano in Toscana.* Pistoia: Tellini, [1974]. 327 p.
          Rev. F. Cardini, *ASI*, 131 (1973, c1975), 287-289; [M. Bertagna], *SF*, 72 (1975), 376-378.

1121   Matanić, A. "De duplici activitate S. Iacobi de Marchia in regno et vicaria franciscali Bosniae." *AFH*, 53 (1960), 111-127.

1122   Mosti, R. "L'eresia dei 'fraticelli' nel territorio di Tivoli." *Atti e memorie della Società tiburtina di storia e d'arte*, 38 (1965), 41-110.

1123   Odierna, A. "Il problema della libertà umana in Pier di Giovanni Olivi." Diss. Università Cattolica del Sacro Cuore, Milan, 1974. —

1124   "Un opuscule de Pierre Jean Olieu: 'Lo cavalier armat." *BLE*, 62 (1961), 201-204.

1125   Parrini, R. "I maestri di Parigi contro i mendicanti." *Eretici e ribelli del XIII e XIV sec.* Ed. D. Maselli. Pistoia: Tellini, [1974]. p. 121-133.

1126   Partee, C. "Peter John Olivi: historical and doctrinal study." *FS*, 20 (1960), 215-260.

1127   Paul, J. "Hugues de Digne." *Franciscains d'Oc.* p. 69-97. See 1089.

1128   ——. "Narbonne et la querelle de la pauvreté." *Narbonne: archéologie et histoire.* Montpellier: [Fédération historique du Languedoc méditerranéen et du Roussillon], 1973. II, 157-162.

1129   Peano, P. "Ministres provinciaux de Provence et spirituels." *Franciscains d'Oc.* p. 41-65. See 1089.

1130   Phelps, J. M. "A study of renewal ideas in the writings of the early Franciscans: 1210-1256." Diss. Univ. Of California, Los Angeles. *DAI*, 33A (1972), 1628.

1131   Poggi, S. "I fraticelli in Toscana." *Eretici e ribelli del XIII e XIV sec.* Ed. D. Maselli. Pistoia: Tellini, [1974]. p. 253-283.

1132   Potkowski, E. "Heretic Stephan of Marchia." *SM*, 13 (1972), 281-290, ill.

1133   Russo, F. "I fraticelli in Calabria nel secolo XIV: fatti e personaggi." *Miscellanea francescana*, 65 (1965), 349-368.

1134   Sacchetti Sassetti, A. "Giovanni da Capestrano e Lorenzo da Rieti, inquisitori in Sabina." *AFH*, 57 (1964), 200-204.

1135   Scalisi, G. *L'idea di chiesa negli spirituali e nei fraticelli.* Studi e testi francescani, 52. Rome and Vicenza: Libreria internazionale edizioni francescane, 1973. 95 p.
        Rev. [M. Bertagna], *SF*, 72 (1975), 385-386.

1136   Schneider, T. *Die Einheit des Menschen. Die anthropologische Formel "anima forma corporis" im sogenannten Korrektorienstreit und bei Petrus Johannis Olivi: ein Beitrag zur Vorgeschichte des Konzils von Vienne.* Beiträge zur Geschichte der Philosophie und Theologie des Mittelalters, n.s. 8. Münster: Aschendorff, c1973. vi, 288 p.
        Rev. W. J. Hoye, *TR*, 70 (1974), 299-301; I. Manzano, *Antonianum*, 48 (1973), 411-412; V. Capanága, *Revista española de teología*, 34 (1974), 287-288.

1137   Schwarz, W. "Si trovano in Dante echi delle opinioni teologiche di Pietro Olivi? – Dante e i Templari." *Atti del Congresso internazionale di studi danteschi ... 20-27 aprile 1965.* Florence: Sansoni, 1965-66. II, 147-149.

1138   Silvestri, G. "'Chi erano gli spirituali': a proposito di un convegno internazionale." *Laurentianum*, 18 (1977), 189-205.

1139   Simoncioli, F. "Breve prospetto delle principali teorie filosofiche di Pier di Giovanni Olivi alla luce della recente indagine di Efrem Bettoni." *SF*, 59 (1962), 47-60.

1140   Simoni, P. "Il problema degli universali nel pensiero di Pier di Giovanni Olivi." Diss. Università Cattolica del Sacro Cuore, Milan, 1971. —

1141   Sisto, A. "Pietro di Giovanni Olivi, il B. Venturino da Bergamo e S. Vincenzo Ferreri." *RSLR*, 1 (1965), 268-273.

1142   Spicciani, A. "Gli scritti sul capitale e sull'interesse di fra Pietro di Giovanni Olivi: fonti per la storia del pensiero economico medioevale." *SF*, 73 (1976), 289-325.

1143   Stadter, E. "Das Glaubensproblem in seiner Bedeutung für die Ethik bei Petrus Johannis Olivi OFM (†1298). Ein Beitrag zur Geschichte der Ethik und Religionsphilosophie des Mittelalters." *FSt*, 42 (1960), 225-296.

1144   ——. "Offenbarung und Heilsgeschichte nach Petrus Johannis Olivi." *FSt*, 44 (1962), 1-12, 129-191.

1145 ——. "Das Problem der Theologie bei Petrus Johannis Olivi OFM, auf Grund gedruckter und ungedruckter Quellen dargestellt." *FSt*, 43 (1961), 113-170.

1146 ——. "Die spiritualistische Geschichtstheologie als Voraussetzung für das Verständnis von *fides* und *auctoritas* bei Petrus Johannis Olivi." *FSt*, 48 (1966), 243-253.

1147 Stephens, J. N. "Heresy in medieval and renaissance Florence." *Past and present*, 54 (1972), 25-60. See 1045.

1148 Todeschini, G. "'Oeconomica franciscana' II: Pietro di Giovanni Olivi come fonte per la storia dell'etica-economica medievale." *RSLR*, 13 (1977), 461-494.

1149 Vallin, P. "Note à propos du *De remediis contra temptationes spirituales*." *RAM*, 45 (1969), 453-455.

1150 Van Dick, W. C. "La représentation de saint François d'Assise dans les écrits des spirituels." *Franciscains d'Oc.* p. 203-230. See 1089.

1151 Vicaire, M. H., trans. "Pierre Jean-Olieu: Épître aux fils de Charles II de Naples, en l'an 1295." *Franciscains d'Oc.* p. 127-138. See 1089.

1152 Vigueras, B. "De intentionalitate in Petri Joannis Olivi doctrina eiusque relatione cum moderna philosophia." Diss. Pontificium Athenaeum Antonianum, Rome. 1963. ——

1153 Weakland, J. E. "Pope John XXII and the beatific vision controversy." *Annuale mediaevale*, 9 (1968), 76-84.

1154 West, D. C. "The re-formed church and the Friars Minor: the moderate Joachite position of Fra Salimbene." *AFH*, 64 (1971), 273-284.

Part Ten

The Free Spirit

Entries 1155 to 1167

1155 Clark, J. P. H. "Walter Hilton and 'liberty of spirit'." *The Downside review*, 96 (1978), 61-78.

1156 Doiron, M., ed. "Margaret Porete, 'The mirror of simple souls': a Middle English translation." With appendix, "The glosses by 'M.N.' and Richard Methley to 'The mirror of simple souls'," by E. Colledge and R. Guarnieri. *Archivio italiano per la storia della pietà*, 5 (1968), 241-355, 357-382.

1157 ——. "The Middle English translation of 'Le mirouer des simples ames'." *Dr. L. Reypens-Album*. Studiën en tekstuitgaven van Ons geestelijk erf, 16. Antwerp: Ruusbroec-Genootschap, 1964. p. 131-152.

1158 Erbstösser, M., and E. Werner. *Ideologische Probleme des mittelalterlichen Plebejertums: die freigeistige Häresie und ihre sozialen Wurzeln*. Forschungen zur mittelalterlichen Geschichte, 7. Berlin: Akademie-Verlag, 1960. 163 p. ill.
  Rev. A. Mens, *RBPH*, 41 (1963), 574-576; A. Gerlich, *HZ*, 196 (1963), 394-396.

1159 Guarnieri, R. "Il movimento del libero spirito: testi e documenti. I. Il movimento del libero spirito dalle origini al secolo XVI. II. Il *Miroir des simples âmes* di Margherita Porete. III. Appendici." *Archivio italiano per la storia della pietà*, 4 (1965), 351-708, ill.
  Rev. S. de Campagnola, *CF*, 37 (1967), 417-419; E. Colledge, *MÆ*, 37 (1968), 240-242; R. Manselli, *RSLR*, 3 (1967), 147-156; M. Rosada, *RSCI*, 22 (1968), 204-207; B. Spaapen, *RAM*, 42 (1966), 423-437, and Ons geestelijk erf, 40 (1966), 369-391.

1160 Hofmann, G. "Die Brüder und Schwestern des Freien Geistes zur Zeit Heinrich Seuses." *Seuse Studien: gesammelte Beiträge zum 600. Todestag*. Ed. E. Filthaut. Cologne, 1966. p. 9-32. ——

1161 Lerner, R. E. "The heresy of the free spirit in the thirteenth century." Diss. Princeton Univ. *DAI*, 25A (1965), 6557.

1162   ———. *The heresy of the free spirit in the later middle ages.* Berkeley, Los Angeles,
         London: University of California Press, 1972. xv, 257 p.
         Rev. W. L. Wakefield, *CH*, 41 (1972), 540; E. L. McLaughlin, *Speculum,*
         49 (1974), 747-751; M. d'Alatri, *CF*, 44 (1974), 429-431; P. de Vooght, *RHE,*
         68 (1973), 875-881; K.-V. Selge, *DAEM,* 31 (1975), 203-205; M. A.
         Orcasitas, *CD,* 186 (1973), 421-422; P. Grand, *BTAM,* 11 (1973), 525-527; C.
         C. de Bruin, *TG,* 86 (1973), 325-327; J. W. O'Malley, *Review for religious,*
         31 (1972), 880; H. S. Offler, *EHR,* 89 (1974), 165; M. D. Lambert, *History,*
         59 (1974), 92-93.
1163   ———. "The image of mixed liquids in late medieval mystical thought." *CH,* 40
         (1971), 397-411.
1164   ———. "A note on the university career of Jacques Fournier, o.cist., later Pope
         Benedict XII." *Analecta cisterciensia,* 30 (1974), 66-69.
1165   McLaughlin, E. C. "The heresy of the Free Spirit and late medieval mysticism."
         MH, n.s. 4 (1973), 37-54.
1166   ———. "The heresy of the Free spirit: a study in medieval religious life." Diss.
         Harvard Univ., 1967-68. —
1167   Orcibal, J. "Le 'Miroir des simples âmes' et la 'secte' du libre esprit." *RHR,* 176
         (1969), 35-60.

Part Eleven

Wyclif and the Wycliffite Bible

A. *Wyclif (Entries 1168 to 1257)*

1168   Aston, M. "John Wycliffe's reformation reputation." *Past and present*, 30 (1965), 23-51.

1169   Auksi, P. "Wyclif's sermons and the plain style." *ARG*, 66 (1975), 5-23. [Incl. Ger. summary]

1170   Benrath, G. A. "Stand und Aufgaben der Wyclif-Forschung." *TLZ*, 92 (1967), 261-264.

1171   ——. "Traditionsbewußtsein, Schriftverständnis und Schriftprinzip bei Wyclif." *Antiqui und moderni*. Ed. A. Zimmermann. Miscellanea mediaevalia, 9. Berlin and New York: de Gruyter, 1974. p. 359-382.

1172   ——. "Wyclif und Hus." *ZTK*, 62 (1965), 196-216.

1173   Beonio-Brocchieri Fumagalli, M. *Wyclif: il comunismo dei predestinati.* [Florence]: Sansoni, c1975. 99 p.

1174   Block, E. A. *John Wyclif: radical dissenter.* Humanities monograph series, 1, no. 1. San Diego: San Diego State University Press, 1962. 58 p.
       Rev. H. Hargreaves, *Modern language review*, 59 (1964), 98.

1175   Boor, F. de. *Wyclifs Simoniebegriff: die theologischen und kirchenpolitischen Grundlagen der Kirchenkritik John Wyclifs.* Arbeiten zur Kirchengeschichte und Religionswissenschaft, 3. Halle: Niemeyer, 1970. 184 p.
       Rev. P. de Vooght, *RHE*, 67 (1972), 932-933; G. A. Benrath, *ZSSRG*, kan. Abt., 89 (1972), 444-446; A. Molnár, *TLZ*, 99 (1974), 775-776; M. Wilks, *JEH*, 24 (1973), 70-71; J. R. Wright, *ATR*, 55 (1973), 370-371; W. Zeller, *ZRGG*, 25 (1973), 279-280.

1176   Boussard, J. "Wyclif et l'église anglaise au xive siècle." *Annuaire de l'École pratique des hautes études, ive section*, 105 (1973), 429-432.

1177   Breck, A. duP., ed. *Johannis Wyclif Tractatus de trinitate.* [Boulder]: University of Colorado Press, 1962. liv, 196 p.
       Rev. H. A. Oberman, *Speculum*, 41 (1966), 315-317.

1178   Butrym, A. J. "An edition, with commentary, of the Wyclifite tracts contained in
       MS Trinity College, Dublin, C.V.6." Diss. Rutgers Univ., State Univ. of
       New Jersey. *DAI*, 32A (1972), 5174-5175.

1179   Crompton, J. "Fasciculi zizaniorum." *JEH*, 12 (1961), 35-45, 155-166.

1180   ———. "John Wyclif: a study in mythology." *Transactions of the Leicestershire
       archaeological and historical society*, 42 (1966-67), 6-34.

1181   Dahmus, J. H. "John Wyclif and the English government." *Speculum*, 35 (1960),
       51-68.

1182   ———. *The prosecution of John Wyclyf*. New Haven and London, 1952. Rpt.
       [Hamden]: Archon, 1970. xi, 167 p.

1183   Daly, L. J. *The political theory of John Wyclif*. Chicago: Loyola University Press,
       1962. xi, 168 p.
       Rev. C. S. Meyer, *JCS*, 6 (1964), 241-243; J. B. Morrall, *CHR*, 49 (1963), 93-
       94; S. H. Thomson, *Speculum*, 40 (1965), 343-344.

1184   ———. "Walter Burley and John Wyclif on some aspects of kingship." *Mélanges
       Eugène Tisserant*. Studi e testi, 231-237. Vatican: Biblioteca Vaticana,
       1964. IV, 163-184.

1185   ———. "Wyclif's political theory: a century of study." *MH*, n.s. 4 (1973), 177-187.

1186   Davidson, C. "Wyclif and the Middle English sermon." *Universitas* (Detroit),
       3 (1965-66), 92-99.

1187   Doyle, E. "William Woodford, O.F.M., and John Wyclif's *De religione*." *Speculum*,
       52 (1977), 329-336.

1188   ———. "William Woodford's 'De dominio civili clericorum' against John Wyclif."
       AFH, 66 (1973), 49-109.

1189   Dyson, T. "Wyclif reviewed." *CQR*, 168 (1967), 423-433.

1190   Eckermann, W. "Augustinus Favaroni von Rom und Johannes Wyclif: der
       Ansatz ihrer Lehre über die Kirche." *Scientia Augustiniana* (Festschrift
       Adolar Zumkeller). Ed. C. P. Mayer and W. Eckermann. Cassiciacum, 30.
       Würzburg: Augustinus-Verlag, 1975. p. 323-348.

1191   Farr, W. E. "John Wyclif as Legal Reformer." Diss. Univ. of Washington. *DAI*,
       32A (1971), 2585.

1192   ———. *John Wyclif as legal reformer*. Studies in the history of Christian thought,
       10. Leiden: Brill, 1974. ix, 187 p.
       Rev. M. Wilks, *JEH*, 27 (1976), 432-433; O. J. de Jong, *Nederlands
       theologisch tijdschrift*, 30 (1976), 232-233; H. Junghans, *TLZ*, 101 (1976),
       592-594; E. C. Tatnall, *CH*, 44 (1975), 534-535; A. Hudson, *JTS*, 27 (1976),
       246; J. Séguy, *ASSR*, 40 (1975), 211-212; A. K. McHardy, *The expository
       times*, 86 (1975), 347-348; J. F. Hitchcock, *TS*, 37 (1976), 184; C. W.
       Brockwell, Jr., *Journal of church and state*, 20 (1978), 551-552; A.
       Patschovsky, *DAEM*, 34 (1978), 683-684.

1193   Fisher, J. H. "Wyclif, Langland, Gower, and the *Pearl* poet on the subject of
       aristocracy." *Studies in medieval literature in honor of Professor Albert*

Croll Baugh. Ed. M. Leach. Philadelphia: University of Pennsylvania Press, c1961. p. 139-157.

1194 Fox, M. "John Wyclif and the Mass." *HJ*, 3 (1962), 232-240.

1195 Fraker, C. F. "The theme of predestination in the *Cancionero de Baena.*" *Bulletin of Hispanic studies*, 51 (1974), 228-243.

1196 Gilbert, N. W. "Ockham, Wyclif, and the 'via moderna'." *Antiqui und moderni.* Ed. A. Zimmermann. Miscellanea mediaevalia, 9. Berlin and New York: de Gruyter, 1974. p. 85-125.

1197 Gilchrist, J. "The social doctrine of John Wycliff." Canadian historical association, *Historical papers 1969*, p. 157-165.

1198 Hargreaves, H. "Wyclif's prose." *Essays and studies* (London), 19 (1966), 1-17.

1199 Hudson, A. "Contributions to a bibliography of Wycliffite writings." *N&Q*, 20 (1973), 443-453.

1200 Hurley, M. "'Scriptura sola': Wyclif and his critics." *Traditio*, 16 (1960), 275-352. Rpt. New York: Fordham University Press, 1960.
Rev. J. Vella, *Divus Thomas*, 67 (1964), 102-105; B. Smalley, *EHR*, 78 (1963), 161-162; J. Beumer, *Scholastik*, 36 (1961), 593. See 1281.

1201 Jurschax, G. M. "Chaucer and fourteenth-century English thought." Diss. Loyola University, Chicago. *DAI*, 33A (1972), 1685.

1202 Kaminsky, H. "Wyclifism as ideology of revolution." *CH*, 32 (1963), 57-74.

1203 Kaňák, M. *John Viklef: život a dílo anglického Husova předchůdce.* [Incl. sources trans. in collab. with K. Červený.] Prague: Blahoslav, 1973. 233 p. ill. [John Wyclif: life and work of the English precursor of Hus]
Rev. P. de Vooght, *RHE*, 70 (1975), 359.

1204 ——. "K nové anglické literatuře o Wyclifovi." *AUC Hist*, 10, no. 2 (1969), 67-76. [Survey-review of recent British and American works on Wyclif]

1205 Kellogg, A. L., and E. W. Talbert. "The Wyclifite *Pater noster* and *Ten commandments*, with special reference to English mss. 85 and 90 in the John Rylands Library." *Bulletin of the John Rylands Library*, 42 (1960), 345-377.

1206 Knapp, P. A. "John Wyclif and the horned patriarchs." *American notes and queries*, 14 (1976), 66-67.

1207 Dickie [Knapp], P. A. "The style of John Wyclif's English sermons." Diss. Univ. of Pittsburgh. *DAI*, 27A (1966), 1028.

1208 Knapp, P. A. *The style of John Wyclif's English sermons.* De proprietatibus litterarum, series practica, 16. The Hague and Paris: Mouton, 1977. 116 p.
Rev. A. Hudson, *N&Q*, 25 (1978), 359; J. H. Fisher, *Speculum*, 54 (1979), 161-162.

1209 Leff, G. "John Wyclif: the path to dissent." *Proceedings of the British Academy*, 52 (1966 [1967]), 143-180.

1210 ——. "Ockham and Wyclif on the eucharist." *Reading medieval studies*, 2 (1976), 1-13.

1211 ——. "Wyclif and Hus: a doctrinal comparison." *Bulletin of the John Rylands Library*, 50 (1968), 387-410.

1212 ——. "Wyclif and the Augustinian tradition, with special reference to his *De trinitate*." *MH*, n.s. 1 (1970), 29-39.

1213 Lewis, J. *The history of the life and sufferings of the reverend and learned John Wiclif*, D.D. Oxford, 1820. Rpt. New York: AMS, 1973. xxxii, 389, [+ 11] p.

1214 McFarlane, K. B. *John Wycliffe and the beginnings of English nonconformity*. London and New York, 1952. Rpt. as *The origins of religious dissent in England* (New York: Collier, 1966), 220 p. Also rpt. as *Wycliffe and English nonconformity* (Harmondsworth: Penguin, 1972), xvii, 188 p.

1215 McHardy, A. K. "John Wycliffe's mission to Bruges: a financial footnote." *JTS*, 24 (1973), 521-522.

1216 McVeigh, T. A. "Chaucer's portraits of the Pardoner and Summoner and Wyclif's *Tractatus de simonia*." *Classical folia*, 29 (1975), 54-58.

1217 Mallard, W. "Clarity and dilemma – the *Forty sermons* of John Wyclif." *Contemporary reflections on the medieval Christian tradition: essays in honor of Ray C. Petry*. Ed. G. H. Shriver. Durham, N.C.: Duke University Press, 1974. p. 19-38.

1218 ——. "Dating the *Sermones quadraginta* of John Wyclif." *MH*, 17 (1966), 86-105.

1219 Mantello, F. A. C. "The endleaves of Trinity College Cambridge Ms 0.4.43 and John Wyclif's *Responsiones ad argumenta cuiusdam emuli veritatis*." *Speculum*, 54 (1979), 100-103.

1220 Molnár, A. "K Viklefově teologii." *TPKR*, 31 (1964), 19-23. Trans., "Recent literature on Wyclif's theology," *CV*, 7 (1964), 186-192.

1221 Molnar, E. S. "Marsilius of Padua, Wyclyf and Hus." *ATR*, 44 (1962), 33-43.

1222 Mudroch, V. "John Wyclyf and Richard Flemyng, bishop of Lincoln: gleanings from German sources." *BIHR*, 37 (1964), 239-245.

1223 ——. "John Wyclif's *Postilla* in fifteenth-century Bohemia." *Canadian journal of theology*, 10 (1964), 118-123.

1224 ——. "The Wyclyf tradition." Diss. University of Toronto, 1960. 296 p. —

1225 Paull, M. R. "Mahomet and the conversion of the heathen in *Piers Plowman*." *ELN*, 10 (1972), 1-8.

1226 Robson, J. A. *Wyclif and the Oxford schools: the relation of the 'Summa de ente' to scholastic debates at Oxford in the later fourteenth century*. Cambridge studies in medieval life and thought, n.s. 8. Cambridge: Cambridge University Press, 1961. xiii, 268 p.
     Rev. M. Deanesly, *CQR*, 163 (1962), 252-253; A. B. Emden, *N&Q*, 9 (1962), 114-115; J. M. Fletcher, *HibbJ*, 60 (1961-62), 179-180; M. Hurley, *The month*, 27 (1962), 50-52; G. Leff, *EHR*, 77 (1962), 721-723; J. E. McCristal, *JRH*, 2 (1963), 254-257; J. B. Morrall, *TS*, 23 (1962), 332-334; H. A.

Oberman, *TLZ*, 89 (1964), 546-550; B. Smalley, *MÆ*, 30 (1961), 200-203; E. R. H[ardy], *ATR*, 44 (1962), 449-450; S. H. Thompson, *Speculum*, 38 (1963), 497-499; J. A. Weisheipl, *CHR*, 48 (1963), 236-237; H. Weisweiler, *Scholastik*, 39 (1964), 605; C. R. Young, *AHR*, 67 (1962), 468-469; Anon., *TLS*, 9 March 1962, p. 172; S. Sousedík, *FČ*, 18 (1970), 113-116; G. A. Barrois, *The Princeton seminary bulletin*, 55, no. 2 (1962), 68.

1227 Rosenberg, A. "Wiclif und Hus." *Die Wahrheit der Ketzer*. Ed. H. J. Schultz. Stuttgart and Berlin: Kreuz-Verlag, c1968. p. 89-98, 268-276, ill.

1228 Sankey, R. W. "A rhetorical study of selected English sermons of John Wycliff." Diss. Northwestern University. *DAI*, 30A (1970), 5098-5099.

1229 Saprykin, I. M. "Vzgliady Jona Wiclifa na obshchnost' imushchestva i ravenstvo." *Srednie veka*, 34 (1971), 163-190. [Incl. summary, "John Wyclif's conception of common property and equality"]

1230 Šmahel, F. "*Universalia realia sunt heresis seminaria*: filosofie pražského extremního realismu ve světle doktrinálně institucionální kritiky." *ČČH*, 16 (1968), 797-818. [Incl. summary, p. 817-818, "... Die Philosophie des extremen Prager Realismus im Lichte einer doktrinär institutionalen Kritik"]

1231 Stacey, J. *John Wyclif and reform*. Philadelphia: Westminster; London: Lutterworth, 1964. 169 p.
Rev. N. V. Hope, *Theology today*, 22 (1965), 142-143; G. A. Benrath, *ARG*, 59 (1968), 106-107; M. A. Schmidt, *CH*, 34 (1965), 460-462; G. Hinson, *Review and expositor*, 62 (1965), 235-236.

1232 ———. "John Wyclif and the ministry of the word." *The London quarterly and Holborn review*, 190 (1965), 50-54.

1233 ———. "The piety of John Wyclif." *The expository times*, 73 (August 1962), 327-329.

1234 Stalder, R. "Le concept de l'église selon le *De ecclesia* de Wiclif." *Bijdragen*, 23 (1962), 38-51, 287-302.

1235 Studzinski, R. J. "John Wyclif and the sacrament of penance." Diss. Fordham Univ. *DAI*, 38A (1977), 2210.

1236 Talbert, E. W., and S. H. Thomson. "Wyclyf and his followers." *A manual of the writings in Middle English, 1050-1500*, 2. Ed. J. B. Severs. [New Haven]: Connecticut academy of arts and sciences, 1970. p. 354-380, 517-533.

1237 Tatnall, E. C. "Church and state according to John Wyclyf." Diss. Univ. of Colorado. *DAI*, 26A (1966), 5393-5394.

1238 ———. "The condemnation of John Wyclif at the council of Constance." *Councils and assemblies*. Ed. G. J. Cuming and D. Baker. Studies in church history, 7. Cambridge: Cambridge University Press, 1971. p. 209-218.

1239 ———. "John Wyclif and *ecclesia anglicana*." *JEH*, 20 (1969), 19-43.

1240 Terasawa, Y. "A rhetorical spoken style of M.E.: the case of Wyclif's sermon translation." *Studies in English literature* (Tokyo), 1968 English number, p. 61-81.

1241   Thomson, S. H. "John Wyclyf." *Reformers in profile.* Ed. B. A. Gerrish. Philadelphia: Fortress Press, c1967. p. 12-39.

1242   ——. "A note on Peter Payne and Wyclyf." *MH*, 16 (1964), 60-63, ill.

1243   Trevelyan, G. M. *England in the age of Wycliffe.* London, 1899. Rpt. New York: Harper and Row, 1963; Totowa, N.J.: Rowman and Littlefield, 1973. xvi, 380 p. London 1900 ed. rpt. New York: AMS, 1975. London 1912 ed. rpt. New York and London: Johnson; Frankfurt am Main: Minerva, 1966.

1244   Vaughan, R. *The life and opinions of John de Wycliffe, D.D., illustrated principally from his unpublished manuscripts.* 2nd ed. London, 1831. Rpt. New York: AMS, [1973]. 2 v.

1245   Vermaseren, B. A. "Nieuwe studies over Wyclif en Huss." *TG*, 76 (1963), 190-212.

1246   Warner, A. R. "Infinitive marking in the Wyclifite sermons." *English studies,* 56 (1975), 207-214.

1247   Wawn, A. N. "Chaucer, Wyclif and the court of Apollo." *ELN*, 10 (1972), 15-20.

1248   Welch, J. N. "Concepts relating to civil rule in the works of St. Augustine and John Wyclif." Diss. St. Louis Univ. *DAI*, 25A (1964), 423.

1249   Wendelborn, G. "Das Verhältnis von Schrift und Vernunft im Werk John Wiclifs." Diss. Universität Rostock, 1964. 320 p. —

1250   ——. "Zur Einordnung Wyclifs." *Standpunkt*, 6, nos. 3-4 (1978), 75 ff. —

1251   Whitney, J. P. "A note on the work of the Wyclif society." *Essays in history presented to Reginald Lane Poole.* Ed. H. W. C. Davis. Oxford, 1927. Rpt. Freeport, N.Y.: Books for Libraries, [1967]. p. 98-114.

1252   Wilks, M. J. "The early Oxford Wyclif: papalist or nominalist?" *The church and academic learning.* Ed. G. J. Cuming. Studies in church history, 5. Leiden: Brill, 1969. p. 69-98.

1253   ——. "*Reformatio regni*: Wyclif and Hus as leaders of the religious protest movements." *Schism, heresy and religious protest* (1972). p. 109-130. See 120.

1254   ——. "Predestination, property, and power: Wyclif's theory of dominion and grace." *Studies in church history*, 2. Ed. G. J. Cuming. [London]: Nelson, [1965]. p. 220-236.

1255   Winn, H. E., ed. *Wyclif: select English writings.* London, 1929. Rpt. New York: AMS, 1976. xl, 179 p.

1256   Workman, H. B. *John Wyclif: a study of the English medieval church.* Oxford, 1926. Rpt. Hamden, Conn.: Archon, 1966. 2 v. in 1.
        Rev. J. Crompton, *JEH*, 18 (1967), 263-266.

1257   Wyclif, J. *Wyclif's Latin works.* London, 1882-1922. Rpt. New York and London: Johnson; Frankfurt am Main: Minerva, 1966. 23 v. in 36. [v. 23: rpt. of G. M. Trevelyan, *England in the age of Wycliffe.* See no. 1243.]

B. *The Wycliffite Bible (Entries 1258 to 1282)*

1258   Benrath, G. A. *Wyclifs Bibelkommentar.* Arbeiten zur Kirchengeschichte, 36.
        Berlin: de Gruyter, 1966. xii, 415 p.
        Rev. J. Noret, *AB*, 86 (1968), 215-216; R. Cegna, *RSLR*, 5 (1969), 460-461;
        S. Wenzel, *Speculum*, 43 (1968), 121-123; W. Fellmann, *ZRGG*, 21 (1969),
        176-178; P. de Vooght, *RHE*, 62 (1967), 830-834; C. L. Gage-Brown, *CQR*,
        168 (1967), 259-260; J. Crompton, *JEH*, 18 (1967), 263-266; H. Karpp, *TLZ*,
        93 (1968), 43-45; G. Wendelborn, *DLZ*, 89 (1968), 1006-1009; D. Braun,
        TZ, 24 (1968), 229-230; P. Prigent, *RHPR*, 48 (1968), 404; B. Smalley, *ZKG*,
        78 (1967), 175-176; A. Molnár, *ARG*, 59 (1968), 241-244, and *CV*, 12
        (1969), 92.
1259   Davis, D. G., Jr. "The Bible of John Wyclif: production and circulation." *Biblio-*
        theca sacra, 128 (1971), 16-26.
1260   Deanesly, M. *The Lollard Bible and other medieval biblical versions.* Cambridge:
        Cambridge University Press, 1920. Rpt. 1966, with new prefatory note.
        xx [errata, xxi-xxiii], 483 p.
        Rev. J. Crompton, *JEH*, 18 (1967), 263-266; G. Huelin, *CQR*, 168 (1967),
        531-532; F. F. Bruce, *Evangelical quarterly*, 39 (1967), 184-185.
1261   Fowler, D. C. "John Trevisa and the English Bible." *Modern philology*, 58 (1960),
        81-98.
1262   Fristedt, S. L. "The dating of the earliest manuscript of the Wycliffite Bible."
        Studier i modern språkvetenskap, n.s. 1 (1960), 79-85.
1263   ———. "New light on John Wycliffe and the first full English Bible." *Studier i*
        modern språkvetenskap, n.s. 3 (1968), 61-86.
1264   ———. "A note on some obscurities in the history of the Lollard Bible:
        amplification of *The Wycliffe Bible. Part II.*" *Studier i modern språkveten-*
        skap, n.s. 4 (1972), 38-45.
1265   ———. "Spanish influence on Lollard translation: amplification of *The Wycliffe*
        Bible, part III." *Studier i modern språkvetenskap*, n.s. 5 (1975), 5-10.
1266   ———. "A weird manuscript enigma in the British Museum." *Studier i modern*
        språkvetenskap, n.s. 2 (1964), 116-121, ill.
1267   ———. *The Wycliffite Bible* (pt. 1: The principal problems connected with Forshall
        and Madden's edition. pt. 2: The origin of the first revision as presented in
        De salutaribus documentis. pt. 3: Relationships of Trevisa and the Spanish
        medieval bibles.) Stockholm studies in English, 4, 21, 28. Stockholm:
        Almqvist and Wiksell, 1953-73. 3 v. ill.
        Rev. B. Danielsson, *SN*, 44 (1972), 188-195; M.-M. Dubois, *MA*, 78 (1972),
        582-583; H. Hargreaves, *The yearbook of English studies*, 1 (1971), 218-
        219; A. Hudson, *MÆ*, 40 (1971), 204-205, and 44 (1975), 179-181.
1268   Hargreaves, H. "From Bede to Wyclif: medieval English Bible translations."
        Bulletin of the John Rylands Library, 48 (1965), 118-140.

1269 ——. "The marginal glosses to the Wycliffite New Testament." *SN*, 33 (1961),
       285-300.

1270 Herold, V. "Johannis Wyclif De universalibus (Summa de ente, Libri primi
       tractatus sextus). Edice úvodní části traktátu." *FČ*, 18 (1970), 999-1009.

1271 Knapp, P. A. "John Wyclif as Bible translator: the texts for the English sermons."
       Speculum, 46 (1971), 713-720.

1272 Lindberg, C. "The manuscripts and versions of the Wycliffite bible: a preliminary
       survey." *SN*, 42 (1970), 333-347.

1273 ——, ed. *The Middle English bible: prefatory epistles of St. Jerome.* Oslo, Bergen
       and Tromsø: Universitetsforlaget, 1978. 172 p.

1274 ——, ed. *MS. Bodley 959: Genesis – Baruch 3.20 in the earlier version of the
       Wycliffite Bible.* Acta Universitatis Stockholmiensis/Stockholm studies in
       English, 6, 8, 10, 13, 20, 29. Stockholm: Almqvist and Wiksell, 1959-
       1973. 6 v. [v. 6 has title, *The earlier version of the Wycliffite Bible: Baruch
       3.20 – end of OT edited from MS Christ Church 145*]
       Rev. B. Danielsson, *SN*, 42 (1970), 498-503; B. Cottle, *Journal of English
       and Germanic philology*, 59 (1960), 565; 61 (1962), 372-373; 63 (1964),
       331-332; 65 (1966), 708-709; 69 (1970), 515-517; M. Lehnert, *Zeitschrift
       für Anglistik und Amerikanistik*, 9 (1961), 414-415; 12 (1964), 54-55; F. C.
       de Vries, *Neophilologus*, 51 (1967), 101-102; E. Colledge, *The modern
       language review*, 55 (1960), 588-589; 58 (1963), 457-458; 59 (1964), 624;
       M. C. Seymour, *The modern language review*, 61 (1966), 484-485; H.
       Marcus, *Archiv für das Studium der neueren Sprachen*, 196 (1960), 343;
       P. Bacquet, *Études anglaises*, 14 (1961), 51; H. Käsmann, *Anglia*, 80
       (1962), 329-333; 81 (1963), 475-477; H. Hargreaves, *RES*, 12 (1961), 71-72;
       13 (1962), 437; 16 (1965), 105-106; 18 (1967), 235; J. Söderlind, *Leuvense
       bijdragen*, 65 (1976), 264-266; P. Gradon, *MÆ*, 30 (1961), 198-200; 33
       (1964), 150-151; 37 (1968), 213; 40 (1971), 201-203; A. Hudson, *MÆ*, 44
       (1975), 179-181; J. H. Dahmus, *Speculum*, 35 (1960), 309-310; H.
       Hargreaves, *The yearbook of English studies*, 7 (1977), 203-205; M.
       Görlach, *Archiv für das Studium der neueren Sprachen und Literaturen*,
       213 (1976), 399-401.

1275 Mallard, W. "John Wiclif and the tradition of biblical authority." *CH*, 30 (1961),
       50-60.

1276 McIntosh, A. "Some linguistic reflections of a Wycliffite." *Franciplegius:
       medieval and linguistic studies in honor of Francis Peabody Magoun, jr.*
       Ed. J. B. Bessinger, jr., and R. P. Creed. New York: New York University
       Press, 1965. p. 290-293.

1277 Minnis, A. J. *"Authorial intention" and "literal sense" in the exegetical theories of
       Richard FitzRalph and John Wyclif: an essay in the medieval history of
       biblical hermeneutics.* Proceedings of the Royal Irish Academy, 75, sect.
       C, no. 1. Dublin: Royal Irish Academy, 1975. 31 p.

1278   Reilly, R. "A Middle English summary of the Bible: an edition of Trinity College (Oxon) MS 93." Diss. Univ. of Washington. *DAI*, 27A (1967), 4229.

1279   Smalley, B. "The Bible and eternity: John Wyclif's dilemma." *Journal of the Warburg and Courtauld Institutes*, 27 (1964), 73-89.

1280   ——. "Wyclif's *Postilla* on the Old Testament and his *Principium*." *Oxford studies presented to Daniel Callus.* Oxford historical society, n.s. 16. Oxford: Oxford historical society, 1964. p. 253-296.

1281   Vooght, P. de. "Wiclif ét la *Scriptura sola*." *ETL*, 39 (1963), 50-86. See 1200.

1282   Wilks, M. "Misleading manuscripts: Wyclif and the non-Wycliffite Bible." *The materials, sources and methods of ecclesiastical history.* Ed. D. Baker. Studies in church history, 11. Oxford: Blackwell, 1975. p. 147-161.

Part Twelve

Lollards

Entries 1283 to 1337

1283 Aston, M. "Lollardy and literacy." *History*, 62 (1977), 347-371.

1284 ——. "Lollardy and sedition, 1381-1431." *Past and present*, 17 (1960), 1-44.

1285 ——. "Lollardy and the reformation: survival or revival?" *History*, 49 (1964), 149-170.

1286 Brockwell, C. W. "Bishop Reginald Pecock and the crisis and challenge of the laity in the English church in the fifteenth century." Diss. Duke Univ. *DAI*, 32A (1972), 5883-5884.

1287 Crompton, J. "Leicestershire Lollards." *Transactions of the Leicestershire archaeological and historical society*, 44 (1968-69), 11-44.

1288 Davis, J. "John Wyclif's reformation reputation." *The churchman*, 83 (1969), 97-102. [Critique of recent studies by M. Aston]

1289 Davis, J. F. "Lollards, reformers and St. Thomas of Canterbury." *University of Birmingham historical journal*, 9 (1963), 1-15.

1290 ——. "Lollard survival and the textile industry in the south-east of England." *Studies in church history*, 3. Ed. G. J. Cuming. Leiden: Brill, 1966. p. 191-201.

1291 Fiehler, R. "Sir John Oldcastle, the original of Falstaff." Diss. Univ. of Texas, Austin. *DAI*, 31A (1970), 2341-2342.

1292 Fines, J. "William Thorpe: an early Lollard." *History today*, 18 (1968), 495-503, ill.

1293 Foreville, R. "Manifestations de Lollardisme à Exeter en 1421? D'après une lettre 'extravagante' de Henri Chichele." *MA*, 69 (1963), 691-706.

1294 Gairdner, J. *Lollardy and the reformation in England: an historical survey.* 4 v. London, 1908-1913. Rpt. New York: Burt Franklin, [1964].

1295 Geodecka, B. "Ideologia ludowego ruchu lollardów." *PH*, 61 (1970), 381-387. [Incl. summary, p. 387, "L'idéologie du mouvement populaire des Lollards"]

1296 Härtel, H. "Lollardische Lehrelemente im 14. und 15. Jh.." Diss. Universität Göttingen, 1969. —

1297 Haines, R. M. "'Wilde wittes and wilfulnes': John Swetstock's attack on those 'poyswunmongeres,' the Lollards." *Popular belief and practice.* Ed. G. J. Cuming and D. Baker. Studies in church history, 8. Cambridge: Cambridge University Press, 1972. p. 143-153.

1298 Hargreaves, H. "Sir John Oldcastle and Wycliffite views on clerical marriage." *MÆ*, 42 (1973), 141-146.

1299 Heidtmann, P. "Wycliffe and the Lollards: a reforming heretical sect at the end of the fourteenth century." *History today*, 20 (1970), 724-732, ill.

1300 Heyworth, P. L. "The earliest black-letter editions of *Jack Upland.*" *The Huntington Library quarterly*, 30 (1967), 307-314.

1301 ——, ed. *Jack Upland, Friar Daw's reply and Upland's rejoinder.* London and Oxford: Oxford University Press, 1968. xii, 176 p.
Rev. *TLS*, 14 August 1969, p. 913; A. Bruten, *RES*, 21 (1970), 194-195; G. L. Harriss, *EHR*, 85 (1970), 611; R. H. Robbins, *N&Q*, 17 (1970), 266-267; D. Knowles, *MÆ*, 39 (1970), 228-230.

1302 ——. "*Jack Upland's rejoinder*, a Lollard interpolator and *Piers Plowman* B.X. 249f." *MÆ*, 36 (1967), 242-248.

1303 ——. "ME *alumere* and *snowcrie*: two ghosts." *English philological studies*, 10 (1967), 57-61.

1304 Holdstock, J. R. "The origins of subversive literature in English." Diss. Univ. of California, Davis. *DAI*, 33A (1973), 5681.

1305 Hudson, A. "The debate on Bible translation, Oxford 1401." *EHR*, 90 (1975), 1-18.

1306 ——. "The examination of Lollards." *BIHR*, 46 (1973), 145-159.

1307 ——. "The expurgation of a Lollard sermon-cycle." *JTS*, 22 (1971), 451-465.

1308 ——. "A Lollard compilation and the dissemination of Wycliffite thought." *JTS*, 23 (1972), 65-81.

1309 ——. "A Lollard compilation in England and Bohemia." *JTS*, 25 (1974), 129-140.

1310 ——. "A Lollard Mass." *JTS*, 23 (1972), 407-419.

1311 ——. "A Lollard quaternion." *RES*, 22 (1971), 435-442.

1312 ——. "A Lollard sermon-cycle and its implications." *MÆ*, 40 (1971), 142-156.

1313 ——. "A neglected Wycliffite text." *JEH*, 29 (1978), 257-279.

1314 ——, ed. *Selections from English Wycliffite writings.* Cambridge, etc.: Cambridge University Press, 1978. xii, 234 p.
Rev. A. K. McHardy, *Expository times*, 90 (1978), 28; J. Dahmus, *Manuscripta*, 23 (1979), 52-53; S. Wenzel, *N&Q*, 26 (1979), 63-64; J. A. F. Thomson, *History*, 64 (1979), 88-89; R. F. S. Hamer, *JTS*, 30 (1979), 355-356; B. Boyd, *JEGP*, 77 (1978), 587; O. S. Pickering, *Archiv für das Studium der neueren Sprachen und Literaturen*, 216 (1979), 171-174; P. B. Taylor, *English studies*, 60 (1979), 523-524; R. G. Davies, *EHR*, 94 (1979), 628.

1315 ——. "Some aspects of Lollard book production." *Schism, heresy and religious protest* (1972). p. 147-157. See 120.

1316 Jones, W. R. "Lollards and images: the defense of religious art in later medieval England." *Journal of the history of ideas*, 34 (1973), 27-50.

1317 Kightly, C. "The early Lollards: a survey of popular Lollard activity in England, 1382-1428." Diss. Univ. of York, England, 1975. vi, 612 [i.e. 624] p.

1318 Kurze, D. "Die festländischen Lollarden: zur Geschichte der religiösen Bewegungen im ausgehenden Mittelalter." *AKG*, 47 (1965), 48-76.

1319 Kuznetsov, E. V. "Dvizhenie lollardov v Anglii (konets XIV-XV v.)." *Uchen'ie zapiski Gor'kovskogo Gos. Universiteta*, istoricheskaia seriia, 95 (1971), 25-286. [Lollard movement in England in the 14th and 15th centuries] — Rev. N. I. Bassovskaya, *Srednie veka*, 38 (1975), 293-296; I. N. Ossinovsky, *Srednie veka*, 38 (1975), 296-299.

1320 Logan, F. D. "Another cry of heresy at Oxford: the case of Dr John Holand, 1416." *The church and academic learning*. Ed. G. J. Cuming. Studies in church history, 5. Leiden: Brill, 1969. p. 99-113.

1321 Luxton, I. "The Lichfield court book: a postscript." *BIHR*, 44 (1971), 120-125.

1322 McFarlane, K. B. *Lancastrian kings and Lollard knights*. Oxford: Clarendon Press, 1972. 261 p.
     Rev. M. Aston, *CHR*, 62 (1976), 106-108; V. J. Scattergood, *MÆ*, 43 (1974), 210-212; J. M. W. Bean, *Speculum*, 49 (1974), 582-584; P. Contamine, *MA*, 81 (1975), 346-347; C. M. Barron, *JEH*, 24 (1973), 414-417; B. Wilkinson, *AHR*, 79 (1974), 1529.

1323 McHardy, A. K. "Bishop Buckingham and the Lollards of Lincoln diocese." *Schism, heresy and religious protest* (1972). p. 131-145. See 120.

1324 Manning, B. L. *The people's faith in the time of Wyclif*. 2nd ed. (rpt.), with new intro. by A. R. Bridbury. Hassocks: Harvester; Totowa, N.J.: Rowman and Littlefield, 1975. x, vii-xvi, 196 p. [Orig. publ. Cambridge, 1919]

1325 Parker, G. H. W. *The morning star: Wycliffe and the dawn of the reformation*. [Exeter]: Paternoster, c1965; Grand Rapids: Eerdmans, [1966]. 248 p.
     Rev. J. W. O'Malley, *TS*, 27 (1966), 472-473; R. W. Scribner, *JRH*, 4 (1967), 354-357; E. W. Gritsch, *Dialog*, 5 (1966), 235-236; N. V. Hope, *Theology today*, 24 (1967), 263-264; W. S. Reid, *Christianity today*, 10 (1966), 1007-1008; G. S. M. Walker, *The evangelical quarterly*, 38 (1966), 61-62; G. M. Marsden, *The Westminster theological journal*, 29 (1966), 81-83; H. Zwaanstra, *Calvin theological journal*, 2 (1967), 104-106; J. D. Mosteller, *Foundations* (Amer. Baptist Hist. Soc.), 9 (1966), 347-348.

1326 Pichette, K. H. "Chaucer's Lollard friend, Sir Richard Stury." Diss. Univ. of Colorado. *DAI*, 29A (1969), 3584.

1326A Robbins, R. H. "Dissent in Middle English literature: the spirit of (Thirteen) Seventy-six." *MH*, n.s. 9 (1979), 25-51.

1327 Scattergood, V. J. "*The two ways*: an unpublished religious treatise by Sir John Clanvowe." *English philological studies*, 10 (1967), 33-56.

1328 ——, ed. *The works of Sir John Clanvowe*. Cambridge: D. S. Brewer; Totowa, N.J.: Rowman and Littlefield, [1975]. 96 p.
      Rev. N. F. Blake, *N&Q*, 23 (1976), 116-117; R. H. Robbins, *Anglia*, 95 (1977), 520-522.

1329 Schofield, A. N. E. D. "England and the council of Basel." *AHC*, 5 (1973), 1-117.

1330 Scoufos, A. L. "Nashe, Jonson, and the Oldcastle problem." *Modern philology*, 65 (1968), 307-324.

1331 Thomson, J. A. F. "John Foxe and some sources for Lollard history: notes for a critical appraisal." *Studies in church history*, 2. Ed. G. J. Cuming. [London]: Nelson, [1965]. p. 251-257.

1332 ——. *The later Lollards, 1414-1520*. Oxford: Oxford University Press, 1965. xi, 272 p.
      Rev. I. R. Abbott, *AHR*, 72 (1967), 561-562; M. Aston, *History*, 53 (1968), 86-88; T. Dahlerup, *Historisk tidsskrift*, ser. 12, 2 (1966-67), 555-556; H. Dauphin, *RHE*, 62 (1967), 672-673; M. Deanesly, *JEH*, 17 (1966), 265-266; A. G. Dickens, *MÆ*, 36 (1967), 299-301; G. G. Krodel, *HZ*, 205 (1967), 683-684; M. L. Loane, *JR*, 46 (1966), 410-411; M. McKisack, *JTS*, 17 (1966), 505-507; S. H. Thomson, *Speculum*, 41 (1966), 774-775; B. R. White, *The Baptist quarterly*, 21 (1966), 334-335; G. E. Duffield, *The churchman*, 80 (1966), 46-47.

1333 ——. "A Lollard rising in Kent: 1431 or 1438?" *BIHR*, 37 (1964), 100-102.

1334 Walsh, K. "The manuscripts of archbishop Richard FitzRalph of Armagh in the Österreichische Nationalbibliothek, Vienna." *Römische historische Mitteilungen*, 18 (1976), 67-75.

1335 Wawn, A. N. "The genesis of *The Plowman's tale*." *The yearbook of English studies*, 2 (1972), 21-40.

1336 Welch, E. "Some Suffolk Lollards." *Proceedings of the Suffolk institute of archaeology*, 29 (1962 [1963]), 154-165.

1337 Wilson, E. "A supplementary note to an edition of Sir John Clanvowe's treatise *The two ways*." *English philological studies*, 11 (1968), 55-56.

Part Thirteen

Jan Hus

Entries 1338 to 1489

A. *Life of Hus* (*Entries 1338 to 1432*)

1338   Bartoš, F. M. "Apologie de M. Jean Huss contre son apologiste." *CV*, 8 (1965), 65-74. [Review essay based mainly on 1960 ed. of P. de Vooght, *L'hérésie de Jean Huss*] Reply by de Vooght in *CV*, 8 (1965), 235-238, and further comment by Bartoš in *CV*, 9 (1966), 175-180.

1339   ——. "Co víme o Husovi nového." *JSH*, 39 (1970), 126-132. [Incl. summary, p. 131-132, "Was wissen wir Neues über Hus?"]

1340   ——. "Hus' trial and the two French bibles." *CV*, 9 (1966), 108-111.

1341   ——. "Leben in Deutschland noch Nachfahren von Hussens Bruder?" *CV*, 14 (1971), 165-168.

1342   ——. "Na obranu M. Jana proti jeho obránci." *Hus stále živý*. Ed. M. Kaňák. Prague, 1965. p. 104-116.

1343   ——. "Několik problémů a naděje husovského badání." *Husův sborník*. p. 6-19. See 1358.

1344   Bourguet, P. "La Bible de Souvigny et le procès de Jean Hus." *CV*, 8 (1965), 187.

1345   Bychyns'kyĭ, Z. *Jonas Husas: reformacijos pradininkas, Vytauto Didž. bendralaikis. Istoriniai biografinė studija*. Trans. M. Plepys. Lietuviu evangeliku spaudos centro, leidinys 2. Chicago: [L.E.S.C.], 1970. 198 p. ill. Orig. publ. as *Ivan Hus: ches'kiĭ muchenik, ĭogo zhitie, nauki i smert'* (Pittsburgh, 1916; Toronto and Winnipeg, 1955). [John Hus: predecessor of the reformation and contemporary of Vytautas the Great]

1346   Čapek, J. B. "Hus ve vztahu k realismu a nominalismu." *FČ*, 15 (1967), 153-158. [Hus's relation to realism and nominalism]

1347   ——. "Hus ve vztahu k realismu a nominalismu." *Husův sborník*. p. 25-34. See 1358.

1348   Crowder, C. M. D. "Constance acta in English libraries." *Das Konzil von*

Konstanz: Beiträge zu seiner Geschichte und Theologie. Ed. A. Franzen and W. Müller. Freiburg, Basel, Vienna: Herder, 1964. p. 477-517.

1349 Dachsel, J. Jan Hus: ein Bild seines Lebens und Wirkens. With texts of Hus's letters (autumn 1414 – July 1415) trans. in collab. with F. Potměšil. Berlin: Evangelische Verlagsanstalt, 1964. 228 p. See 1624.
Rev. A. Molnár, cv, 8 (1965), 80.

1350 Delius, W. "Luther und Huss." Luther-Jahrbuch, 38 (1971), 9-25.

1351 Dobiáš, F. M. "Calvin, Luther a Hus." Husův sborník. p. 132-139. See 1358.

1352 Flegl, M. "Hus v pojetí Palackého a Karafiáta." KR, 35 (1968), 228-231. [Hus as viewed by Palacký and Karafiát]

1353 ——. "Z dějin úcty k památkám na Husův život a působení." Husův sborník. p. 155-162. See 1358.

1354 Friedenthal, R. Ketzer und Rebell: Jan Hus und das Jahrhundert der Revolutionskriege. Munich: Piper, c1972. 478 p.
Rev. J. Ehlers, HZ, 218 (1974), 660-662; A. Molnár, cv, 16 (1973), 216-217.

1355 Graf, G. "Albert Hauck über Jan Hus: zur Selbstkritik der Reformationshistoriographie." ZKG, 83 (1972), 34-51.

1356 Hendrix, S. H. "'We are all Hussites'? Hus and Luther revisited." ARG, 65 (1974), 134-161. [Incl. Ger. summary]

1357 [Heřmanský, F., trans.] Petra z Mladoňovic, Zpráva o mistru Janu Husovi v Kostnici. Intro. by Z. Fiala. Prague: Universita Karlova, 1965. 243 p. [Czech trans. of Relatio de magistri Joannis Hus causa, with intro. in Czech, English, and German]. See 1382.

1358 Husův sborník: soubor prací k 550. výročí m. Jana Husa. Ed. R. Říčan, with collab. of M. Flegl. Prague: Komenského evangelická fakulta bohoslovecká, 1966. 201 p.

1359 Jílek, F. "Mezinárodní význam Husovy pravopisné reformy." Husův sborník. p. 57-60. See 1358.

1360 Kadlec, J. "Johannes Hus in neuem Licht?" TPQ, 118 (1970), 163-168.

1361 Kalivoda, R. "Hus a Viklef." FČ, 14 (1966), 253-264. [Hus and Wyclif]

1362 ——. "Hus, husovská a husitská tradice." Novinářský sborník, 1965, 472-482. ——

1363 Kaňák, M. "Důležitější biografická a bibliografická data o mistru Janu Husovi." Hus stále živý. Prague, 1965. p. 127-144.

1364 ——. "Hus a Viklef." Husův sborník. p. 48-56. See 1358.

1365 ——, ed. Hus stále živý: sborník studií k 550. výročí Husova upálení. Prague, 1965. 144 p. [Collection of studies on the 550th anniversary of Hus's death]
Rev. A. Molnár, cv, 9 (1966), 111-112.

1366 ——. "K pramenům názorů Husovych." Hus stále živý. Prague, 1965. p. 9-19.

1367 Kejř, J. "Právo a právní prameny v Husově díle." Husův sborník. p. 84-95. Incl. discussion by E. Michálek. See 1358.

1368   ———. "Zur Entstehungsgeschichte des Hussitentums." *Die Welt zur Zeit des Konstanzer Konzils.* Vorträge und Forschungen, 9. Constance and Stuttgart: Thorbecke, c1965. p. 47-61.

1369   Kišš, I. "Luther und Hus." *CV*, 8 (1965), 239-250.

1370   Kitts, E. J. *Pope John the Twenty-third and Master John Hus of Bohemia.* London, 1910. Rpt. New York: AMS, 1978. xxx, 446 p. ill.

1371   Laptěva, L. P. "Jan Hus v ruské historiografii v 19. a na počátku 20. století." With Russian summary. *Slovanské historické studie*, 9 (1972), 37-91. English summary by R. E. Weltsch in *Historical abstracts*, 20A (1974), no. 22: "Jan Hus in Russian historiography in the 19th and at the beginning of the 20th century."

1372   Lipatnikova, G. I. "Ian Hus i studenti Praz'kogo universitetu." *Ukrains'ke slov'ianoznavstvo*, 6 (1972), 16-22. [Hus and the students at the University of Prague]

1373   Lohse, B. "Luther und Huss." *Luther: Zeitschrift der Luther-Gesellschaft*, 36 (1965), 108-122.

1374   Ludolphy, I. "Johann Huss." *Luther: Zeitschrift der Luther-Gesellschaft*, 36 (1965), 97-107.

1375   Lützow, F., Graf von. *The life and times of master John Hus.* London and New York, 1909. Rpt. New York: AMS, 1978. xiii, 398 p.

1376   Macek, J. *Jan Hus.* Prague: Svobodné Slovo, 1961. 207 p. ill.

1377   ———. "Jean Hus et son époque." Trans. K. Trojanová. *Historica*, 13 (1966), 51-80.

1378   Machilek, F. "Ergebnisse und Aufgaben moderner Hus-Forschung. Zu einer neuen Biographie des Johannes Hus." *ZOF*, 22 (1973), 302-330.

1379   ———. "Hus in Konstanz: zu einer deutschen Übersetzung der Relatio de Magistro Johanne Hus des Peter von Mladoňovic." *ZRGG*, 18 (1966), 163-170. See 1383.

1380   Machovec, M. *Bude katolická církev rehabilitovat Jana Husa?* [Prague]: Nakl. politické literatury, 1963. 2nd ed. 1965. 133 p. [Incl. summary, "Wird die katholische Kirche Jan Hus rehabilitieren?" and extract from P. de Vooght]

1381   Misset-Hopes, S. "Jean Hus." *CEC*, 21, no. 46 (1970), 45-51.

1382   Mladoňovic, P. *John Hus at the Council of Constance.* Trans. M. Spinka. Records of civilization, Sources and studies, 73. New York and London: Columbia University Press, 1965. xii, 327 p. Trans. of *Relatio de magistri Joannis Hus causa.* See 1357.
          Rev. P. Brock, *CHR*, 55 (1969), 80-81; J. Ficek, *Christianity today*, 10 (1966), 36-38; J. Gill, *JEH*, 17 (1966), 261-262; M. Harvey, *HJ*, 8 (1967), 97-98; F. G. Heymann, *ARG*, 59 (1968), 110-111; H. Kaminsky, *JR*, 47 (1967), 76-77; F. Oakley, *Speculum*, 42 (1967), 190-191; A. N. E. D. Schofield, *SEER*, 45 (1967), 556-558; M. Wilks, *JTS*, 17 (1966), 504-505; S. H.

Thomson, *AHR*, 72 (1967), 560-561; G. E. Rothenberg, *The historian*, 29 (1966), 88-89; J. H. Kromminga, *Calvin theological journal*, 2 (1967), 257-258; F. Seibt, *ARG*, 64 (1973), 315-316; B. Thompson, *The Drew gateway*, 37, nos. 1-2 (1966-67), 46-48; G. E. Duffield, *The churchman*, 80 (1966), 57-58.

1383 ———. *Hus in Konstanz: der Bericht des Peter von Mladoniowitz*. Trans. J. Bujnoch. Slavische Geschichtsschreiber, 3. Graz, Vienna, and Cologne: Styria, 1963. 295 p.

Rev. F. Machilek, *ZRGG*, 18 (1966), 163-170.

1384 ———. *Zpráva o mistru Janu Husovi v Kostnici*. Prague: Universita Karlova, 1965. 246 p. ill. Trans. of *Relatio de magistro Johanne Hus* by F. Heřmanský, with intro. in Czech, English, and German by Z. Fiala.

1385 Molnár, A. "Hus auf dem Konstanzer Konzil." *Materialdienst des Konfessions-kundlichen Instituts Bensheim*, 16 (1965), 41-45. —

1386 ———. "Hus et son appel à Jésus-Christ." *CV*, 8 (1965), 95-104.

1387 ———. "Husovo místo v evropské reformaci." *ČČH*, 14 (1966), 1-14. [Incl. summary, "L'apport de Jean Hus à la réforme européenne"]

1388 ———. "Husovo odvolání ke Kristu." *Husův sborník*. p. 73-83. See 1358.

1389 ———. *Jan Hus, testimone della verità*. Ritratti storici, 6. Turin: Claudiana, c1973. 253 p. ill. Trans., *Jean Hus, témoin de la vérité* (Paris and Lausanne: Les Bergers et les Mages, 1978), 268 p.

1390 ———. "John Hus – witness to the truth." *The reformed and Presbyterian world*, 28 (1965), 252-257.

1391 ———. "Les réponses de Jean Huss aux quarante-cinq articles." *RTAM*, 31 (1964), 85-99.

1392 ———. "Gli studi su Jan Hus nel 550° anniversario della morte." Trans. G. Rochat. *Nuova rivista storica*, 49 (1965), 696-699.

1393 Mols, R. "Réhabilitation de Jean Hus?" *NRT*, 83 (1961), 960-966.

1394 Myln'ikov, A. S. "Kniga, kotoruiu derzhal Ian Hus." *Kniga*, 32 (1976), 176-177. [The book held by Hus]

1395 Nečas, J., and V. Starý. *Master John Hus and the town of Husinec*. Trans. J. Ondryášová. [Prague: Svépomoc, 1969.] 19 p. ill.

1396 Nuttall, G. F. "Dante and Hus." *The London quarterly and Holborn review*, 190 (1965), 291-295.

1397 Oberg, R. E. "Kutna Hora: influências morais e políticas no julgamento do mestre João Hus." *Revista de história* (São Paulo), 42, no. 85 (1971), 33-47.

1398 Palacký, F., ed. *Documenta mag. Joannis Hus vitam, doctrinam, causam in Constantiensi concilio actam et controversias de religione in Bohemia annis 1403-1418 motas illustrantia*. Prague, 1869. Rpt. Osnabrück: Biblio-Verlag, 1966. xvi, 768 p.

1399 Pilny, J. *La fin de Jean Hus*. Geneva: Perret-Gentil, 1970. 61 p.

1400 *Pravda vítězí: pamětní tisk k 550. výročí upálení mistra Jana Husa.* [Prague: Svobodné Slovo, 1965.] 63 p. ill. [Truth conquers: memorial volume on the occasion of the 550th anniversary of the burning of Hus]

1401 Říčan, R. "Hus a čeští evangelíci." *Husův sborník.* p. 167-199. See 1358.

1402 Riemeck, R. *Jan Hus: Reformation 100 Jahre vor Luther.* Frankfurt am Main: Stimme-Verlag, 1966. 187 p. [Incl. suppl., "Die drei Reden, die Hus in Konstanz nicht halten durfte"]

1403 Schofield, A. N. E. D. "The case of Jan Hus." *IER*, 109 (1968), 394-406.

1404 Segert, S. "Husův zájem o hebrejský jazyk." *Husův sborník.* p. 69-72. See 1358.

1405 Seibt, F. "Geistige Reformbewegungen zur Zeit des Konstanzer Konzils." *Die Welt zur Zeit des Konstanzer Konzils.* Vorträge und Forschungen, 9. Constance and Stuttgart: Thorbecke, c1965. p. 31-46.

1406 ———. "Hus und wir Deutschen. Zum 600. Geburtstag eines großen Bekenners." *Kirche im Osten,* 13 (1970), 74-103.

1407 ———. *Jan Hus: das Konstanzer Gericht im Urteil der Geschichte.* Carl Friedrich von Siemens Stiftung, Themen, 15. [Munich: Siemens Stiftung, 1973.] 54 p. ill.

1408 ———. "Nullus est Dominus...." *Geschichte in der Gesellschaft: Festschrift für Karl Bosl.* Ed. F. Prinz, et al. Stuttgart: Hiersemann, 1974. p. 393-408.

1409 Sita, K. "M. Jan Hus a české probuzenecké hnutí v XIX. století." *Husův sborník.* p. 140-144. See 1358.

1410 Šmahel, F. *Hranice pravdy.* Prague: Magnet, 1969. 189 p. ill. [The stake of truth — Constance and the burning of Hus]

1411 Smolík, J. "Die Wahrheit in der Geschichte: zur Ekklesiologie von Jan Hus." *Evangelische Theologie,* 32 (1972), 268-276. See 1474.

1412 Sousedík, S. "Huss et la doctrine eucharistique 'rémanentiste'." *Divinitas,* 21 (1977), 383-407.

1413 Špét, J. "Účast university a Národního muzea na Husových oslavách před půl stoletím." *Husův sborník.* p. 145-154. See 1358.

1414 Spinka, M. *John Hus: a biography.* Princeton: Princeton University Press, 1968. [viii], 344 p.
    Rev. P. de Vooght, *RHE*, 65 (1970), 183-185; R. Cegna, *RSLR*, 7 (1971), 521-524; F. Rapp, *MA*, 79 (1973), 178-180; S. H. Thomson, *ARG*, 61 (1970), 290-292; O. Odložilík, *Speculum*, 44 (1969), 663-664; A. Molnár, *CV*, 12 (1969), 172; E. Stoye, *JEH*, 21 (1970), 265-267; R. Mols, *NRT*, 92 (1970), 1115; R. T. Handy, *Christianity today*, 13, no. 22 (1 August 1969), 16-17; L. Nemec, *TS*, 30 (1969), 379, and *CHR*, 57 (1971), 499-500; H. W. Pipkin, *JCS*, 13 (1971), 530-531; M. Kanák, *CH*, 39 (1970), 114-115; J. M. Lochman, *Union Seminary quarterly review*, 25 (1969), 75-78.

1415 ———. *John Hus and the Czech reform.* Chicago, c1941. Rpt. Hamden, Conn.: Archon, 1966. vii, 81 p.

1416 ——. *John Hus' concept of the church*. Princeton: Princeton University Press, 1966. ix, 432 p.

Rev. R. Bennett, *History*, 53 (1968), 90-91; M. Deanesly, *CQR*, 168 (1967), 261; J. P. Dolan, *Manuscripta*, 10 (1966), 175-176; J. Durkan, *New Blackfriars*, 48 (1966-67), 329; M. S. Fousek, *CH*, 36 (1967), 88-89; H. Kaminsky, *JR*, 47 (1967), 76-77; A. Molnár, *CV*, 9 (1966), 207-208; O. Odlozilík, *AHR*, 72 (1966), 165-166; R. C. Petry, *Speculum*, 43 (1968), 191-192; A. N. E. D. Schofield, *SEER*, 45 (1967), 556-558; E. Stoye, *JEH*, 21 (1970), 265-267; B. Töpfer, *ZG*, 16 (1968), 384-386; P. de Vooght, *RHE*, 62 (1967), 140-142; M. J. Wilks, *JTS*, 18 (1967), 521-524; E. W. Gritsch, *LW*, 14 (1967), 123; L. Nemec, *TS*, 27 (1966), 683-685, and *CHR*, 55 (1969), 78-80; J. L. Ficek, *Christianity today*, 10, no. 23 (2 September 1966), 42-43; F. L. Battles, *The Hartford quarterly*, 7, no. 2 (1967), 76-77; J. L. Garrett, *Review and expositor*, 66 (1969), 443-444; B. Thompson, *The Drew gateway*, 37, nos. 1-2 (1966-67), 46-48.

1417 Thils, G. "Le traité de l'église au XVe siècle: à propos de *L'hérésie de Jean Huss* et *Hussiana* de P. de Vooght." *ETL*, 38 (1962), 523-533. See 1420, 1422.

1418 Trtík, Z. "K otázce filosofického realismu Husova." *Náboženská revue*. 1971. ——

1419 Vidmanová, A. "Nova Hussiana." *LF*, 90 (1967), 75-78. [Review of recent literature]

1420 Vooght, P. de. *L'hérésie de Jean Huss*. Bibliothèque de la Revue d'histoire ecclésiastique, 34. Louvain: Bibliothèque de l'Université, 1960. xix, 494 p.

Rev. M. Cappuyns, *RHE*, 57 (1962), 191-193; B. Chudoba, *CHR*, 47 (1961), 367-368; J. Lecler, *RSR*, 50 (1962), 445-450; D. Mansilla, *Hispania sacra*, 13 (1960), 237-239; J.-P. Massaut, *RBPH*, 40 (1962), 155-161; G. Miccoli, *SM*, 3rd ser., 3 (1962), 189-196; R. Mols, *NRT*, 83 (1961), 960-966; J. Strakoš, *CHR*, 49 (1963), 94-96; O. Odlozilík, *AHR*, 67 (1962), 384-386; S. H. Thomson, *Speculum*, 38 (1963), 116-121; L. Waeber, *ZSKG*, 55 (1961), 229-232; E. Winter, *DLZ*, 83 (1962), 519-522; G. Thils, *ETL*, 38 (1962), 523-533. See 1421.

1421 ——. *L'hérésie de Jean Huss*. Bibliothèque de la Revue d'histoire ecclésiastique, 34bis and 35bis. Louvain: Bibliothèque de l'Université, 1975. xxii, 1032 p. in 2 v. [2nd ed., rvsd., of 1420 and 1422]

Rev. L. H. Zuck, *CH*, 46 (1977), 114-115; F. Šmahel, *AHC*, 9 (1977), 425-427; A. Molnár, *RHE*, 72 (1977), 736-738; M. Pacaut, *RH*, 261 (1979), 259.

1422 ——. *Hussiana*. Bibliothèque de la Revue d'histoire ecclésiastique, 35. Louvain: Bibliothèque de l'Université, 1960. vii, 450 p. See 1421.

Rev. M. Cappuyns, *RHE*, 57 (1962), 191-193; B. Chudoba, *CHR*, 47 (1961), 367-368; J. Lecler, *RSR*, 50 (1962), 445-450; D. Mansilla, *Hispania sacra*, 13 (1960), 237-239; G. Miccoli, *SM*, 3rd ser., 3 (1962), 189-196; J. Strakoš, *CHR*, 49 (1963), 94-96; O. Odlozilík, *AHR*, 67 (1962), 384-386; S. H. Thomson, *Speculum*, 38 (1963), 116-121; L. Waeber, *ZSKG*, 55 (1961),

232-235; R. Mols, *NRT*, 83 (1961), 960-966; E. Winter, *DLZ*, 83 (1962), 519-522; J.-P. Massaut, *RBPH*, 40 (1962), 155-161; G. Thils, *ETL*, 38 (1962), 523-533.

1423 ——. "Jan Hus: heretic or martyr?" Trans. W. H. Zawadzki. *The tablet*, 223 (1969), 99-100, ill.

1424 ——. "Jan Hus im Lichte des 2. Vatikanischen Konzils." *Kirchenblatt für die reformierte Schweiz*, 121 (1965), 340-341.

1425 ——. "Jean Huss à l'heure de l'œcuménisme." *Irénikon*, 42 (1969), 293-313.

1426 ——. "Jean Huss à l'heure du marxisme-léninisme." *RHE*, 57 (1962), 493-500.

1427 ——. "Jean Huss, aujourd'hui." *Bohemia: Jahrbuch des Collegium Carolinum*, 12 (1971), 34-52. [Incl. Ger. summary]

1428 ——. "Jean Huss au Symposium hussianum pragense." *Istina*, 11 (1965-66), 41-60. Trans. "Jan Hus beim Symposium hussianum pragense (August 1965)." *TPQ*, 114 (1966), 81-95.

1429 ——. "Jean Huss et ses juges." *Das Konzil von Konstanz: Beiträge zu seiner Geschichte und Theologie*. Ed. A. Franzen and W. Müller. Freiburg, Basel, Vienna: Herder, 1964. p. 152-173.

1430 ——. Jean Huss peut-il être réhabilité?" *Revue générale belge*, 99, no. 2 (1963), 31-39.

1431 ——. "Obscurités anciennes autour de Jean Huss." *RHE*, 66 (1971), 137-145.

1432 Zelinka, T. Č. "Přátelé Husovi v bechyňském kraji." *Husův sborník*. p. 103-110. See 1358.

B. *Hus' Writings* (*Entries 1433 to 1489*)

1433 Bartoš, F. M. "Hus a jeho účast na staročeské bibli." *Strahovská knihovna*, 3 (1968), 86-115. [Incl. summary, "Hus und seine Beteiligung an der alttschechischen Bibel"]

1434 ——. "Hus' commentary on the Sentences of Peter Lombard." *CV*, 3 (1960), 145-157.

1435 ——. "Problém Husových tzv. Betlemských kázání." *Husův sborník*. p. 42-47. See 1358.

1436 ——, and P. Spunar. *Soupis pramenů k literární činnosti M. Jana Husa a M. Jeronýma Pražského*. Prague: Historický ústav Českoslov. akad. věd, 1965. 369 p.

1437 Bouzková, H. "Die Nebensätze in den Predigten von Johannes Hus." *Acta universitatis carolinae*, 1970, Philosophica et historica, 1: Graecolatina pragensia, 4, p. 15-18.

1438 Cedlová, M. "K Husovu autorství jeho Výkladu Summy naturalium Alberta Velikého." *Husův sborník*. p. 35-41. See 1358.

1439 Červený, K. "Překlad několika Husových latinských kázání." *Hus stále živý*. Ed. M. Kaňák. Prague, 1965. p. 69-86.

1440   Chatillon, F. "L'image de l'étalon hennissant mise à profit par Jean Huss." *Revue du moyen âge latin*, 23 (1967 [1976-77]), 126-128.

1441   Danhelka, J. "Poškození budyšinského husovského kodexu a jejich svědectví." *Z kralické tvrze*, 3 (1969), 18-22. [Implications of the damage to MS Bautzen fol. 51] —

1442   Dobiáš, F. M., and A. Molnár, trans. *Mistr Jan Hus, O církvi*. Intro. J. Hrabák. Památky staré literatury české, 29. Prague: Československá Akademie Věd, 1965. 311 p. [Hus's *De ecclesia*]
         Rev. L. Brož, *CV*, 8 (1965), 181; A. Vidmanová, *LF*, 88 (1965), 237.

1443   ——, and ——, ed. and trans. *Mistr Jan Hus, Sermo de pace – Řeč o míru*. Prague: Kalich, 1963. 93 p.
         Rev. L. Brož, *CV*, 7 (1964), 316; A. Vidmanová, *LF*, 88 (1965), 237-239.

1444   Ebertová, A. "Sociálně theologická problematika v díle Husově." *Hus stále živý*. Ed. M. Kaňák. Prague, 1965. p. 87-103.

1445   Fiala, Z. "K výkladu slov sutor a sartor v studii A. Vidmanové 'Krejčí a ševci v Husově listu z Kostnice'." *ČČH*, 16 (1968), 525-526. [On the interpretation of the words *sutor* and *sartor* in A. Vidmanová's "Tailors and shoemakers in Hus's letter from Constance." See 1485.]

1446   Flajšhans, W., ed. *Mag. Jo. Hus Opera omnia*. Prague, 1903-1908. Rpt. Osnabrück: Biblio-Verlag, 1966. 3 v.

1447   Fleischmannová, E. "Větné vsuvky v Husově traktátu O manželství." *LF*, 88 (1965), 225-231. [Incl. summary, "Syntaktische Parenthese im Traktat 'Über die Ehe' von Johannes Hus"]

1448   Gregor, A. "M. Jan Hus, milovník a znalec českého jazyka." *Husův sborník*. p. 61-68. See 1358.

1449   Havránek, B. "Český jazyk Husův." *Slovo a slovesnost*, 27 (1966), 1-16. [Incl. summary, "La langue tchèque de Hus"]

1450   Horský, R. "Kazatelské a pastýřské dílo M. Jana Husi." *Hus stále živý*. Ed. M. Kaňák. Prague, 1965. p. 45-68.

1451   Hus, J. *'Dat boeken van deme repe'; 'De uthlegghinge ouer den louen,' aus dem Tschechischen ins Niederdeutsche übertragen von Johann von Lübeck*. Nikolaus Ludwig von Zinzendorf: Materialen und Dokumente, I, 2. Rpt. of Lübeck [ca. 1480] ed., with intro. by A. Molnár. Hildesheim and New York: Olms, 1971. [vi p. + 199 f.]

1452   ——. *Passio domini nostri Iesu Cristi*. Ed. A. Vidmanová-Schmidtová. Magistri Iohannis Hus opera omnia, 8. Prague: Academia scientiarum bohemoslovaca, 1973. 277 p. ill.
         Rev. P. Spunar, *Zprávy jednoty klasických filologů*, 16 (1974), 69-71.

1453   ——. *Polemica*. Ed. J. Eršil. Magistri Iohannis Hus opera omnia, 22. Prague: Academia scientiarum bohemoslovaca, 1966. 513 p.
         Rev. F. M. Bartoš, *CV*, 9 (1966), 298-300; A. Segovia, *Archivo teológico granadino*, 30 (1967), 433-434.

1454 ———. *Postilla adumbrata*. Ed. A. Molnár. Magistri Iohannis Hus opera omnia, 13. Prague: Academia scientiarum bohemoslovaca, 1975. 663 p. ill. Rev. S. Hoyer, *ZG*, 25 (1977), 612.

1455 ———. *Sermones de tempore qui Collecta dicuntur*. Ed. A. Schmidtová. Magistri Iohannis Hus opera omnia, 7. Prague: Academia scientiarum bohemoslovenica, 1959. 623 p. ill.

1456 ———. *Výklady*. Ed. A. Molnár. Magistri Iohannis Hus opera omnia, 1: Expositiones bohemicae. Prague: Nakladatelství Československé Akademie Věd, 1975. 714 p.

1457 Kamínková, E. *Husova Betlémská kázání a jejich dvě recense*. Acta Universitatis Carolinae, Philosophica et historica, 1963: Monographia 2. Prague: Universita Karlova, 1963. 85 p. [Incl. Lat. and Ger. summaries, "De magistri Iohannis Hus sermonum in capella Bethlehem recensionibus duabus"]

1458 ———. "Je Hus autorem traktátu Exercicium rethorice?" *LF*, 88 (1965), 387-392. [Incl. summary, "Exercicium rethorice an magistri Iohannis Hus opus sit"]

1459 ———. "Rým v Husových latinských proslovech." *LF*, 88 (1965), 182-191. [Incl. summary, "Der Reim in den lateinischen Reden von J. Hus"]

1460 Kouba, J. "Jan Hus und das geistliche Lied." *Jahrbuch für Liturgik und Hymnologie*, 14 (1969), 190-196.

1461 Lützow, F., Graf von. *A history of Bohemian literature*. London and New York, 1899. Rpt. Port Washington, N.Y., and London: Kennikat, 1970. xii, 425 p.

1462 Mánek, J. "Husův spor o autoritu." *Hus stále živý*. Ed. M. Kaňák. Prague, 1965. p. 20-37.

1463 Michálek, E. "K biblickým citátům v Husově české nedělní Postile." *LF*, 93 (1970), 21-28. [Incl. summary, "Ad bibliorum in Hussii Postilla bohemica sententias"]

1463A ———. "K frazeologické složce v Husově slovní zásobě." *LF*, 88 (1965), 192-197. [Incl. summary, "K voprosy izycheniia frazeologii v iazyke Iana Husa"]

1463B Molnar, E. C. S. "The liturgical reforms of John Hus." *Speculum*, 41 (1966), 297-303.

1464 Nechutová, J. "Husovo kázání 'Dixit Martha' a Mikuláše z Drážďan traktát 'De purgatorio' (k otázce Husovy literární původnosti)." *LF*, 88 (1965), 147-157. [Incl. summary, "Die Predigt von Hus 'Dixit Martha' und der Traktat Nikolaus von Dresden 'De purgatorio' – zur Frage der literarischen Ursprünglichkeit bei Hus"]

1465 ———. "M. Štěpán z Pálče v Husově korespondenci." *LF*, 93 (1970), 29-36. [Incl. summary, "Quid M. Iohannes Hus in epistulis suis de M. Stephano Páleč existimaverit"]

1466 Němec, I. "Husův podíl na slovním bohatství staré češtiny v oblasti slovesa." *LF*,

88 (1965), 198-203. [Incl. summary, "Vklad Iana Husa v leksikal'noe bogatstvo drevnecheshskogo iazyka (v oblasti glagola)"]

1467 Nováková, J. "Ještě k Husovým hexametrům." *LF*, 88 (1965), 176-181. [Incl. summary, "Hexametrorum hussianorum coronis"]

1468 Říčan, R. "Husova česká postila a postila Petra Chelčického." *Husův sborník.* p. 111-131. See 1358.

1469 Riedlinger, H. "Ekklesiologie und Christologie bei Johannes Hus: die Gnadenfülle Christi und die Kirche in seinem Kommentar zur Distinctio XIII des dritten Buchs der Sentenzen." *Von Konstanz nach Trient ... Festgabe für August Franzen.* Ed. R. Bäumer. Munich, Paderborn, Vienna: Schöningh, 1972. p. 47-55.

1470 Ryba, B. "Nový rukopis Husova Výkladu na Lombarda." *Strahovská knihovna*, 2 (1967), 27-30. [Incl. summary, "Eine neue Handschrift des lateinischen Lombardkommentars von Mag. Joh. Hus"]

1471 Schamschula, W. "De ablatione temporalium a clericis: ein Beitrag zur Hus-Bibliographie." *Zeitschrift für slavische Philologie*, 39 (1976), 166-172.

1472 ——, trans. *Jan Hus: Schriften zur Glaubensreform und Briefe der Jahre 1414-1415.* Frankfurt am Main: Insel, c1969. 195 p.

1473 Schröpfer, J. *Hussens Traktat "Orthographia bohemica": die Herkunft des diakritischen Systems in der Schreibung slavischer Sprachen und die älteste zusammenhängende Beschreibung slavischer Laute.* Slavistische Studienbücher, 4. Wiesbaden: Harrassowitz, 1968. 143 p.
    Rev. A. Vidmanová, *MB*, 1 (1969), 166-172.

1474 Smolík, J. "Truth in history according to Hus' conception." *CV*, 15 (1972), 97-109.

1475 Spinka, M., trans. *The letters of John Hus.* Manchester: Manchester University Press; Totowa, N.J.: Rowman and Littlefield, c1972. ix, 233 p.
    Rev. O. Odlozilík, *CHR*, 62 (1976), 109-110; J. W. O'Malley, *Review for religious*, 32 (1973), 684.

1476 Stejskal, K. "Die Orthographia Hussens und das slawische Kloster in Prag – Emaus." *MB*, 3 (1970), 265-277. Trans., "Husova Ortographia a slovanský klášter v Praze – Emauzích," *JSH*, 41 (1972), 35-40.

1477 Trtík, Z. "Husův odkaz a oba principy reformace." *Hus stále živý.* Ed. M. Kaňák. Prague, 1965. p. 38-44.

1478 ——. "Jan Hus als philosophischer Realist." *TZ*, 28 (1972), 263-275.

1479 Vidmanová, A. "Autentičnost Husových citátů." *FČ*, 18 (1970), 1018-1024. [The authenticity of Hus's quotations]

1480 ——. "Autoritäten und Wiclif in Hussens homiletischen Schriften." *Antiqui und moderni.* Ed. A. Zimmermann. Miscellanea mediaevalia, 9. Berlin and New York: de Gruyter, 1974. p. 383-393.

1481 ——. "Husova tzv. postilla De tempore (1408/9)." *LF*, 94 (1971), 7-22. [Incl. summary, "M. Iohannis Hus opus postilla De tempore (1408/9) nuncupatum"]

1482   ——. "Husovo Leccionarium bipartitum ve světle textové kritiky." *LF*, 98 (1975),
        199-207. [Incl. summary, "Hussens Leccionarium bipartitum im Lichte
        der Textkritik"]

1483   Vidmanová-Schmidtová, A. "Husovy hexametry." *LF*, 88 (1965), 158-175. [Incl.
        summary, "Hussens Hexameter"]

1484   Vidmanová, A. "K autorství Husovy Passio domini nostri Iesu Christi." *LF*, 91
        (1968), 116-132. [Incl. summary, "Scripseritne M. Iohannes Hus 'Passio-
        nem domini nostri Iesu Cristi'?"]

1485   ——. "Krejčí a ševci v Husově listu z Kostnice." *Zprávy jednoty klasických
        filologů*, 9 (1967), 135-138. [Tailors and shoemakers in Hus's letter from
        Constance. See also 1445]

1486   ——. "Kursus u Husa." *LF*, 88 (1965), 380-386. [Incl. summary, "Hussens
        Kursus"]

1487   Vincenz, A. de. "Zu einigen Fragen der Interpretationen der *Orthographia
        bohemica*." *Forschung und Lehre: Abschiedsschrift zu Joh. Schröpfers
        Emeritierung und Festgruß zu seinem 65. Geburtstag.* Hamburg: Slavi-
        sches Seminar, c1975. p. 428-443.

1488   Vooght, P. de, [and J. Pilny]. "Un classique de la littérature spirituelle: la *Dcerka*
        de Jean Huss." *RHS*, 48 (1972), 275-314.

1489   Zeman, A. "K biblickému textu Husovy Postily." *LF*, 101 (1978), 13-16. [Incl.
        summary, "Observationes ad textum biblicum Postillae bohemicae M.
        Johannis Hus pertinentes"]

Part Fourteen

Hussites

ENTRIES 1490 TO 1784

A. *General (Entries 1490 to 1680)*

1490 Bartoš, F. M. "Bojovníci a státníci husitští a Universita Karlova." *AUC Hist*, 12 (1972), 7-65. [Incl. summary, p. 65, "Die hussitischen Kämpfer und Staatsmänner und die Karlsuniversität"]

1491 ——. "Dva hejtmané táborského bratrstva." *JSH*, 33 (1964), 83-88.

1492 ——. "An English cardinal and the Hussite revolution." *CV*, 6 (1963), 47-52.

1493 ——. "Hus, Lollardism and devotio moderna in the fight for a national bible." *CV*, 3 (1960), 247-254.

1494 ——. *Husitská revoluce*. Prague: Nakl. Československé Akademie Věd, 1965-1966. 2 v.
Rev. F. Šmahel, *ČČH*, 14 (1966), 568-571; P. de Vooght, *RHE*, 62 (1967), 724-725; A. Molnár, *CV*, 9 (1966), 287-292, and *Nuova rivista storica*, 51 (1967), 184-191; M. Spinka, *CH*, 34 (1965), 460, and 36 (1967), 475-476; [L. Brož], *CV*, 9 (1966), 104.

1495 ——. "Husitská revoluce v zápase o mír." *KR*, 27 (1960), 74-78.

1496 ——. "Konec táborských 'pikartů'." *JSH*, 41 (1972), 41-44. [Incl. summary, p. 44, "Das Ende der Pikharten von Tábor"]

1497 ——. "Das Reformprogramm des Mag. Johannes Cardinalis von Bergreichenstein, des Gesandten der Karls-Universität in Prag, für das Konzil zu Konstanz." *Festschrift für Hermann Heimpel zum 70. Geburtstag*. Veröffentlichungen des Max-Planck-Instituts für Geschichte, 36. Göttingen: Vandenhoeck and Ruprecht, 1971-1972. II, 652-685.

1498 ——. "Z dějin Karlovy university v době husitské." *JSH*, 40 (1971), 54-63, 115-122. [Incl. summaries, "Zur Geschichte der Karlsuniversität während der hussitischen Revolution"]

1499 [——.] "Verzeichnis der Veröffentlichungen von F. M. Bartoš 1959-1969." *MB*, 1 (1969), 237-247.

1500   Betts, R. R. *Essays in Czech history*. London: University of London, Athlone
          Press; New York: Oxford University Press, 1969. xvi, 315 p.
          Rev. F. G. Heymann, *Speculum*, 47 (1972), 282-284; R. Cegna, *RSLR*, 7
          (1971), 188-189; A. Molnár, *CV*, 12 (1969), 233; H. S. Offler, *JTS*, 21 (1970),
          238-240; F. Rapp, *MA*, 80 (1973), 362-365; M. Fousek, *CHR*, 59 (1973),
          338-339.

1501   Bezděková, Z. "Práce táborského Spolku pro postavení Husova pomníku v
          propagaci a bádání o husitství." *JSH*, 35 (1966), 110-112.

1502   Bylina, S. "Husyci na Łużycach w relacji śląskich kronikarzy xv wieku."
          Polsko-łużyckie stosunki kulturalne. Ed. J. Śliziński. Wrocław, Warsaw,
          and Kraków: Zakład Narodowy im. Ossolińskich, 1970. p. 221-226. [Incl.
          summary, "Les hussites en Lusace vus par les chroniqueurs silésiens du
          xvᵉ siècle"]

1503   Čapek, J. B. "K vývoji a problematice bratrstva Orebského." *JSH*, 35 (1966),
          92-109.

1504   Cegna, R. "Contributo allo studio delle fonti sull'Ussitimo: la ricerca della 'Ec-
          clesia spiritualis' nel medioevo cattolico." *Studi źródłoznawcze*, 20 (1974
          [1976]), 163-182. [Incl. Polish summary]

1505   ——. "Początki utrakwizmu w Czechach w latach 1412-1415." *PH*, 69 (1978),
          103-114. [The origins of utraquism in Bohemia, 1412-1415]

1506   ——. "L'Ussitismo piemontese nel '400: appunti ed ipotesi per uno studio
          organico." *RSLR*, 7 (1971), 3-69.

1507   ——. "Il volto cattolico della contestazione ussito-valdese e le sue origini
          germaniche." *BSSV*, 136 (1974), 37-42.

1508   Cinke, V. "Eine Randglosse zu Seibts Hussitica." *MB*, 1 (1969), 107-113. See 1640.

1509   Cook, W. R. "The eucharist in Hussite theology." *ARG*, 66 (1975), 23-35. [Incl.
          Ger. summary]

1510   ——. "John Wyclif and Hussite theology 1415-1436." *CH*, 42 (1973), 335-349.

1511   ——. "The Kutná Hora meeting of May, 1420: a last attempt to preserve peace
          in Bohemia." *CV*, 17 (1974), 183-191.

1512   ——. "La transsubstantiation, clef théologique de la fragmentation du mouve-
          ment hussite." *Irénikon*, 49 (1976), 323-332.

1513   Décsy, G., ed. *Der Münchener Kodex, II: Das ungarische Hussiten-Evangeliar aus
          dem 15. Jahrhundert*. Wiesbaden: Harrassowitz, 1966. xvii, 125 p. [V. 1,
          containing facsimile, publ. in 1958 as *Der Münchener Kodex: ein
          ungarisches Sprachdenkmal aus dem Jahre 1466*, ed. J. von Farkas.
          See also 1616.]

1514   Denis, E. *Huss et la guerre des hussites*. Paris, 1930. Rpt. New York: AMS, 1978.
          xii, 506 p.

1515   Fišer, F. "Hodinkové oficium svátku mistra Jana Husa." *Časopis Národního
          muzea* (Prague), 135, no. 2 (1966), 81-98. [Incl. summary, "Officium
          horarum festi Ioannis Hus"]

1516 Flegl, M. "K otázce původu bratra Řehoře." *KR*, 41 (1974), 219-223. [The lineage of brother Řehoř (Gregory of Kunwald)]

1517 Frinta, A. "O stížném listu z roku 1415." *JSH*, 36 (1967), 157-158, ill. [Incl. summary, p. 158, "Über die Protestschrift aus dem Jahre 1415"]

1518 Garbacík, J., and A. Strzelecka. "Uniwersytet Jagielloński wobec problemów husyckich w xv w. (próba wprowadzenia w zagadnienie)." *AUC Hist*, 5 (1964), 7-52.

1519 Gindely, A. *Geschichte der Böhmischen Brüder*. Prague, 1861. Rpt. Osnabrück: Biblio, 1968. 2 v. [v. 1: 1450-1564]

1520 Girke-Schreiber, J. "Die böhmische Devotio moderna." *Bohemia sacra: das Christentum in Böhmen 973-1973*. Ed. F. Seibt. Düsseldorf: Schwann, 1974. p. 81-91, 564-565.

1521 Graus, F. "Krize středověku a husitství." *ČČH*, 17 (1969), 507-526. Ger. summary, p. 525-526: "Die Krise des Mittelalters und das Hussitentum." Eng. trans. by J. J. Heaney, "The crisis of the middle ages and the Hussites," in *The reformation in medieval perspective*, ed. S. E. Ozment (Chicago: Quadrangle, 1971), p. 76-103.

1522 Guy, A. "Jean Hus et le communisme chrétien de Bohême." Toulouse, Université, Faculté des lettres, *Annales*, 5, no. 2 (1969), 3-21.

1523 Hallauer, H. "Das Glaubengespräch mit den Hussiten." *Nikolaus von Kues als Promotor der Oekumene*. Ed. R. Haubst. Mitteilungen und Forschungsbeiträge der Cusanus-Gesellschaft, 9. Mainz: Matthias Grünewald, 1971. p. 53-75.

1524 Heck, R. *Tabor a kandydatura jagiellońska w Czechach (1438-1444)*. Prace Wrocławskiego towarzystwa naukowego, A, 98. Wrocław: Zakład Narodowy im. Ossolińskich, 1964. 263 p. [Incl. Ger. summary]

1525 Heimpel, H., ed. *Drei Inquisitions-Verfahren aus dem Jahre 1425: Akten der Prozesse gegen die deutschen Hussiten Johannes Drändorf und Peter Turnau sowie gegen Drändorfs Diener Martin Borchard*. Veröffentlichungen des Max-Planck-Instituts für Geschichte, 24. Göttingen: Vandenhoeck and Ruprecht, 1969. 265 p. ill.
Rev. K.-V. Selge, *HZ*, 210 (1970), 128-130; M. Spinka, *CHR*, 57 (1971), 501-503; P. de Vooght, *RHE*, 65 (1970), 896-898; G. May, *ZSSRG*, kan. Abt., 88 (1971), 378-386; W. H. Struck, *Hessisches Jahrbuch für Landesgeschichte*, 18 (1970), 348-353; A. Triller, *Zeitschrift für die Geschichte und Altertumskunde Ermlands*, 35 (1971), 219-222.

1525A Heřman, J., and V. Sadek. "Hebrejský pramen o husitech." *Dějiny a současnost*, 5, no. 9 (1963), 5-8, ill.

1526 Heymann, F. G. "The background of the Hussite revolution." *Man, state, and society in East European history*. Ed. S. Fischer-Galati. New York, Washington, London: Praeger, c1970. p. 15-33. Rpt. from Heymann's *John Žižka and the Hussite revolution* (Princeton, 1955), p. 36-60.

1527 ——. "The crusades against the Hussites." *A history of the crusades*, 3: *The fourteenth and fifteenth centuries*. Ed. H. W. Hazard. [Madison and London]: University of Wisconsin Press, c1975. p. 586-646 + map.

1528 ——. "The Hussite revolution and reformation and its impact on Germany." *Festschrift für Hermann Heimpel zum 70. Geburtstag*. Veröffentlichungen des Max-Planck-Instituts für Geschichte, 36. Göttingen: Vandenhoeck and Ruprecht, 1971-1972. II, 610-626.

1529 ——. "The Hussite revolution and the German peasants' war: an historical comparison." *MH*, n.s. 1 (1970), 141-159.

1530 ——. "The Hussite-Utraquist church in the fifteenth and sixteenth centuries." *ARG*, 52 (1961), 1-16.

1531 Höfler, K., ed. *Geschichtschreiber der husitischen Bewegung in Böhmen*. Fontes rerum austriacarum, 1st ser., 2, 6, 7. Vienna, 1856-1866. Rpt. Graz: Akademische Druck- und Verlagsanstalt; New York: Johnson Reprint, 1969-1970. 3 v.

1532 Höß, I. "Die hussitische Revolution." *Geschichte in Wissenschaft und Unterricht*, 16 (1965), 207-217.

1533 Hoffmann, F. *Jihlava v husitské revoluci*. Havlíčkův Brod: Krajské nakl., 1961. 251 p. ill. [Jihlava and the Hussite revolution]

1534 ——. "K počátkům Tábora." *ČČH*, 15 (1967), 103-120. [Origins of the Hussite town of Tabor]

1535 Holmes, G. A. "Cardinal Beaufort and the crusade against the Hussites." *EHR*, 88 (1973), 721-750.

1536 Hoyer, S. "Die Auswirkungen der hussitischen revolutionären Bewegung auf Deutschland als Forschungsgegenstand." *Jahrbuch für die Geschichte der UdSSR und der volksdemokratischen Länder Europas*, 9 (1966), 313-325.

1537 ——. "Nicolaus Rutze und die Verbreitung hussitischer Gedanken im Hanseraum." *Neue hansische Studien*. Ed. K. Fritze, et al. Forschungen zur mittelalterlichen Geschichte, 17. Berlin: Akademie-Verlag, 1970. p. 157-170.

1538 Hrubý, K. "Senior communitas – eine revolutionäre Institution der Prager hussitischen Bürgerschaft." Trans. M. Glettler. *Bohemia: Jahrbuch des Collegium Carolinum*, 13 (1972), 9-43.

1539 ——. "Sociologický model husitské revoluce v hranicích politického systému pražských měst." *Sociologický časopis*, 3 (1967), 575-590.

1540 ——. "Struktury a postoje husitských skupin pražského politického systému." *AUC Hist*, 9, no. 1 (1968), 29-78. [Incl. summary, "Die Struktur und die Stellung der hussitischen Gruppen im Prager politischen System"]

1541 Hub, R. "Vylíčení husitského revolučního hnutí v západoněmeckých učebnicích." *JSH*, 33 (1964), 88-97.

1542 Ionescu-Nişcov, T. "Husitica v rumunské historiografii." *ČČH*, 14 (1966), 104-115. [Hussitica in Romanian historiography]

1543   Ivanov, I. F. "Stanovlenie marksistskoĭ kontseptsii gusitskogo naslediia v
       mezhvoennoi Cheksoslovakii." *Sovetskoe slavianovedenie*, 1977, no. 2,
       27-38. [The formation of the Marxist concept of the Hussites' heritage in
       interwar Czechoslovakia]

1544   Jeschke, J. B. "K theologickým předpokladům Husovy reformace." *Husův
       sborník*. p. 20-24. See 1358.

1545   Kadlec, J. "Die Bibel im mittelalterlichen Böhmen." *Archives d'histoire doctrinale
       et littéraire du moyen âge*, 31 (1964), 89-109.

1546   ——. "Czeska katolicka emigracja okresu husytyzmu na ziemiach polskich i na
       Śląsku." *Zeszyty naukowe Katolickiego uniwersytetu lubelskiego*, 19, no. 4
       (1976), 27-36. ——

1547   Kalivoda, R. *Husitská ideologie*. Prague: Československà Akademie Věd, 1961.
       560 p. Ger. summary by M. Quotidian, p. 513-528: "Die hussitische
       Ideologie." Trans. H. Thorwart and M. Glettler, *Revolution und Ideologie:
       der Hussitismus*, with revisions (Cologne and Vienna: Böhlau, 1976), xiii,
       397 p.
       Rev. P. de Vooght, *RHE*, 57 (1962), 493-500; B. Töpfer, *ZG*, 11 (1963), 146-
       147; M. Machovec, *FČ*, 10 (1962), 398-419, with reply by Kalivoda in 11
       (1963), 228-263, and discussion by J. Kudrna, et al. in 10 (1962), 790-824;
       F. Kavka, *JSH*, 32 (1963), 187-189; A. Molnár, *BSSV*, 112 (1962), 78-80.
       Rev. (trans.) J. Klassen, *AHR*, 82 (1977), 623; F. Graus, *HZ*, 225 (1977), 147-
       150; H. Kaminsky, *Speculum*, 53 (1978), 386-389; L. Nemec, *CHR*, 65
       (1979), 467-468.

1548   ——. "Husitskà revoluce a poděbradská epocha." *FČ*, 13 (1965), 387-393. [The
       Hussite revolution and the epoch of George Poděbrady]

1549   ——. "Seibtova Hussitica a husitská revoluce." *AUC Hist*, 8, no. 2 (1967), 61-83.
       Trans. J. Wehle, "Seibt's *Hussitica* und die hussitische Revolution," in
       Historica, 14 (1967), 225-246. See 1640.

1550   ——, and A. Kolesnyk, eds. *Das hussitische Denken im Lichte seiner Quellen*.
       Intro. R. Kalivoda. Texts trans. M. Becker, H. Koblischke, A. Kolesnyk,
       and I. Pape. Berlin: Akademie-Verlag, 1969. 467 p.
       Rev. A. Molnár, *CV*, 13 (1970), 201-205; S. Hoyer, *DLZ*, 92 (1971), 143-
       146; S. Wollgast, *Deutsche Zeitschrift für Philosophie*, 19 (1971), 806-809;
       T. Ionescu-Nişcov, *Studii şi materiale de istorie medie*, 6 (1973), 417-420.

1551   Kaminsky, H. "Chiliasm and the Hussite revolution." *CH*, 26 (1957), 43-71. Rpt. in
       S. L. Thrupp, ed., *Change in medieval society: Europe north of the Alps,
       1050-1500* (New York: Appleton-Century-Crofts, 1964), p. 249-278.

1552   ——. "The free spirit in the Hussite revolution." *Millennial dreams in action:
       studies in revolutionary religious movements*. Ed. S. L. Thrupp. New York:
       Schocken, [1970]. p. 166-186.

1553   ——. *A history of the Hussite revolution*. Berkeley and Los Angeles: University of
       California Press, 1967. xv, 580 p. ill.

Rev. R. Bennett, *History*, 53 (1968), 90-91; P. Brock, *CHR*, 56 (1970), 369-370; M. Fousek, *Slavic review*, 29 (1970), 502-503; F. G. Heymann, *Speculum*, 44 (1969), 147-150; S. Hoyer, *ZG*, 18 (1970), 114-116; C. Manschreck, *Journal of ecumenical studies*, 5 (1968), 404-405; A. Molnár, *MB*, 1 (1969), 360-366; J. Nemec, *Thought*, 44 (1969), 147-148; L. Nemec, *TS*, 29 (1968), 131-134; F. Šmahel, *ČČH*, 16 (1968), 901-904; P. de Vooght, *RHE*, 63 (1968), 543-547; F. Seibt, *HZ*, 210 (1970), 409-412, and *DAEM*, 25 (1969), 288-289.

1554 ——. "The Prague insurrection of 30 July 1419." *MH*, 17 (1966), 106-126.

1555 ——. "The religion of Hussite Tabor." *The Czechoslovak contribution to world culture*. Ed. M. Rechcigl. The Hague, London, Paris: Mouton, 1964. p. 210-223.

1556 ——. "The University of Prague in the Hussite revolution: the role of the masters." *Universities in politics*. Ed. J. W. Baldwin and R. A. Goldthwaite. Baltimore and London: Johns Hopkins Press, c1972. p. 79-106. Rev. J. Hlaváček, *AUC Hist*, 15, no. 2 (1975), 103-104.

1557 Kavka, F. "The Hussite movement and the Czech reformation." *Cahiers d'histoire mondiale*, 5 (1960), 830-856.

1558 ——. "Ze zahraniční literatury o husitství." *JSH*, 32 (1963), 92-94. [Review of recent literature on Hussites]

1559 Kejř, J. "Die Entstehung der Stadtverfassung von Tabor." *Festschrift für Hermann Heimpel zum 70. Geburtstag*. Veröffentlichungen des Max-Planck-Instituts für Geschichte, 36. Göttingen: Vandenhoeck and Ruprecht, 1971-1972. II, 686-712.

1560 ——. "Das Hussitentum und das kanonische Recht." *Proceedings of the third international congress of medieval canon law, Strasbourg, 3-6 September 1968*. Ed. S. Kuttner. Monumenta iuris canonici, series C, subsidia 4. Vatican City, 1971. p. 191-204.

1561 ——. "Ke zdrojům husitských názorů na teorii soudních důkazů." *Právněhistorické studie*, 11 (1965), 9-15. [Incl. summary, "Zu den Quellen hussitischer Ansichten über die Theorie gerichtlicher Beweise"]

1562 ——. *Kvodlibetní disputace na pražské universitě*. Sbírka pramenů a příruček k dějinám University Karlovy, 6. Prague: Universita Karlova, 1971. 206 p. [Incl. summary, "Les disputes quodlibétiques à l'université de Prague"]

1563 ——. "O formě disputace na pražské universitě." *Strahovská knihovna*, 5/6 (1970-71), 181-189. [Incl. summary, "Über die Form der Disputation an der Prager Universität"]

1564 ——. *Stát, církev a společnost v disputacích na pražské universitě v době Husově a husitské*. Rozpravy ČSAV, 74, no. 14. Prague: ČSAV, 1964. 63 p. Rev. F. Kavka, *Právněhistorické studie*, 11 (1965), 257-260.

1565 Klassen, J. M. "The Czech nobility's use of the right of patronage on behalf of the Hussite reform movement." *Slavic review*, 34 (1975), 341-359.

1566 ——. *The nobility and the making of the Hussite revolution.* East European monographs, 47. Boulder, Colo: East European Quarterly, 1978. 186 p. —
Rev. W. Cook, *AHR*, 84 (1979), 1035-1036.

1567 ——. "Noble patronage and politics in the Hussite revolution." Diss. Univ. of Washington. *DAI*, 34A (1973), 2492-2493.

1568 ——. "Ownership of church patronage and the Czech nobility's support for Hussitism." *ARG*, 66 (1975), 36-49. [Incl. Ger. summary]

1569 Köpstein, H. "Über die Teilnahme von Deutschen an der hussitischen revolutionären Bewegung – speziell in Böhmen." *ZG*, 11 (1963), 116-145.

1570 Kolár, J., and E. Pražák. "Redatace husitských památek." *Dějiny a současnost*, 10, no. 9 (1968), 19-21. [The redating of Hussite literature]

1571 Kolbuszewski, S. "Le mouvement wicléfiste en Pologne au xve siècle." *Geschichte der Ost- und Westkirche in ihren wechselseitigen Beziehungen.* Annales Instituti slavici, I, 3. Wiesbaden: Harrassowitz, 1967. p. 138-141.

1572 Kornell, K. "Economic problems of Bohemia in the early xvth century and the Hussite attempts at their solution." Thesis, Univ. of Wales, Aberystwyth, [1970]. [iii], 126 p.

1573 Krása, J. "Studie o rukopisech husitské doby." *Umění*, 22 (1974), 17-50, ill. [Incl. summary, "Die Handschriften der Hussitenzeit"]

1574 Krchňák, A. *Čechové na basilejském sněmu.* Rome: Křesťanskà akademie, 1967. 274 p.

1575 Krejci, J. "The meaning of Hussitism." *JRH*, 8 (1974), 3-20.

1576 Křesadlo, K. "K dějinám města Slaného do porážky husitské revoluce." *Středočeský sborník historický*, 8 (1973), 55-69. [On the history of Slaný until the defeat of the Hussite revolution]

1577 Lacaze, Y. "Philippe le Bon et le problème hussite: un projet de croisade bourguignon en 1428-1429." *RH*, 241 (1969), 69-98.

1578 Laptěva, L. P. "Hus a Viklef." *JSH*, 40 (1971), 162-180. [Incl. summary, "Hus und Wiclef: Erklärung ihrer wechselseitigen Beziehung in der russischen Historiographie des 19. und Anfang des 20. Jahrhunderts"]

1579 Laptěvová, L. P. "K hodnocení husitského revolučního hnutí současnou západní historiografii." *JSH*, 33 (1964), 198-204.

1580 Lavicka, L. "*L'espion turc*, le monde slave et le hussitisme." *XVIIe siècle*, 110-111 (1976), 75-92.

1581 Lipatnikova, G. I. "K izucheniiu gusitskogo dvizheniia russkoĭ dorevoliutsionnoĭ istoriografii." *Voprosy istorii slavian*, 1 (1963), 69-92. [The study of the Hussite movement by Russian historians before 1917]

1582 Macek, J. "Die böhmische und die deutsche radikale Reformation bis zum Jahre 1525." *ZKG*, 85 (1974), 149-173.

1583 ——. "Giovanni Hus e la riforma boema." *BISIM*, 78 (1967), 45-73.

1584 ——. *Die Hussitenbewegung in Böhmen*. Trans. E. Jiřiček. 2nd ed. Prague: Orbis,
       1965. 135 p. Trans. V. Fried and I. Milner, *The Hussite movement in
       Bohemia*, ed. E. Lauer (London: Lawrence and Wishart), viii, 119 p.
       Trans. M. Aynonin, *Le mouvement hussite en Bohème* (Prague: Orbis,
       1965), 134 p.
       Rev. H. Bodensieck, *ZOF*, 18 (1969), 111-114.

1585 ——. *Jean Hus et les traditions hussites (xvᵉ-xixᵉ siècles)*. Civilisations et men-
       talités. [Paris]: Plon, c1973. 390 p. ill.
       Rev. H. Desroche, *ASSR*, 40 (1975), 249; N. Coulet, *ETR*, 51 (1976), 127-
       128; P. de Vooght, *RHE*, 70 (1975), 125-128; J. Solé, *Annales*, 31 (1976),
       529-531; F. Graus, *Zeitschrift für historische Forschung*, 1 (1974),
       244-245.

1586 ——. "Naissance et fond de la réforme (en marge du livre de J. Delumeau,
       Naissance et affirmation de la réforme)." Trans. K. Trojanová. *Historica*,
       14 (1967), 247-269.

1587 Machilek, F. "Böhmen, Polen und die hussitische Revolution." *ZOF*, 23 (1974),
       401-430.

1588 ——. "Heilserwartung und Revolution der Táboriten 1419/21." *Festiva Lanx:
       Studien zum mittelalterlichen Geistesleben*. Festschrift Johannes Spörl. Ed.
       K. Schnith. Munich: Salesianische Offizin, c1966. p. 67-94.

1589 ——. *Ludolf von Sagan und seine Stellung in der Auseinandersetzung um Konzi-
       liarismus und Hussitismus*. Wissenschaftliche Materialien und Beiträge
       zur Geschichte und Landeskunde der böhmischen Länder, 8. Munich: R.
       Lerche, 1967. vii, 256 p.
       Rev. W. Brandmüller, *DAEM*, 25 (1969), 289; H. Heimpel, *ZSSRG*, Kan. Abt.,
       87 (1970), 470-471; R. Bäumer, *Römische Quartalschrift*, 65 (1970), 250-
       251; H. Kaminsky, *Speculum*, 44 (1969), 310-311; D. Kurze, *ZKG*, 81
       (1970), 267; P. de Vooght, *RHE*, 63 (1968), 999-1002; L. Juhnke, *Zeitschrift
       für die Geschichte und Altertumskunde Ermlands*, 33 (1969), 381-383.

1590 Machovcová, M., and M. Machovec. *Utopie blouznivců a sektářů*. Prague: Nakl.
       Československé Akademie Věd, 1960. 526 p. [Radical and sectarian
       concepts of utopia]
       Rev. A. Molnár, *CV*, 4 (1961), 273-279.

1591 Madre, A. "Kardinal Branda an Nikolaus von Dinkelsbühl: eine Anweisung zur
       Kreuzzugspredigt gegen die Hussiten." *Von Konstanz nach Trient ... Fest-
       gabe für August Franzen*. Ed. R. Bäumer. Munich, Paderborn, Vienna:
       Schöningh, 1972. p. 87-100.

1592 Marečková, D. "Leningradský zlomek staročeské veršované skladby husitské."
       Sborník Národního Muzea v Praze, ser. C, 12 (1967), 65-84. [Incl.
       summary, "Fragment de Léningrad d'une poésie en vieux tchèque de
       l'époque hussite"]

1593   Maresch, L. "Hussitismus, ein Versuch der begrifflichen Erläuterung." *Translatio studii: manuscript and library studies honoring Oliver L. Kapsner*, O.S.B. Ed. J. G. Plante. Collegeville, Minn.: St. John's University Press, 1973. p. 260-269.

1594   Mikulka, J. "Polacy w Czechach i ich rola w rozwoju husytyzmu." *Odrodzenie i reformacja w Polsce*, 11 (1966), 5-27. [Incl. summary, "Die Polen in Böhmen und die Rolle, die sie in der Entwicklung des Hussitismus spielten"]

1595   ———. *Polské země a herese v době před reformací.* Práce z dějin východní Evropy, 1; Heretická hnutí ve východní Evropě, 1. Prague: Ústav dějin východní Evropy, ČSAV, 1969. 144 p. [Poland and heresy before the reformation]
        Rev. S. Bylina, *Odrodzenie i reformacja w Polsce*, 17 (1972), 217-220.

1596   Molnár, A. "Apocalypse XII dans l'interprétation hussite." *RHPR*, 45 (1965), 212-231.

1597   ———. "Aspects de la continuité de pensée dans la réforme tchèque." *CV*, 15 (1972), 27-50, 111-125.

1598   ———. "Bratrský synod ve Lhotce u Rychnova." *Bratrský sborník*. Ed. R. Říčan. Prague: Komenského evangelická fakulta bohoslovecká, 1967. p. 15-37.

1599   ———. "Cola di Rienzo, Petrarca e le origini della riforma hussita." *Protestantesimo*, 19 (1964), 214-223.

1600   ———. "Ecclesiological aspects of the first reformation." *CV*, 11 (1968), 221-231.

1601   ———. "Endzeit und Reformation." *Heidelberger Jahrbücher*, 9 (1965), 73-80.

1602   ———. "L'évolution de la théologie hussite." *RHPR*, 43 (1963), 133-171.

1603   ———. "Die Funktion der Kirche in der böhmischen Reformation." *CV*, 17 (1974), 15-24.

1604   ———. "Hnutí svobodného ducha a husitství." *KR*, 30 (1963), 37-39.

1605   ———. "Der Hussitismus als christliche Reformbewegung." *Bohemia sacra: das Christentum in Böhmen 973-1973*. Ed. F. Seibt. Düsseldorf: Schwann, 1974. p. 92-109, 565-566.

1606   ———. *Jan Hus, testimone della verità*. Pref. L. Santini. Turin: Claudiana, 1973. 255 p. ill.
        Rev. P. de Vooght, *RHE*, 70 (1975), 328-329; J. I. Tellechea Idígoras, *Salmanticensis*, 22 (1975), 387; J. Séguy, *ASSR*, 37 (1974), 244-245; L. B. Pascoe, *CH*, 43 (1974), 537; L. Nemec, *CHR*, 63 (1977), 459-460; J.-M. Léonard, *ETR*, 49 (1974), 442-443; J. Gill, *JEH*, 26 (1975), 200; L. Brož, *CV*, 16 (1973), 296-297; J.-M. Thiriet, *RHPR*, 56 (1976), 434-435; F. Machilek, *AHC*, 8 (1976), 658-659; E. Pacho, *Ephemerides carmeliticae*, 27 (1976), 532.

1607   ———. "Nad uvodnimi kapitolami Biskupcovy táborské konfese." *TPKR*, 28 (1961), 67-72. —

1608   ———. "Non-violence et théologie de la révolution chez les hussites du xvème siècle." *Lumière et vie*, 18, no. 91 (jan.-fév. 1969), 33-46.

1609   ———. "Ohlas Táborské konfese u románských valdenských." *Strahovská knihovna*, 5/6 (1970-71), 201-208. [Incl. summary, "L'écho de la confession de foi taborite auprès des vaudois des Alpes"]

1610   ———. "Une protestation demi-millénaire." *cv*, 10 (1967), 1-3.

1611   ———. "Die Rassenfrage im Lichte der böhmischen Reformation." *cv*, 17 (1974), 266-268.

1612   ———. "Zwischen Revolution und Krieg." *cv*, 10 (1967), 33-44.

1613   Nechutová, J. "K předhusitské a Husově eklesiologii." *Sborník prací filosofické fakulty Brněnské University*, B 19 (1972), 97-102. [Incl. summary, "Zur vorhussitischen Ekklesiologie und zu der Ekklesiologie von Hus"]

1614   ———. "Nové pohledy na úlohu valdenství v utváření husitského myšlení." *Husův sborník*. p. 96-102. See 1358.

1615   Niederländer, R. "Die *Chronica Hussitarum* des Andreas von Regensburg als eine wesentliche Quelle für die Geschichte der Hussitenkriege." *Liber ad magistrum: Festgabe Johannes Spörl*. Munich: Historisches Seminar der Universität, 1964. p. 83-88. —

1616   Nyíri, A., ed. and trans. *A Müncheni Kódex 1466-ból*. Codices hungarici, 7. Budapest: Akadémiai Kiadó, 1971. 402 p. ill. [The Munich Codex (1466) of the NT, said to be from the Hungarian Hussite Bible. With Latin trans.]

1617   Oberdorffer, K. "Die Reformation in Böhmen und das späte Hussitentum." *Bohemia: Jahrbuch des Collegium Carolinum*, 6 (1965), 123-145.

1618   Odložilík, O. "A church in a hostile state: the Unity of Czech brethren." *Central European history*, 6 (1973), 111-127.

1619   ———. "Životopisec husitského krále." *Křesťanské listy a Husův lid*, 23, no. 64 (1962), 161-165. —

1620   Palacký, F., ed. *Urkundliche Beiträge zur Geschichte des Hussitenkrieges*. Prague, 1873-1874. Rpt. Osnabrück: Biblio-Verlag, 1966. 2 v.

1621   Panaitescu, P. P. "Husitismul şi cultura slavonă în Moldava." *Romanoslavica*, 10 (1964), 275-287.

1622   Pitter, P. *Geistige Revolution im Herzen Europas: Quellen der tschechischen Erneuerung*. Zürich and Stuttgart: Rotapfel, c1968.

1623   Polívka, M. "Problematika husitství v české historické literatuře z let 1972-1974." *čČH*, 24 (1976), 278-290. [Review of scholarship]

1624   Potměšil, F. "Kniha Joachima Dachsela o Husovi." *Husův sborník*. p. 163-166. [On Joachim Dachsel's *Jan Hus*] See 1349, 1358.

1625   Pražák, E. "K interpretaci veršované satiry Zbarvení mnichové." *Strahovská knihovna*, 5/6 (1970-71), 191-200. [Incl. summary, "Zur Interpretation der Satire in Versen Zbarvení mnichové (gefärbten Mönche)"]

1626   ———. "O datování husitského veršovaného traktátu Proti poutím." *LF*, 91 (1968),

297-302. [Incl. summary, "Über die Datierung des hussitischen Traktats Gegen die Wallfahrten"]

1627   Rejchrtová, N. "Czech utraquism at the time of Václav Koranda the younger and the visual arts." *CV*, 20 (1977), 157-170, 233-244.

1628   Říčan, R. "The seventy-fifth birthday of F. M. Bartoš, historian of Hussitism." *CV*, 7 (1964), 155-160.

1629   Roubic, A. "Přerov za husitství a do nástupu Pernštejnů (v letech 1412-1475)." *Dějiny města Přerova*. Přerov: Městský Národní Výbor, 1970-1971. II, 147-170. [Přerov during the Hussite period and before the time of the Pernsteins]

1630   Růžička, V. "Cesta Dr. K. Farského za Husem a husitstvím (několik dokumentů a svědectví)." *Hus stále živý*. Ed. M. Kaňák. Prague, 1965. p. 117-126.

1631   Ryba, B. "Strahovské Zjevenie: český husitský výklad na Apokalypsu a jeho latinská lollardská předloha Johna Purveye." *Strahovská knihovna*, 1 (1966), 7-27. [Incl. summary, "Strahover Offenbarung: eine tschechische hussitische Exegese der Apokalypse und ihre lateinische lollardische Vorlage des John Purvey"]

1632   Scherbaum, E. "Das hussitische Böhmen bei Thomas Ebendorfer." Diss. Universität Wien, 1972. —

1633   Schlesinger, G. *Die Hussiten in Franken. Der Hussiteneinfall unter Prokop dem Großen im Winter 1429/30, seine Auswirkungen sowie sein Niederschlag in der Geschichtschreibung.* Die Plassenburg: Schriften für Heimatforschung und Kulturpflege in Ostfranken, 34. Kulmbach: Stadtarchiv, Freunde der Plassenburg, 1974. 233 p.

1634   Schmidt, H. *Hus und Hussitismus in der tschechischen Literatur des XIX. und XX. Jahrhunderts.* Slavistische Beiträge, 36. Munich: Sagner, 1969. 296 p.
        Rev. V. Viktora, *LF*, 94 (1971), 253-255.

1635   Schofield, A. N. E. D. "An English version of some events in Bohemia during 1434." *SEER*, 42 (1964), 312-331.

1636   Seibt, F. "Die Hussitenzeit als Kulturepoche." *HZ*, 195 (1962), 21-62.

1637   ——. "Die hussitische Revolution." *Zwischen Frankfurt und Prag: Vorträge der wissenschaftlichen Tagung des Collegium Carolinum in Frankfurt/M am 7. und 8. Juni 1962.* Munich: Robert Lerche, 1963. p. 75-102.

1638   ——. "Die hussitische Revolution und der deutsche Bauernkrieg." *HZ*, n.s., suppl. 4 (1975), 47-61.

1639   ——. "Die hussitische Revolution und die europäische Gesellschaft." *Cultus pacis.* Ed. V. Vaněček. Prague: Academia, 1966. p. 21-33.

1640   ——. *Hussitica: zur Struktur einer Revolution.* Beihefte zum Archiv für Kulturgeschichte, 8. Cologne and Graz: Böhlau, 1965. vii, 205 p.
        Rev. H. Bodensieck, *ZOF*, 18 (1969), 111-114; A. Borst, *ZKG*, 78 (1967), 176-178; F. G. Heymann, *ARG*, 59 (1968), 107-110; R. Kalivoda, *Historica*, 14 (1967), 225-246; H. Kaminsky, *Speculum*, 42 (1967), 756-758; E.

Lemberg, *HZ*, 206 (1968), 396-398; J. Mikulka, *Slavia*, 37 (1968), 527-529; E. Pásztor, *SM*, 3rd ser., 9 (1968), 441-443; H. Slapnicka, *ZSSRG*, Germ. Abt., 84 (1967), 469-470; P. de Vooght, *RHE*, 62 (1967), 142-143; H. Ebner, *MIÖG*, 75 (1967), 457-458; J. Macek, *ČČH*, 15 (1967), 225-231; K. F. Richter, *Zeitschrift für bayerische Landesgeschichte*, 30 (1967), 989-991; J. Bujnoch, *Jahrbücher für Geschichte Osteuropas*, 15 (1967), 149-150.

1641 ——. "Tabor und die europäischen Revolutionen." *Bohemia: Jahrbuch des Collegium Carolinum*, 14 (1973), 33-42.

1642 Serczyk, J. "Husytyzm na Mazowszu w drugiej połowie xv wieku." *Studia z dziejów kościoła katolickiego*, 1, no. 1 (1960), 161-179. [Hussitism in Mazury in the latter half of the 15th century]

1643 Šidak, J. "Jedan nov prilog poznavanju hrvatsko-čeških odnosa u Husovo doba." *Slovo*, 9/10 (1960), 198-200.

1644 Šmahel, F. "Circa universalia sunt dubitationes non pauce I-III. Studie a texty k pražskému sporu o universalia realia." *FČ*, 18 (1970), 987-998. [Studies and texts concerning the Prague disputations over "universalia realia"]

1645 ——. "'Doctor evangelicus super omnes evangelistas': Wyclif's fortune in Hussite Bohemia." *BIHR*, 43 (1970), 16-34.

1646 ——. *Idea národa v husitských Čechách*. České Budějovice: Růže, 1971. 229 p. ill. [The idea of nationalism in Hussite Bohemia]

1647 ——. "The idea of the 'nation' in Hussite Bohemia: an analytical study of the ideological and political aspects of the national question in Hussite Bohemia from the end of the 14th century to the eighties of the 15th century." Trans. R. F. Samsour. *Historica*, 16 (1969 for 1968), 143-247; 17 (1969), 93-197.

1648 ——. "Le mouvement des étudiants à Prague dans les années 1408-1412." Trans. K. Trojanová. *Historica*, 14 (1967), 33-75.

1649 ——. "Počátky studentské nonkonformity." *Dějiny a současnost*, 11, no. 4 (1969), 33-37, ill. [The beginnings of student nonconformity]

1650 ——. "Tábor a husitské revoluce: problémy interpretace." *JSH*, 40, suppl. (1971), 9-21. [Tabor and the Hussite revolution: problems of interpretation]

1651 Souček, B. *Česká apokalypsa v husitství: z dějin textu Zjeveni Janova – od Konstantina ke Komenskému. Úvodem k vydání Nového zákona Táborského*. [Prague]: Českobratrská Církev Evangelická, 1967. 206 p. [Incl. summary, "The Czech Apocalypse of the Hussites"]

1652 Sousedík, S. "Pojem 'distinctio formalis' u českých realistů v době Husově." *FČ*, 18 (1970), 1024-1029. [The concept of "distinctio formalis" according to the Czech realists in the time of Hus]

1653 Spunar, P. "Antihussitische Verse aus Schlesien." *Basler Zeitschrift für Geschichte und Altertumskunde*, 74 (1974), 189-200.

1654 Šváb, M. "Ein neu erkanntes Hussitenlied in einem Erfurter Kodex." *Zeitschrift für Slawistik*, 20 (1975), 391-401, ill.

1655   Svejkovský, F. "Akrostich Trcho a další stopy působnosti protihusitského básníka
       Jakuba Trcha." *ČČH*, 16 (1968), 585-594. [The acrostic TRCHO and further
       traces of the activity of Jacob Trch, anti-Hussite poet]

1656   ——. "Musejní rukopis XIV E 7 jako pramen k dějinám hudby z doby husitské."
       Acta universitatis carolinae, 1965, Philosophica et historica, 2, p. 45-55.
       [Incl. summary, "Das Manuskript XIV E 7 aus der Bibliothek des Prager
       Nationalmuseums als Quelle für die Musikgeschichte in der Zeit der
       Hussitenbewegung"]

1657   ——, ed. *Veršované skladby doby husitské.* Památky staré literatury české, 26.
       Prague: Nakl. Československé Akademie Věd, 1963. 225 p.

1658   Sygusch, K. C. "Die Auseinandersetzung der Oberlausitz mit dem Hussitismus.
       Unter besonderer Berücksichtigung ihrer Kirchengeschichte." Diss. Uni-
       versität Leipzig, 1966. —

1659   Talley, T. J. "A Hussite Latin gradual of the xvth century." *Bulletin of the General
       theological seminary*, 48, no. 5 (1962), 8-13, ill. —

1660   Töpfer, B. "Fragen der hussitischen revolutionären Bewegung." *ZG*, 11 (1963),
       146-167.

1661   Tourn, G. "Prima e seconda riforma, un dialogo mancato." *Protestantesimo*, 29
       (1974), 129-148.

1662   Vantuch, A. "La participation liégeoise à la croisade contre les hussites en 1421,
       d'après Jean de Stavelot." *Liège et Bourgogne.* Actes du colloque tenu à
       Liège les 28, 29 et 30 octobre 1968. [Liège: Université de Liège; Paris:
       Belles Lettres, 1972.] p. 45-54.

1663   Varsik, B. "Husiti a reformácia na Slovensku." *Historické štúdie*, 14 (1969),
       217-222. [Hussites and the reformation in Slovakia]

1664   ——. *Husitské revolučné hnutie a Slovensko.* Publikácie Slovenskej historickej
       spoločnosti pri Slovenskej akadémii vied, 9. Bratislava: Vydavateľstvo
       Slovenskej akadémie vied, 1965. 374 p. [Incl. summary, "Die hussitische
       revolutionäre Bewegung und die Slowakei"]
       Rev. L. Hosák, *ZG*, 14 (1966), 1021-1022; F. Kavka, *ČČH*, 14 (1966),
       571-574.

1665   Vidmanová, A. "K středolatinské textové kritice." *LF*, 94 (1971), 184-192. [Incl.
       Latin summary. Review-essay on recent editions of Jakoubek of Stříbro,
       Nicholas of Dresden, and John of Příbram]

1666   Vooght, P. de. "La confrontation des thèses hussites et romaines au concile de
       Bâle (janvier-avril 1433)." *RTAM*, 37 (1970), 97-137, 254-291.

1667   ——. "L'hérésie des taborites sur l'eucharistie (1418-1421)." *Irénikon*, 35 (1962),
       340-350.

1668   ——. "De Hussiten." *Spiegel historiael*, 4 (1969), 273-277.

1669   ——. "Les hussites et la 'Reformatio Sigismundi'." *Von Konstanz nach Trient ...
       Festgabe für August Franzen.* Ed. R. Bäumer. Munich, Paderborn,
       Vienna: Schöningh, 1972. p. 199-214.

1670 ——. "La notion d''Église-assemblée des prédestinés' dans la théologie hussite primitive." *CV*, 13 (1970), 119-136.

1671 Werner, E. "Antihussitisches Pamphlet oder taboritischer Traktat? Eine Datie-rungsfrage." *Wissenschaftliche Zeitschrift der Karl-Marx-Universität Leipzig*, Gesellschafts- und sprachwissenschaftliche Reihe, 9 (1959-60), 579-581.

1672 ——. *Der Kirchenbegriff bei Jan Hus, Jakoubek von Mies, Jan Želivský und den linken Taboriten.* Sitzungsberichte der Deutschen Akademie der Wissen-schaften zu Berlin, Klasse für Philosophie, Geschichte, Staats-, Rechts- und Wirtschaftswissenschaften, 1967, no. 10. Berlin: Akademie-Verlag, 1967. 73 p.

Rev. E. Pásztor, *SM*, 3rd ser., 8 (1967), 1187-1189; H. Mohr, *DLZ*, 90 (1969), 533-535.

1673 ——. "Popular ideologies in late mediaeval Europe: Taborite chiliasm and its antecedents." *Comparative studies in society and history*, 2 (1960), 344-363.

1674 Winter, E. *Frühhumanismus: seine Entwicklung in Böhmen und deren europäi-sche Bedeutung für die Kirchenreformbestrebungen im 14. Jahrhundert.* Beiträge zur Geschichte des religiösen und wissenschaftlichen Denkens, 3. Berlin: Akademie-Verlag, 1964. 239 p.

Rev. F. Seibt, *ZOF*, 15 (1966), 567-570; A. Molnár, *Nuova rivista storica*, 49 (1965), 449-450; G. Mühlpfordt, *DLZ*, 86 (1965), 1004-1007; F. Šmahel, *ČČH*, 14 (1966), 70-73; B. Töpfer, *ZG*, 13 (1965), 336-339.

1675 Zapletal, F. *Přerov za válek husitských.* Přerov: Městský Národní Výbor, 1965. 60 p.

1676 Zelinka, T. Č, "Dějinná půda husitství na Jindřichohradecku." *JSH*, 35 (1966), 85-91.

1677 Zeman, J. K. "Anabaptism: a replay of medieval themes or a prelude to the modern age?" *The Mennonite quarterly review*, 50 (1976), 259-271.

1678 ——. *The Hussite movement and the reformation in Bohemia, Moravia and Slovakia (1350-1650): a bibliographical study guide (with particular reference to resources in North America).* Reformation in central Europe, 1. Ann Arbor: Michigan Slavic Publications, for Center for Reformation Research, c1977 [1978]. xxxvi, 390 p.

Rev. L. Gross, *The Mennonite quarterly review*, 53 (1979), 258-259; *ČČH*, 27 (1979), 453.

1679 ——. "Restitution and dissent in the late medieval renewal movements: the Waldensians, the Hussites and the Bohemian Brethren." *JAAR*, 44 (1976), 7-27.

1680 ——. "The rise of religious liberty in the Czech reformation." *Central European history*, 6 (1973), 128-147.

B. *Individuals Connected wth the Hussites* *(Entries 1681 to 1784)*

Note: entries are arranged alphabetically by individual.

ANDREW GAŁKA Z DOBČINA

1681   Bartoš, F. M. "Osudy polského husity v Táboře a v Čechách." *JSH*, 41 (1972), 111-114. [Incl. summary, "Schicksal eines polnischen Hussiten in Tábor und in Böhmen (Andreas Gałka von Dobčina)"]

ARSEN, JOHANN

1682   Šmahel, F. "Ein unbekanntes Prager Quodlibet von ca. 1400 des Magisters Johann Arsen von Langenfeld." *DAEM*, 33 (1977), 199-215.

BEAUFORT, HENRY

1683   Schnith, K. "Kardinal Heinrich Beaufort und der Hussitenkrieg." *Von Konstanz nach Trient ... Festgabe für August Franzen.* Ed. R. Bäumer. Munich, Paderborn, Vienna: Schöningh, 1972. p. 119-138.

CHELČICKÝ, PETER

1684   Bartoš, F. M. "Strahovské Zjevení a záhada jeho původce." *JSH*, 39 (1970), 256-258. [Incl. summary, "Die Apokalypse von Strahov und ihr Verfasser (Chelčický?)"]

1685   Bašus, B. B. "Petr Chelčický – o boji duchovním." *KR*, 27 (1960), 14-21.

1686   Blucha, J. "Tzv. Budapešt'ský rukopis Petra Chelčického." *JSH*, 29 (1960), 77-82.

1687   Chelčický, Peter. *Drobné spisy: O boji duchovním, O církvi svaté, O trojiem lidu řeč, Replika proti Mikuláši Biskupcovi.* Ed. E. Petrů. Památky staré literatury české, 30. Prague: Československé Akademie Věd, 1966. 239 p. ill. [Minor writings: On spiritual warfare, On the holy church, On the triple division of society, Reply to Nicolaus Biskupec]

1687A   Flegl, M. "K problému identifikace Petra Chelčického." *LF*, 102 (1979), 18-25.

1688   Horák, C. "Chelčického metoda myšlení." *KR*, 40 (1973), 29-31 [Chelčický's method of thought]

1689   Kaminsky, H. "Peter Chelčický: treatises on Christianity and the social order." *Studies in medieval and renaissance history*, 1 (1964), 105-179.

1690   Míka, A. *Petr Chelčický.* Prague: Svobodné Slovo, 1963. 223 p. ill.

1691   Molnár, A. "Chelčického valdenská interpretace Řím 13." *KR*, 36 (1969), 206-212. Trans., "Romani 13 nella interpretazione della prima riforma," *Protestantesimo*, 24 (1969), 65-76. Trans., "Romains 13 dans l'interprétation de la première réforme," *ETR*, 46 (1971), 231-240.

1692   ——. "Crisis of the parish." *CV*, 13 (1970), 45-56.

1693   ——. "Frammento inedito di una spiegazione di Chelcický su Rom. 13." *Protestantesimo*, 24 (1969), 76-78.

1694   ———. "Peter Chelčickýs Deutung von Röm 13, 1-7." *TLZ*, 101 (1976), 481-489.

1695   Petrů, E. "K metodě myšlení Petra Chelčického." *LF*, 93 (1970), 120-127. [Incl. summary, "La méthode de la pensée de Petr Chelčický"]

1696   Šmahel, F. "Antiideál mesta v díle Petra Chelčického: příspěvek k sociální kritice středověkého města." *ČČH*, 20 (1972), 71-94. [Incl. summary, "Antiideal der Stadt im Werk Peters von Cheltschitz"]

1697   Vogl, C., trans. *Peter Cheltschizki, 'Das Netz des Glaubens', aus dem Alttschechischen ins Deutsche übertragen.* Dachau bei München, 1924. Rpt., with new intro. by A. Molnár, Hildesheim and New York: Olms, 1970. Nikolaus Ludwig von Zinzendorf: Materialen und Dokumente, I, 5. xii*, xvi, 317 p.

1698   Wagner, M. L. "The life and thought of Petr Chelčický: a radical separatist in Hussite Bohemia." Diss. Chicago Theological Seminary, 1973. —

CONRAD OF WALDHAUSEN

1699   Bylina, S. *Wpływy Konrada Waldhausena na ziemiach polskich w drugiej połowie XIV i pierwszej połowie XV wieku.* Wrocław [etc.]: Zakład Narodowy im. Ossolińskich, Wydawnictwo Polskiej Akademii Nauk, 1966. 120 p. [The influence of Konrad Waldhausen in Polish territories in the second half of the 14th and in the first half of the 15th century]

GREGORY OF KUNWALD

1700   Bartoš, F. M. "Původ a rodina Bratra Řehoře, tvůrce Jednoty bratrské." *JSH*, 39 (1970), 58-66. [Incl. summary, "Die Familie und das private Leben des Schöpfers der Brüder-Unität, Bruder Gregors"]

1701   Flegl, M. "K otázce sociálního původu bratra Řehoře a jeho literárních počátků." *LF*, 100 (1977), 88-94. [On the question of the social origin of Brother Řehoř (Gregory of Kunwald) and his literary beginnings]

JAKOUBEK OF STŘÍBRO

1702   Seibt, F. "Die *revelatio* des Jacobellus von Mies über die Kelchkommunion." *DAEM*, 22 (1966), 618-624.

1703   Urfus, V. "Jakoubek ze Stříbra a Mikuláš z Drážďan jako teoretikové úroku a lichvy." *JSH*, 35 (1966), 199-205. [Jakoubek of Stříbro and Nicholas of Dresden as theorists on interest and usury]

1704   Voogt, P. de. *Jacobellus de Stříbro (†1429), premier théologien du hussitisme.* Bibliothèque de la Revue d'histoire ecclésiastique, 54. Louvain: Bibliothèque de l'Université, 1972. xv, 415 p.
        Rev. W. R. Cook, *CH*, 43 (1974), 397-398; J. Gill, *JEH*, 25 (1974), 205-207; R. Mols, *NRT*, 97 (1975), 741-742; L. Nemec, *CHR*, 62 (1976), 110-112; P. L. Nyhus, *AHR*, 80 (1975), 84; H. Bascour, *RHE*, 70 (1975), 799-800; J. Lecler, *RSR*, 63 (1975), 547-550.

1705 ——. "Jacobellus de Stříbro, le taboritisme hussite et la discussion chrétienne sur la violence." *Rhythmes du monde*, 18 (1970), 140-144.
1706 ——. "Le sermon 'Factum est ut moreretur mendicus' de Jacobellus de Stříbro (nov. 1413)." *RTAM*, 36 (1969), 195-212.

JANOV, MATTHEW OF

1707 Nechutová, J. "De 'Tractatus de corpore Christi' M. Mauritio adscripti fonte Janoviano." *LF*, 93 (1970), 262-270. [Incl. Czech summary]
1708 ——. "Filosofické zdroje díla m. Mateje z Janova." *FČ*, 18 (1970), 1010-1018. [Philosophical sources of the works of Matthew of Janov]
1709 ——. "M. Matej z Janova v odborné literatuře." *Sborník prací filosofické fakulty Brnenské university*, 17 (1972), 119-133. ——

JENŠTEJN, JAN

1710 Weltsch, R. E. *Archbishop John of Jenstein (1348-1400): papalism, humanism and reform in pre-Hussite Prague*. The Hague and Paris: Mouton, 1968. 252 p.
Rev. Z. R. Dittrich, *TG*, 83 (1970), 429-430; J. V. Polc, *MB*, 1 (1969), 162-165.

JEROME OF PRAGUE

1711 Pilný, J. *Jerôme de Prague: un orateur progressiste du moyen âge*. [Geneva]: Perret-Gentil, c1974. 75 p.
1712 Schmitt, C. B. "A fifteenth century Italian translation of Poggio's letter on Jerome of Prague." *ARG*, 58 (1967), 5-15.
1713 Šmahel, F. *Jeronym Pražský* [added title: *Mistr Jeronym Pražský: život revolučního intelektuála*]. Prague: Svobodné Slovo, 1966. 242 p. ill. [Jerome of Prague: the life of a revolutionary intellectual]
1714 ——. "Leben und Werk des Magisters Hieronymus von Prag: Forschung ohne Probleme und Perspektiven?" *Historica*, 13 (1966), 81-111.
1715 ——. "Pramen Jerónymovy Chvály svobodných umění." *Strahovská knihovna*, 5/6 (1970-71), 169-180. [Incl. summary, "De 'Recommendacionis arcium liberalium' magistri Hieronymi Pragensis origine"]
1716 Sousedík, S. "M. Hieronymi Pragensis ex Iohanne Scoto Eriugena excerpta." *LF*, 98 (1975), 4-7.
1717 Watkins, R. N. "The death of Jerome of Prague: divergent views." *Speculum*, 42 (1967), 104-129.

JESENICE, JAN

1718 Kejř, J. "O některých spisech M. Jana z Jesenice." *LF*, 86 (1963), 77-90. [Incl. summary, "Über einige Schriften des Magisters Johannes von Jesenice"]
1719 ——. *Husitský právník M. Jan z Jesenice*. Právněhistorická knižnice, 7. Prague:

Československé Akademie Věd, 1965. 178 p. [Incl. summary, "Der hussitische Rechtsgelehrte Magister Johann von Jesenitz"]
Rev. M. Truc, *Právněhistorické studie*, 11 (1965), 260-262.

1720   Kubalík, J. "Johannes von Ragusa und die hussitische Ekklesiologie." *Theologisch-praktische Quartalschrift*, 125 (1977), 290-295.

Kravar, Pavel

1721   Moonan, L. "Pavel Kravar and some writings once attributed to him." *The Innes review*, 27 (1976), 3-23.

Luke of Prague

1722   Molnár, A. "Luc de Prague à Constantinople." *cv*, 4 (1961), 192-201.
1723   ——. "Études et conversion de Luc de Prague." *cv*, 3 (1960), 255-262.
1724   Trtík, Z. "Moderní prvky v theologii Lukáše Pražského." *Československá církev a Jednota bratrská*. Ed. M. Kaňák. [Prague: Ústřední církevní nakl. 1967. p. 68-81.

Lupáč, Martin

1725   Bartoš, F. M. "Cusanus and the Hussite bishop M. Lupáč." *cv*, 5 (1962), 35-46.
1726   ——. "O rodiště husitského státníka Martina Lupáče." *jsh*, 36 (1967), 159-163. [Incl. summary, "Über den Geburtsort des hussitischen Staatsmannes Martin Lupáč"]
1727   Molnár, A. "'Probacio preceptorum minorum' de Martin Lupáč." *cv*, 9 (1966), 55-62.

Matthew of Hnátnice

1728   Bartoš, F. M. "A delegate of the Hussite church to Constantinople in 1451-1452." *Byzantinoslavica*, 24 (1963), 287-292; 25 (1964), 69-74.

Matthew of Kraków

1729   Kałuża, Z. "Eklezjologia Mateusza z Krakowa (uwagi o *De praxi Romanae curiae*)." *Studia mediewistyczne*, 18, pt. 1 (1977), 51-174.
1730   Seńko, W. *Mateusza z Krakowa "De praxi Romanae curiae."* Wrocław: Zakład Narodowy im. Ossolińskich, 1969. 185 p. Publ. also as *Mateusz z Krakowa "O praktykach Kurii rzymskiej"* (Wrocław, etc.: Panstwowe Wydawnictwo Naukowe, 1970), lxi, 136 p. ill.
Rev. V. Herold, *Fc*, 18 (1970), 1031-1033.

Milíč, Jan

1731   Flegl, M. "Miličova naděje." *kr*, 37 (1970), 41-45. [Milíč's hope]
1732   Herold, V., and M. Mráz. "Jan Milíč z Kroměříže a husitské revoluční myšlení." *Fc*, 22 (1974), 765-785. Trans., "Johann Milíč von Kremsier und das

hussitische revolutionäre Denken," *Mediaevalia philosophica Polonorum*, 21 (1975), 27-52.

1733 ——, and ——, ed. *Iohannis Milicii de Cremsir tres sermones synodales*. Prague: Academia, 1974. 154 p. ill.

1734 ——, and ——. "Johann Milič von Kremsier – ein ideologischer Wegbereiter des Hussitentums und des deutschen Bauernkrieges." *Deutsche Zeitschrift für Philosophie*, 23 (1975), 570-582.

1735 Leszczyńska, B. "Jan Milicz z Kromieryża i jego kontakty z ziemiami polskimi." *Śląski kwartalnik historyczny, Sobótka*, 15 (1960), 15-22. [Incl. summary, "Jan Milicz aus Kroměřiž und seine Kontakte mit Polen"]

MLADOŇOVIC, PETR

1736 Bartoš, F. M. "Osud Husova evangelisty Petra Mladoňovice." *TPKR*, 30 (1963), 79-85.

NICHOLAS OF DRESDEN

1737 ——. "Dvě nové publikace o německém husitovi Mikuláši z Drážďan." *TPKR*, 35 (1968), 85-89. [Review essay on J. Nechutová's recent publications on Nicholas of Dresden]

1738 Cegna, R. "Istanze religiose e sociali in Nicola da Dresda." *RSLR*, 4 (1968), 288-315.

1739 ——, ed. "Nicola della Rosa Nera, detto da Dresda (1380?-1416?): *De reliquiis et De veneratione sanctorum: De purgatorio*." *Mediaevalia philosophica Polonorum*, 23 (1977), 3-171.

1740 Kaminsky, H., D. L. Bilderback, I. Boba, and P. N. Rosenberg, ed. and trans. *Master Nicholas of Dresden: the old color and the new. Selected works contrasting the primitive church and the Roman church*. Transactions of the American philosophical society, 55, pt. 1. Philadelphia: American philosophical society, 1965. 93 p. ill.

1741 Kejř, J. "Z nové literatury o M. Mikuláši z Drážďan." *Právněhistorické studie*, 15 (1971), 221-229. [Incl. summary, "Aus der neuen Literatur über den Mgr. Nicolaus von Dresden"]

1742 Nechutová, J. "Bernard z Clairvaux v díle Mikuláse z Drázdan." *Sborník prací filosofické fakulty Brnenské university*, 10 (1965), 313-320. [Incl. summary, "Bernard von Clairvaux im Werk von Nikolaus von Dresden"]

1743 ——. *Místo Mikuláše z Drážd'an v raném reformačním myšlení: přispěvek k výkladu nauky*. Rozpravy Československé akademie věd, Řada společenských věd, 77, no. 16. Prague: čsav, 1967. 84 p. [Incl. summary, "Der Platz des Nikolaus von Dresden im Denken der frühen Reformation (ein Beitrag zur Erläuterung seiner Lehre)"]
Rev. P. de Vooght, *RHE*, 64 (1969), 116-120.

1744 ——. "Traktát Mikuláse z Drázdán – De imaginibus – a jeho vztah k Mateji z

Janova." *Sborník prací filosofické fakulty Brnenské university*, 9 (1964), 149-162. —

1745   Vooght, P. de, ed. "Le dialogue *De purgatorio* (1415) de Nicolas de Dresde." *RTAM*, 42 (1975), 132-223.

NICHOLAS OF PELHŘIMOV

1746   Molnár, A. "Biskupcův problém revoluce." *KR*, 38 (1971), 9-13. [Nicholas of Pelhřimov's problem of revolution]

1747   ——. "Nicolaus Biskupec de Pelhřimov: *De divisione Scripture sacre multiplici*." *CV*, 13 (1970), 154-170.

1748   ——. "Réformation et révolution: le cas du senior taborite Nicolas Biskupec de Pelhřimov." *CV*, 13 (1970), 137-153.

1749   Peschke, E. "Zur Theologie des Taboriten Nikolaus von Pilgram." *Wissenschaftliche Zeitschrift Martin-Luther-Universität Halle-Wittenberg*, Gesellschafts- und sprachwissenschaftliche Reihe, 19, no. 6 (1970), 153-170.

1750   Vooght, P. de. "Nicolas Biskupec de Pelhřimov et son apport à l'évolution de la méthodologie théologique hussite." *RTAM*, 40 (1973), 175-207.

OLDŘICH OF ROŽMBERK

1751   Pletzer, K. "Prozrazená akce husitů proti Oldřichu z Rožmberka v roce 1422." *JSH*, 31 (1962), 79-83.

PÁLEČ, STEPHEN

1752   Nechutová, J. "M. Štěpán von Páleč und die Hus-Historiographie." *MB*, 3 (1971), 87-122.

1753   Palacz, R. "La 'positio de universalibus' d'Étienne de Palecz." *Mediaevalia philosophica Polonorum*, 14 (1970), 113-129.

1754   ——. "Stefan Palecz." *Materiały i studia do dziejów historii filozofii w Polsce*, 8 (1967), 93-124.

1755   Svatoš, F. "Une figure anti-hussite au sein de la réforme tchèque." *Annuaire de l'Institut de philologie et d'histoire orientales et slaves*, 15 (1958-60), 319-323. [Stephen Páleč]

PAYNE, PETER

1756   Cook, W. R. "Peter Payne and the Waldensians." *BSSV*, 137 (1975), 3-13. [Incl. Italian summary by E. Peyrot]

1757   ——. "Peter Payne, theologian and diplomat of the Hussite revolution." Diss. Cornell Univ. *DAI*, 32A (1972), 6323.

PODĚBRADY, GEORGE

1758   Heymann, F. G. *George of Bohemia: king of heretics*. Princeton: Princeton University Press, 1965. xvi, 671 p. ill.

Rev. C. G. A[ndrae], *Historisk tidskrift* (1967), 284; R. F. Bennett, *History*, 51 (1966), 82-84; P. Brock, *CHR*, 54 (1968), 129-131; V. J. K. Brook, *CQR*, 167 (1966), 393-394; F. L. Carsten, *JEH*, 17 (1966), 121-122; R. Cegna, *RSLR*, 3 (1967), 332-334; J. P. Dolan, *Cithara*, 6, no. 2 (1967), 69-70; H. Kaminsky, *Speculum*, 41 (1966), 543-546; R. Luman, *JR*, 47 (1967), 169-170; E. Merey-Kadar, *JCS*, 9 (1967), 105-107; A. Molnár, *CV*, 9 (1966), 202-204; O. Odložilík, *Renaissance news*, 19 (1966), 31-32; P. J. Schroeder, *Concordia theological monthly*, 37 (1966), 335-336; F. Seibt, *HZ*, 203 (1966), 674-678, and *ARG*, 58 (1967), 106-108; A. A. Strnad, *ZOF*, 18 (1969), 118-120; P. de Vooght, *RHE*, 61 (1966), 879-881; J. Macek, *ČČH*, 13 (1965), 537-540; P. St. Amant, *Review and expositor*, 62 (1965), 490.

1759 ——. "Kirche und 'Ketzerkönig'." *Bohemia sacra: das Christentum in Böhmen 973-1973*. Ed. F. Seibt. Düsseldorf: Schwann, 1974. p. 315-322, 577.

1760 Kalivoda, R. "Die hussitische Revolution und die Podiebrader Epoche." *Cultus pacis*. Ed. V. Vaněček. Prague: Academia, 1966. p. 167-178.

1761 Kavka, F. "La Bohême hussite et les projets de paix de Georges de Podiébrad." *Cultus pacis*. Ed. V. Vaněček. Prague: Academia, 1966. p. 13-20.

1762 Macek, J. "Der Konziliarismus in der böhmischen Reformation – besonders in der Politik Georgs von Podiebrad." *ZKG*, 80 (1969), 312-330.

1763 Odložilík, O. *The Hussite king: Bohemia in European affairs, 1440-1471*. New Brunswick: Rutgers University Press, c1965. ix, 337 p. ill. map.
Rev. A. J. Bannan, *Cithara*, 6, no. 1 (1966), 67-68; R. Bennett, *History*, 53 (1968), 90-91; P. Brock, *CHR*, 54 (1968), 129-131; H. Kaminsky, *Speculum*, 41 (1966), 543-546; A. Molnár, *CV*, 9 (1966), 202-204; F. Seibt, *HZ*, 203 (1966), 674-678; J. Macek, *ČČH*, 15 (1967), 89-91; A. A. Strnad, *ZOF*, 18 (1969), 114-118.

1764 Válka, J. "Husitský král a jeho arcibiskup." *Z kralické tvrze*, 5 (1971), 45-51. —

1765 Vaněček, V., ed. *Cultus pacis: études et documents du "Symposium Pragense Cultus Pacis 1464-1964," commemoratio pacis generalis ante quingentos annos a Georgio Bohemiae rege propositae*. Prague: Academia, 1966. 200 p.

PROCOP OF KLADRUBY

1766 Kadlec, J. "Mistr Prokop z Kladrub." *AUC Hist*, 12 (1972), 91-110. [Incl. summary, "Magister Prokop aus Kladruby"]

RAŇKUV, VOJTĚCH

1767 Kadlec, J. *Leben und Schriften des Prager Magisters Adalbert Rankonis de Ericinio, aus dem Nachlass von Rudolf Holinka und Jan Vilikovský*. Beiträge zur Geschichte der Philosophie und Theologie des Mittelalters, n.s. 4. Münster: Aschendorff, c1971. xvi, 356 p. ill.

Rev. F. Ruello, *RSR*, 61 (1973), 403-405; P. Uiblein, *MIÖG*, 82 (1974), 223-224; P. Spunar, *MB*, 4 (1974), 187-188.

1768 ——. *Mistr Vojtěch Raňkův z Ježova*. Práce z dějin University Karlovy, 7. Prague: Universita Karlova, 1969. 97 p. [Incl. summary, "Maître Vojtěch Raňkův de Ježov"]
Rev. F. Šmahel, *MB*, 3 (1971), 365-366.

Reček, John

1769 Bartoš, F. M. "Der grosse Staatsmann der hussitischen Revolution Illuminator Johann Reček." *MB*, 1 (1969), 116-128.

Rejštejn, Jan

1770 Bartoš, F. M. "Reformní program M. Jana Kardinála z Rejštejna, vyslance Karlovy university pro koncil kostnický." *JSH*, 38 (1969), 99-118. [Incl. summary, "Das Reformprogram des Gesandten der Prager Universität für das Konzil von Konstanz im Jahre 1414"]

Rokycana, John

1771 Šimek, F. "Několik pozoruhodných slov z Rokycanových postil." *Strahovská knihovna*, 5/6 (1970-71), 209-212. [Incl. summary, "Einige bemerkenswerte Wörter aus den Postillen Rokycanas"]

Schwab, Hermann

1772 Kadlec, J. "Hermann Schwab von Mindelheim und sein Apokalypsekommentar." *Scientia Augustiniana* (Festschrift Adolar Zumkeller). Ed. C. P. Mayer and W. Eckermann. Cassiciacum, 30. Würzburg: Augustinus-Verlag, 1975. p. 276-288.

Želivský, Jan

1773 Bylina, S. "Elementy chiliastyczne w poglądach Jana Želivskiego." *PH*, 63 (1972), 241-252. [Incl. summary, "Les éléments chiliastiques dans les idées de Jean Želivsky"]

Žižka, Jan

1774 Bartoš, F. M. "Osudy Žižkových hrobů." *JSH*, 34 (1965), 202-210.
1775 ——. "Žižkův zeť', jeho sestra a děd." *JSH*, 32 (1963), 1-6.
1776 Čapek, J. B. "Vztah Jana Žižky k Bratrstvu orebskému." *KR*, 40 (1974), 184-189. [Žižka's association with the Orebian brethren]
1777 Fišer, F. "Žižkas Schlüssel und weitere Bemerkungen zum Jenaer Kodex." *MB*, 1 (1969), 295-306.
1778 Flegl, M. "Žižka ve světle svých listů." *JSH*, 38 (1969), 169-177. [Incl. summary, "Žižka im Licht seiner Briefe"]

1779 ———. "Žižkův boj s hříchem." *KR*, 36 (1969), 84-86. [Žižka's struggle with sin]

1780 Heymann, F. G. *John Žižka and the Hussite revolution*. New York: Russell and Russell, 1969. [v], 521 p. ill. maps. Orig. publ. Princeton, 1955.

1781 Hůlka, Alois, ed. *O Janu Žižkovi*. České Budějovice: Růže, 1974. 111 p.

1782 Molnár, A. "Zur Frage der Trennung zwischen Jan Žižka und Tábor (zum 550. Todestag Žižkas)." *CV*, 17 (1974), 123-140.

1783 Šmahel, F. *Jan Žižka v Trocnova: život revolučního válečníka*. Prague: Melantrich, 1969. 261 p.

1784 Vlček, E. *Čáslavská Kalva: pravděpodobný pozůstatek Jana Žižky z Trocnova*. Čáslav: Měst. muzeum, 1974. 31 p. —

Part Fifteen

Other Popular Heresies

ENTRIES 1785 TO 1808

1785 Alatri, M. da. "Gli idolatri recanatesi secondo un rotolo vaticano del 1320." *CF*, 33 (1963), 82-105.

1786 Albert, K. "Amalrich von Bena und der mittelalterliche Pantheismus." *Die Auseinandersetzungen an der Pariser Universität im XIII. Jahrhundert*. Ed. A. Zimmermann. Miscellanea mediaevalia, 10. Berlin and New York: de Gruyter, 1976. p. 193-212.

1787 Braekman, M. "Jacob Peyt, hérésie ou révolte sociale en Flandre au XIVe siècle?" *Bulletin de la Société d'histoire du protestantisme belge*, 7 (1978), 313-332.

1788 Cavallari, U. "Eresia e politica: Corrado Venosta e Raimondo della Torre." *Archivio storico lombardo*, 9th ser., 5-6 (1966-67 [1968]), 46-50.

1789 Cecchini, G. "Raniero Fasani et les flagellants." *Mélanges de l'École française de Rome: moyen âge, temps modernes*, 87 (1975), 339-352.

1790 Erbstösser, M. "Die radikalen Geisslergruppen in Thüringen 1349." *Studia z dziejów kultury i ideologii ofiarowane Ewie Maleczyńskiej w 50 rocznicę pracy dydaktycznej i naukowej*. Wrocław, Warsaw, and Kraków: Zakład Narodowy im. Ossolińskich, 1968. p. 142-153.

1791 Fitzthum, M. "Die Irrtümer des Propstes Heinrich Minnike." *Analecta praemonstratensia*, 36 (1960), 128-132.

1792 Frugoni, A. "La devozione dei Bianchi del 1399." *L'attesa dell'età nuova nella spiritualità della fine del medioevo*. Convegni del Centro di studi sulla spiritualità medievale, 3. Todi: Accademia Tudertina, 1962. p. 232-248, ill.

1793 ———. "Sui flagellanti del 1260." *BISIM*, 75 (1963), 211-237.

1794 Goeters, J. F. G. "Johann Ruchrat von Wesel: mittelalterlicher Ketzer oder Vorläufer der Reformation?" *Monatshefte für evangelische Kirchengeschichte des Rheinlandes*, 16 (1967), 184-191.

1795 Heimpel, H. "Der verketzerte Matthäus von Krakau." *Festschrift für Walter Schlesinger*. Cologne and Vienna: Böhlau, 1973-74. II, 443-455.

1796 Henderson, J. "The flagellant movement and flagellant confraternities in central Italy, 1260-1400." *Studies in church history*, 15 (1978), 147-160.

1797 Kauffman, C. M. "Barnaba da Modena and the flagellants of Genoa." *Victoria and Albert Museum bulletin*, 2 (1966), 12-20, ill.

1798 Kieckhefer, R. "Radical tendencies in the flagellant movement of the mid-fourteenth century." *The journal of medieval and renaissance studies*, 4 (1974), 157-176.

1799 Manselli, R. "I passagini." *BISIM*, 75 (1963), 189-210.

1800 Merlo, G. G. "Circolazione di eretici tra Francia e Piemonte nel xiv secolo." *Provence historique*, 27 (1977), 325-334.

1801 Morghen, R. "Ranieri Fasani e il movimento dei disciplinati del 1260." *Civiltà medioevale al Tramonto*. 2nd ed., rvsd. Rome and Bari, 1973. p. 43-62. Orig. publ. in *Risultati e prospettive della ricerca sul movimento dei disciplinati* (Perugia, 1969).

1802 Potkowski, E. "Heretyk Stefan z Marchii." *Polska w świecie*. Warsaw: Państwowe Wydawnictwo Naukowe, 1972. p. 169-178. [The heretic Stephen of the March]

1803 Ramm, B. I. "Elementy narodnogo svobodomysliia v dvizhenii amal'rikan." *Srednie veka*, 25 (1964), 101-112. [Incl. summary, "Sur le mouvement des amauriciens"]

1804 Runge, P., ed. *Die Lieder und Melodien der Geißler des Jahres 1349, nach der Aufzeichnung Hugo's von Reutlingen. Nebst einer Abhandlung über die italienischen Geißlerlieder von Heinrich Schneegans und einem Beitrage zur Geschichte der deutschen und niederländischen Geißler von Heino Pfannenschmid*. Leipzig, 1900. Rpt. Hildesheim: Olms; Wiesbaden: Breitkopf und Härtel, 1969. viii, 222 p.

1805 Székely, G. "Le mouvement des flagellants au 14e siècle, son caractère et ses causes." With discussion. *Hérésies et sociétés* (1968). p. 229-241. See 65.

1806 Vasoli, C. "Une secte hérétique florentine à la fin du 15e siècle: les 'oints'." *Hérésies et sociétés* (1968). p. 259-271. See 65.

1807 Wailes, S. L. "Heresy in Austria: a new look at a medieval source." *Neuphilologische Mitteilungen*, 79 (1978), 97-101.

1808 Woś, J. W. "Le eresie nel commento di Jacopo della Lana al canto ix dell'Inferno dantesco." *Bollettino storico pisano*, 36-38 (1967-69), 71-80.

Part Sixteen

Witchcraft

Entries 1809 to 1868

1809 Alauzier, L. d'. "Sorcellerie à Millau au xve siècle." *Études sur le Rouergue.* Rodez: Société des lettres, sciences et arts de l'Aveyron, 1974. p. 115-124.

1810 Aureggi, O. "Stregoneria retica e tortura giudiziaria." *Bollettino della Società storica valtellinese,* 17 (1963-64), 46-90.

1811 Baschwitz, K. *Hexen und Hexenprozesse: die Geschichte eines Massenwahns und seiner Bekämpfung.* Munich: Rütten und Loening, c1963. 480 p. ill. Abridged ed., *Hexen und Hexenprozesse: die Geschichte eines Massenwahns* (Munich: Deutscher Taschenbuchverlag, 1966), 400 p. Rev. B. Vogler, *RHPR,* 48 (1968), 98-99.

1812 Bayer, V. *Ugovor s đavlom: procesi protiv čarobnjaka u Evropi a napose u Hrvatskoj.* 2nd ed. Zagreb: Zora, 1969. 801 p. ill.

1813 Bohr, C. *L'inquisition en Lorraine.* Metz: [by the author], 1973. x, 53 p. —

1814 Bonney, F. "Autour de Jean Gerson: opinions de théologiens sur les superstitions et la sorcellerie au début du xve siècle." *MA,* 77 (1971), 85-98.

1815 Brucker, G. A. "Sorcery in early renaissance Florence." *Studies in the renaissance,* 10 (1963), 7-24.

1816 Caro Baroja, J. *Las brujas y su mundo.* Madrid: Revista de Occidente, 1961. 375 p. Trans. O. N. V. Glendinning, *The world of witches* (Chicago: University of Chicago Press, 1965), xiv, 313 p. [Numerous later editions and translations]

1817 Cauzons, T. de [pseud.]. *La magie et la sorcellerie en France.* Paris, 1901-1913. Rpt. Osnabrück: Zeller, 1974. 4 v. [v. 2: "Poursuite et châtiment de la magie jusqu'à la réforme protestante..."]

1818 Cohn, M. *Europe's inner demons: an enquiry inspired by the great witch-hunt.* New York: Basic Books; London: Heinemann for Sussex University Press, 1975. xvi, 302 p. ill. Rev. B. P. Copenhaver, *CH,* 44 (1975), 529; E. Janeway, *The Atlantic,* 236 (August 1975), 80-84; R. I. Moore, *History,* 61 (1976), 444-445; J. L.

Nelson, *Religion*, 5 (1975), 179-182; G. Strauss, *Commentary*, 59 (June 1975), 83-86; G. Steiner, *The New Yorker*, 8 September 1975, p. 118-125; A. Lion, *ASSR*, 42 (1976), 222-224; E. W. Monter, *The British journal for the history of science*, 11 (1978), 180.

1819 ——. "Myths and hoaxes of European demonology, I: Was there ever a society of witches?" *Encounter*, 43, no. 6 (December 1974), 26-41, ill.

1820 ——. "Myths and hoaxes of European demonology, II: three forgeries." *Encounter*, 44, no. 1 (January 1975), 11-24.

1821 ——. "The myth of Satan and his human servants." *Witchcraft: confessions and accusations*. Ed. M. Douglas. London [etc.]: Tavistock, c1970. p. 3-16.

1822 Crowe, M. J., ed. *Witchcraft: catalogue of the witchcraft collection in Cornell University Library*. Intro. R. H. Robbins. Millwood, N.Y.: Kraus-Thomson (KTO), 1977. lxxxviii, 653 p. Intro. and pref. by Robbins also publ. as *Witchcraft: an introduction to the literature of witchcraft* (Millwood: KTO, 1978), vi, 121 p.
   Rev. L. S. Thompson, *Germanic notes*, 9 (1978), 17.

1823 Eliade, M. "Some observations on European witchcraft." *History of religions*, 14 (1975), 149-172. Abridged version in his *Occultism, witchcraft, and cultural fashions: essays in comparative religions* (Chicago and London: University of Chicago Press, 1976), p. 69-92.

1824 Filhol, R. "Procès de sorcellerie à Bressuire (août-septembre 1475)." *RHDFE*, 42 (1964), 77-83.

1825 Forbes, T. R. "Perrette the midwife: a fifteenth century witchcraft case." *Bulletin of the history of medicine*, 36 (1962), 124-129.

1826 Gerest, C. "Le démon dans le paysage théologique des chasseurs de sorcières: études d'après le 'Marteau des sorciéres', xve siècle." *Concilium*, 103 (1975), 55-70. —

1827 Gianni, M. "Il *Malleus maleficarum* e il *De pytonicis mulieribus*: due modi d'intendere la stregoneria sul finire del xv secolo." *Studi sul medioevo cristiano offerti a Raffaello Morghen*. Rome: Istituto Storico Italiano per il Medio Evo, 1974. I, 407-426.

1828 Gibson, W. B. *Witchcraft*. New York: Grosset and Dunlap; London: Barker, 1973. 149 p.

1829 Hansen, J., ed. *Quellen und Untersuchungen zur Geschichte des Hexenwahns und der Hexenverfolgung im Mittelalter*. With appendix, "Geschichte des Wortes Hexe," by J. Franck. Bonn, 1901. Rpt. Hildesheim: Georg Olms, 1963. xi, 703 p.

1830 ——. *Zauberwahn, Inquisition und Hexenprozess im Mittelalter, und die Entstehung der grossen Hexenverfolgung*. Historische Bibliothek, 12. Munich, 1900. Rpt. Aalen: Scientia, 1964. xv, 538 p. Trans. of p. 235-277 ("Credenze magiche, eresia e inquisizione") in M. Romanello, ed., *La stregoneria in Europa* (Bologna: Mulino, c1975), p. 69-94.

1831   Harrison, M. *The roots of witchcraft*. London: Muller, 1973. 278 p. ill.

1832   Harvey, M. "Papal witchcraft: the charges against Benedict XIII." *Sanctity and secularity: the church and the world*. Ed. D. Baker. Studies in church history, 10. Oxford: Blackwell, 1973. p. 109-116.

1833   Hohl, C. "Hérésie ou sorcellerie: la Vauderie à Saint-Aubin-Châteauneuf au XVᵉ siècle." *La Puisaye: actes du 39ᵉᵐᵉ Congrès de l'Association bourguignonne des sociétés savantes, Toucy ... 1968*. Puisaye: Association d'études et de recherches du vieux Toucy, [1970]. p. 95-99. —

1834   Horsley, R. A. "Further reflections on witchcraft and European folk religion." *History of religions*, 19 (1979), 71-95.

1835   ——. "Who were the witches? The social roles of the accused in the European witch trials." *JIH*, 9 (1979), 689-715.

1836   Institoris, H., and J. Sprenger. *Malleus maleficarum*. Trans. M. Summers. London, 1928. Rpt. New York: Blom, 1970. xlv, 277 p. [Publ. also in numerous other rpt. editions]

1837   Kelly, H. A. "English kings and the fear of sorcery." *MS*, 39 (1977), 206-238.

1838   ——. *The devil, demonology and witchcraft: the development of Christian beliefs in evil spirits*. Garden City, N.Y.: Doubleday, 1968. vi, 137 p. 2nd ed. 1974.

1839   Kieckhefer, R. *European witch trials: their foundations in popular and learned culture, 1300-1500*. Berkeley and Los Angeles: University of California Press, 1976. x, 181 p.

Rev. R. Cavendish, *Folklore*, 87 (1976), 122; J. E. Weakland, *CH*, 45 (1976), 528-529; N. Cohn, *TLS*, 23 July 1976, 902-903; C. Larner, *EHR*, 92 (1977), 646-647; H. Kamen, *History*, 62 (1977), 315-316; A. Patschovsky, *DAEM*, 33 (1977), 285; J. B. Russell, *Speculum*, 53 (1978), 149-151; B. R. Kreiser, *AHR*, 83 (1978), 151-153; R. W. England, Jr., *The annals of the American academy of political and social science*, 429 (1977), 182-183; G. Zinn, *CH*, 48 (1979), 342-343.

1840   Kors, A. C., and E. Peters, comp. *Witchcraft in Europe, 1100-1700: a documentary history*. Philadelphia: University of Pennsylvania Press, c1972; London: Dent, 1973. viii, 382 p. ill.

Rev. J. B. Russell, *CH*, 41 (1972), 539; D. P. Scaer, *The Springfielder*, 36 (1972), 245-246; R. H. West, *The Georgia review*, 27 (1973), 137-141; H. C. E. Midelfort, *CHR*, 59 (1973), 508-509; B. R. Kreiser, *The library quarterly*, 43 (1973), 269-270; R. H. Schmandt, *The historian*, 35 (1973), 456-457; R. Hughes, *Columbia*, 52, no. 8 (1972), 32.

1841   Leutenbauer, S. *Hexerei- und Zaubereidelikt in der Literatur von 1450 bis 1550*. Münchener Universitätsschriften, Juristische Fakultät, Abhandlungen zur rechtswissenschaftlichen Grundlagenforschung, 3. Berlin: Schweitzer, 1972. xxv, 178 p.

1842   Mammoli, D. [ed. and trans.]. *The record of the trial and condemnation of a witch, Matteuccia di Francesco, at Todi, 20 March 1428.* Res tudertinae, 14. Rome, 1972. 52 p. ill. Rvsd. rpt. of Latin text and glossary by M. Pericoli in *Medicina nei secoli*, 9 (1972), 54-84.

1843   Manselli, R. *Magia e stregoneria nel medio evo.* Turin: Giappichelli, 1976. 224 p.

1844   ———. "Le premesse medioevali della caccia alle streghe." *La stregoneria in Europa (1450-1650).* Ed. M. Romanello. Bologna: Mulino, c1975. p. 39-62.

1845   Merzbacher, F. *Die Hexenprozesse in Franken.* 2nd, rvsd. ed. Munich: Beck, c1970. xii, 257 p., w. maps. Orig. publ. Munich, 1957.

1846   Michelet, J. *Satanism and witchcraft: a study in medieval superstition.* Trans. A. R. Allinson. New York, 1939; rpt. New York: Citadel, 1962. xx, 332 p. Orig. publ. Paris 1862 as *La sorcière*; trans. orig. publ. Paris 1904. Numerous later editions, translations, and reprints.

1847   Midelfort, H. C. E. "Recent witch hunting research, or Where do we go from here?" *The papers of the Bibliographical society of America*, 62 (1968), 373-420.

1848   Monter, E. W. "The historiography of European witchcraft: progress and prospects." *JIH*, 2, no. 3 (Winter 1972), 435-451.

1849   ———. "The pedestal and the stake: courtly love and witchcraft." *Becoming visible: women in European history.* Ed. R. Bridenthal and C. Koonz. Boston [etc.]: Houghton Mifflin, c1977. p. 119-136.

1850   Murray, A. "Medieval origins of the witch hunt." *The Cambridge quarterly*, 7 [1976], 63-74.

1850A   Paravy, P. "À propos de la genèse médiévale des chasses aux sorcières: le traité de Claude Tholosan, juge dauphinois (vers 1436)." *Mélanges de l'École française de Rome: moyen âge – temps modernes*, 91 (1979), 333-379.

1851   Peters, E. *The magician, the witch and the law.* [Philadelphia]: Univ. of Pennsylvania Press, 1978. xviii, 218 p.
        Rev. M. François, *AHR*, 84 (1979), 1030; E. W. Monter, *JIH*, 10 (1979), 338-340.

1852   Potkowski, E. "Haeresis et secta maleficorum: powstanie stereotypu." *Cultus et cognitio: studia z dziejów średniowiecznej kultury* [Festschrift Aleksander Gieysztor]. Warsaw: Państwowe Wydawnictwo Naukowe, 1976. p. 469-483.

1853   Riezler, S. von. *Geschichte der Hexenprozesse in Bayern, im Lichte der allgemeinen Entwicklung dargestellt.* Stuttgart, 1896. Rpt. (with appendix, index, and map by F. Merzbacher) Aalen: Scientia, 1968. x, 404 p.

1854   Robbins, R. H. "The heresy of witchcraft." *The South Atlantic quarterly*, 65 (1966), 532-543.

1855   ———. "The real crime of witchcraft." *California monthly*, 76 (1966), 4-7.

1856 ——. "Yellow cross and green fagot." *The Cornell Library journal* (Winter 1970), p. 3-33, ill.

1857 Romanello, M., ed. *La stregoneria in Europa (1450-1650)*. Bologna: Mulino, c1975. 379 p.

1858 Rose, E. *A razor for a goat: a discussion of certain problems in the history of witchcraft and diabolism*. [Toronto]: University of Toronto Press, c1962. [vii], 257 p.
Rev. R. H. Robbins, *Speculum*, 38 (1963), 499-501.

1859 Rosen, G. "A study of the persecution of witches in Europe as a contribution to the understanding of mass delusions and psychic epidemics." *Journal of health and human behavior*, 1 (1960), 200-211.

1860 Russell, J. B. "Medieval witchcraft and medieval hersy." *On the margin of the visible: sociology, the esoteric, and the occult*. Ed. E. A. Tiryakian. New York, etc.: John Wiley, c1974. p. 179-189.

1861 ——. "Witchcraft and heresies." *Values and the medieval classics in secondary education*. Papers from the Spartanburg Day School conference, 7-8 March 1969. Spartanburg, S.C., 1969. p. 61-74.

1862 ——. *Witchcraft in the middle ages*. Ithaca and London: Cornell University Press, c1972. ix, 394 p.
Rev. L. F. Barmann, *Manuscripta*, 17 (1973), 38-40; R. Manselli, *SM*, 3rd ser., 15 (1974), 894-897; H. C. E. Midelfort, *AHR*, 78 (1973), 1030-1031; J. E. Weakland, *CH*, 42 (1973), 127-128; F. Picó, *TS*, 34 (1973), 341; G. Olsen, *Triumph*, 8, no. 2 (Feb. 1973), 39-41; E. Peters, *CHR*, 60 (1974), 468-470; J. L. Nelson, *Religion*, 4 (1974), 167-168; J. Beckman and F. Lelait, *MA*, 82 (1976), 188-189; R. H. West, *The Georgia review*, 27 (1973), 137-141; R. H. Schmandt, *The historian*, 35 (1973), 456-457; R. Cavendish, *Folklore*, 83 (1972), 345-346; F. Cheyette, *History: reviews of new books*, 1 (1973), 51-52; R. Briggs, *TLS*, 3 January 1975, p. 13-14; G. Leff, *EHR*, 89 (1974), 884-885; B. S. Bachrach, *The annals of the American academy of political and social science*, March 1973, p. 221-222; R. F. Wells, *Social science*, Summer 1973, p. 188-189.

1863 ——, and M. W. Wyndham. "Witchcraft and the demonization of heresy." *Mediaevalia*, 2 (1976), 1-21.

1864 Singer, G. A. "*La vauderie d'Arras*, 1459-1491: an episode of witchcraft in later medieval France." Diss. Univ. of Maryland. *DAI*, 36A (1975), 1021-1022.

1865 Villette, P. "La sorcellerie à Douai." *MSR*, 18 (1961), 123-173.

1866 ——. *La sorcellerie et sa répression dans le nord de la France*. Paris: Pensée universelle, 1976. 283 p.
Rev. H. Platelle, *MSR*, 35 (1978), 73-77.

1867 [Wunderer, R.] *Erotik und Hexenwahn: eine Studie der Entstehung des Hexenwahns in der vorchristlichen Zeit bis zu den Pogromen unserer Vergangenheit*. 3rd ed. Stuttgart: Weltspiegel, 1963. 149 p. ill.

1868   Ziegeler, W. *Möglichkeiten der Kritik am Hexen- und Zauberwesen im ausgehen-*
       den Mittelalter: zeitgenössische Stimmen und ihre soziale Zugehörigkeit.
       Kollektive Einstellungen und sozialer Wandel im Mittelalter, 2. Cologne
       and Vienna: Böhlau, 1973. xi, 231 p.
       Rev. H. Kühnel, *MIÖG*, 83 (1975), 204; J. B. Russell, *Speculum*, 50 (1975),
       751-752; J. Beckman and C. Dulieu-Eckmann, *MA*, 82 (1976), 387-389;
       E. Peters, *CHR*, 63 (1977), 144-145; O. Huth, *Philosophy and history*, 10
       (1977), 255; F. Merzbacher, *Zeitschrift für historische Forschung*, 3 (1976),
       251-253.

Part Seventeen

Repression

ENTRIES 1869 TO 2017

1869   Alatri, M. da. "Accuse di eresia a Spoleto e a Narni negli anni 1259 e 1260." CF, 39 (1969), 419-427.

1870   ——. "Antonio, martello degli eretici?" *Il santo,* 5 (1965), 123-130.

1871   ——. "Archivio, offici e titolari dell'inquisizione toscana verso la fine del duecento." CF, 40 (1970), 169-190.

1872   ——. "Documenti sulla vertenza del 1355/56 tra inquisizione e tudertini." CF, 33 (1963), 267-326.

1873   ——. "Due inchieste papali sugli inquisitori veneti (1302 e 1308)." CF, 39 (1969), 172-187.

1874   ——. "L'eresia nella cronica di Fra Salimbene." CF, 37 (1967), 366-373.

1875   ——. "Inquisitori veneti del duecento." CF, 30 (1960), 398-452.

1876   ——. "L'inquisizione a Firenze negli anni 1344/46 da un'istruttoria contro Pietro da l'Aquila." *Miscellanea Melchor de Pobladura.* Ed. Isidoro de Villapadierna. Bibliotheca seraphico-capuccina, 23-24. Rome: Institutum historicum ord. F.M. Cap., 1964. I, 225-249.

1877   ——. "Un mastodontico processo per eresia a Viterbo nello scorcio del duecento." CF, 42 (1972), 299-308.

1878   ——. "Nuove notizie sull'inquisizione toscana del duecento." CF, 31 (1961), 637-644.

1879   ——. "Un processo dell'inverno 1346-1347 contro gli inquisitori delle Marche." AFH, 71 (1978), 305-338.

1880   ——. "Rileggendo gli atti del processo trentino dell'inverno 1332-1333." CF, 35 (1965), 177-189.

1881   ——. "San Bonaventura, l'eresia, e l'inquisizione." *Miscellanea francescana,* 75 (1975), 305-322.

1882   ——. "Una sentenza assolutoria dell'inquisitore Fra Michele da Firenze (1350)." CF, 34 (1964), 367-372.

1883   ——. "Una sentenza dell'inquisitore Fra Filippo da Mantova (1287)." *CF*, 37 (1967), 142-144.

1884   ——. "Il vescovo e il *negotium fidei* (secoli XII- XIII)." *Vescovi e diocesi in Italia nel medioevo (sec. IX-XIII): Atti del II Convegno di storia della chiesa in Italia (Roma, 5-9 sett. 1961).* Italia sacra, 5. Padua: Antenore, 1964. p. 349-363.

1885   Ancourt, A. "Une victime de l'inquisition à Villefranche en 1273." *Procès-verbaux des séances de la Société des lettres, sciences et arts de l'Aveyron,* 38 (1959-62), 14-18.

1886   Antichi, V. "L'inquisizione a Firenze nel XIV secolo." *Eretici e ribelli del XIII e XIV sec.* Ed. D. Maselli. Pistoia: Tellini, [1974]. p. 213-231.

1887   Arnold of Villanova. *Escritós condenados por la inquisición.* Trans. E. Cánovas and F. Piñero. Biblioteca de visionarios, heterodoxos y marginados, 10. Madrid: Editora Nacional, 1976. 223 p.

1888   Bachelier, E. "L'intransigeance d'un évêque du Puy vis-à-vis des cathares." *Bulletin historique, scientifique, littéraire, artistique et agricole illustré, publié par la Société académique du Puy et de la Haute-Loire,* 45 (1969), 113-114. —

1889   Bath Sheva, A. *Mishpato shel Barukh.* Ramat-Gan: Bar-Ilan University, c1974. xviii, 121 p. ill. [Incl. summary, "The case of Baruch: the earliest report of the trial of a Jew by the inquisition (1320)"]

1890   Bévenot, M. "The inquisition and its antecedents." *HJ,* 7 (1966), 257-268, 381-393; 8 (1967), 52-69, 152-168.

1891   Biener, F. A. *Beiträge zu der Geschichte des Inquisitionsprozesses und der Geschworenengerichte.* Leipzig, 1827. Rpt. Aalen: Scientia, 1965. viii, 320 p.

1892   Biget, J.-L. "Un procès d'inquisition à Albi en 1300." *Le crédo, la morale et l'inquisition.* Cahiers de Fanjeaux, 6. Toulouse: Privat, c1971. p. 273-341.

1893   Bodineau, P. "Un inquisiteur bourgignon (Jean de Beaune) en pays cathare au début du XIVe siècle." *Société d'archéologie de Beaune, Histoire, lettres, sciences et arts: mémoires,* 57 (1973-74), 186-189. —

1894   Bolton, B. "Tradition and temerity: papal attitudes to deviants, 1159-1216." *Schism, heresy and religious protest* (1972). p. 79-91. See 120.

1895   Botineau, P. "Les tribulations de Raymond Barrau, O.P. (1295-1338)." *École française de Rome, Mélanges d'archéologie et d'histoire,* 77 (1965), 475-528.

1896   Brizzolari, C. *L'inquisizione a Genova e in Liguria.* Genoa: ERGA, 1974. 97 p.

1897   Brugues, J. L. "L'inquisition et les frères Prêcheurs." *Documents pour servir à l'histoire de l'ordre de saint Dominique en France,* ser. A, 9 (1974), 25-29. —

1898   Bühler-Reimann, T. "Enquête – inquesta – inquisitio." *ZSSRG,* 92, Kan. Abt. 61 (1975), 53-62.

1899   Cantelar Rodríguez, F. *El matrimonio de herejes: bifurcación del* impedimentum disparis cultus *y divorcio por herejía.* Monografias canónicas Peñafort, 15.

Salamanca: Consejo Superior de Investigaciones Científicas, Instituto San Raimundo de Peñafort, 1972. xxiii, 204 p.

Rev. F. Merzbacher, *AKK*, 143 (1974), 262-264; A. Reuter, *Neue Zeitschrift für Missionswissenschaft*, 29 (1973), 305-306; B. A. Rodríguez, *Revista española de derecho canónico*, 29 (1973), 521-522.

1900   Capitani, O. "Legislazione antiereticale e strumento di costruzione politica nelle decisioni normative di Innocenzo III." *BSSV*, 140 (1976), 31-53.

1901   Carano, R. *Autodafé*. Illustrated by E. Sio. Conegliano: Quadragono, [1975]. [28] p. ill.

1902   Castries, Duke of. "L'inquisition, ce mot que l'église regrette." *Historia*, 352 (1976), 98-107, ill.

1903   Cohn, H. H. "Tortures and confessions: historical sidelights on the psychology of law." *Scripta hierosolymitana*, 21 (1969), 3-27.

1904   Corsi, D. "Per la storia dell'inquisizione a Firenze nella seconda metà del secolo XIII." *BSSV*, 132 (1972), 3-5.

1905   Coulton, G. G. *The inquisition*. London, 1929. Rpt. Folcroft, Pa.: Folcroft, 1974. 80 p.

1906   ——. *Inquisition and liberty*. London, 1938; Boston, 1959. Rpt. Gloucester, Mass.: P. Smith, 1969. [ix], 354 p. ill.

1907   *Le crédo, la morale et l'inquisition*. Cahiers de Fanjeaux, 6. Toulouse: Privat, c1971. 435 p. ill.

Rev. A. Vauchez, *ASSR*, 35 (1973), 184-185, and 36 (1973), 155-156; H. Maisonneuve, *MSR*, 29 (1972), 149-151, and *RHE*, 68 (1973), 167-173; G. Lobrichon *RHS*, 51 (1975), 300-303; F. Simoni Balis-Crema, *SM*, 3rd ser., 13 (1972), 1077-1081; G. May, *ZSSRG*, Kan. Abt., 90 (1973), 437-441; E. Griffe, *BLE*, 75 (1974), 233-235; N. Coulet, *ETR*, 47 (1972), 487-491; R. Mols, *NRT*, 94 (1972), 876-877; M. Reynaud, *Cahiers d'histoire*, 18 (1973), 94-95.

1908   Davis, G. W., ed. *The inquisition at Albi, 1299-1300: text of register and analysis*. Studies in history, economics and public law, 538. New York, 1948. Rpt. New York: Octagon (Farrar, Straus, and Giroux), 1974. 322 p.

1909   Delhaye, P. "L'*ignorantia juris* et la situation morale de l'hérétique dans l'église ancienne et médiévale." *Études d'histoire du droit canonique dédiées à Gabriel Le Bras*. Paris: Sirey, 1965. II, 1131-1141.

1909A Delpoux, C. "L'inquisition à Narbonne." *CEC*, 30, no. 84 (1979), 29-37.

1910   Dossat, Y. "Le 'bûcher de Montségur' et les bûchers de l'inquisition." *Le crédo, la morale et l'inquisition*. Cahiers de Fanjeaux, 6. Toulouse: Privat, c1971. p. 361-378.

1911   ——. "Les débuts de l'inquisition à Montpellier et en Provence." *BPH*, 1961 (1963), 561-579.

1912   ——. "Une figure d'inquisiteur: Bernard de Caux." *Le crédo, la morale et l'inquisition*. Cahiers de Fanjeaux, 6. Toulouse: Privat, c1971. p. 253-272.

1913 ——. "Gui Foucois, enquêteur-réformateur, archevêque et pape (Clément IV)." *Les évêques, les clercs et le roi (1250-1300).* Cahiers de Fanjeaux, 7. Toulouse: Privat, c1972. p. 23-47, ill.

1914 ——. "Le massacre d'Avignonet." *Le crédo, la morale et l'inquisition.* Cahiers de Fanjeaux, 6. Toulouse: Privat, c1971. p. 343-359.

1915 ——. "Les origines de la querelle entre Prêcheurs et Mineurs provencaux: Bernard Délicieux." *Franciscains d'Oc.* p. 315-354. See 1089.

1916 ——. "La répression de l'hérésie par les évêques." *Le crédo, la morale et l'inquisition.* Cahiers de Fanjeaux, 6. Toulouse: Privat, c1971. p. 217-251.

1917 Duvernoy, J. "L'acception: 'haereticus' (*iretge*) = 'parfait cathare' en Languedoc au XIIIe siècle." *The concept of heresy in the middle ages* (1976). p. 198-210. See 25.

1918 ——. "Un extrait du manuscrit Vat. no. 4030 de la Bibliothèque Vaticane: enquête sur Bertrand de Tays." *Société ariégeoise, sciences, lettres et arts: bulletin annuel,* 19 (1960-61), 37-45.

1919 ——, ed. and trans. *Inquisition à Pamiers: interrogatoires de Jacques Fournier, 1318-1325.* Toulouse: Privat, c1966. 239 p. ill.
    Rev. M.-R. Mayeux, *RHEF*, 54 (1968), 95-98.

1920 ——, ed. *Le registre d'inquisition de Jacques Fournier, évêque de Pamiers (1318-1325).* Bibliothèque méridionale, 2nd ser., 41. Toulouse: Privat, 1965. 3 v.
    Rev. A. Dondaine, *RHR*, 178 (1970), 49-56; D. Walther, *CH*, 35 (1966), 467.

1921 Ebels-Hoving, B. "Traditie en vernieuwing in de ketterbestrijding van Innocentius III: de *Exposition en proie.*" *TG*, 88 (1975), 151-168.

1922 Emery, R. W. *Heresy and inquisition in Narbonne.* Studies in history, economics and public law, 480. New York, 1941. Rpt. New York: AMS, 1967. 184 p.

1923 Erbstösser, M. "Ein neues Inquisitionsprotokoll zu den sozial-religiösen Bewegungen in Thüringen Mitte des 14. Jahrhunderts." *Wissenschaftliche Zeitschrift der Karl-Marx-Universität Leipzig,* Gesellschafts- und sprachwissenschaftliche Reihe, 14 (1965), 379-388.

1924 Eymeric, N., and F. Peña. *Le manuel des inquisiteurs.* Intro., trans. L. Sala-Molins. Le savoir historique, 8. Paris and The Hague: Mouton, c1973. 249 p.
    Rev. J.-C. Schmitt, *ASSR*, 20 (1975), 211; O. de Saint-Blanquat, *BEC*, 135 (1977), 190-191.

1925 Ferlus, J. "L'inquisition médiévale en Languedoc. 'Que fut-elle en réalité?'" *Société ariégeoise, sciences, lettres et arts: bulletin annuel,* 23 (1967), 117-128.

1926 Flatten, H. *Der Häresieverdacht im Codex iuris canonici.* Kanonistische Studien und Texte, 21. Amsterdam: Schippers, 1963. 338 p.
    Rev. L. Hofmann, *Trierer theologische Zeitschrift,* 74 (1965), 313-314; G. May, *ZSSRG,* Kan. Abt., 82 (1965), 306-309; B. Primetshofer, *TPQ,* 114 (1966), 387-388.

1927 Förg, L. *Die Ketzerverfolgung in Deutschland unter Gregor ix. Ihre Herkunft, ihre Bedeutung und ihre rechtlichen Grundlagen.* Historische Studien, 218. Berlin, 1932. Rpt. Vaduz: Kraus, 1965. 98 p.

1928 Foreville, R. "Les statuts synodaux et le renouveau pastoral du xiiie siècle dans le midi de la France." *Le crédo, la morale et l'inquisition.* Cahiers de Fanjeaux, 6. Toulouse: Privat, c1971. p. 119-150.

1929 Fort i Cogul, E. *Catalunya i la inquisició.* Barcelona: Aedos, [1973]. 333 p. ill.

1930 Garrigue, G. "Marques distinctives des hérétiques du midi de la France au xiiie et xive siècles." *CEC,* 25, no. 62 (1974), 53-58.

1931 Gartner, G. "Mittelalterliche Ketzerprozesse in Steyr." *Auftrag und Verwirklichung.* Ed. F. Loidl. Wiener Beiträge zur Theologie, 44. Vienna: Wiener Dom-Verlag, 1974. p. 123-133.

1932 Giordano, N. "L'esecuzione in effigie (relaxo in statua): contributo alla storia della procedura inquisitoriale." *Archivio storico siciliano,* 18 (1968), 217-266.

1933 Giunta, F. "Die Politik Friedrichs ii. gegen die Ketzer." *Stupor mundi: zur Geschichte Friedrichs ii. von Hohenstaufen.* Ed. G. Wolf. Darmstadt: Wissenschaftliche Buchgesellschaft, 1966. p. 289-295. Trans. by G. Opitz from *Atti del Convegno internazionale di studi federiciani 1950* (Palermo, 1952), p. 91-95.

1934 Gonnet, G. "Sul concilio di Verona." *BSSV,* 140 (1976), 21-30.

1935 Grauwen, W. M. "Was de inquisiteur Koenraad van Marburg (†1233) een premonstratenzer?" *Analecta praemonstratensia,* 52 (1976), 212-224.

1936 Grigulevich, I. R. *Istoriia inkvizitsii (xiii-xx vv.).* Moscow: Nauka, 1970. 447 p. ill. Trans. H. Mohr, *Ketzer − Hexen − Inquisitoren: Geschichte der Inquisition (13.-20. Jahrhundert)* (Berlin: Akademie-Verlag, 1976), 2 v., ill. Rev. (German trans.) K. Schwurack, *ZG,* 26 (1978), 932.

1937 Grundmann, H. "Ketzerverhöre des Spätmittelalters als quellenkritisches Problem." *DAEM,* 21 (1965), 519-575. Rpt. in H. Grundmann, *Ausgewählte Aufsätze,* I (Stuttgart: Hiersemann, 1976), 364-416.

1938 Gy, P.-M. "Le précepte de la confession annuelle (Latran iv, c. 12) et la détection des hérétiques: S. Bonaventure et S. Thomas contre S. Raymond de Peñafort." *RSPT,* 58 (1974), 444-450.

1939 Hageneder, O. "Der Häresiebegriff bei den Juristen des 12. und 13. Jahrhunderts." *The concept of heresy in the middle ages* (1976). p. 42-103. See 25.

1940 Halaga, O. R. "Spätmittelalter als s.g. Krisenepoche im Lichte der Inquisition in Ungarn." *MB,* 3 (1971), 193-208.

1941 Hayward, F. *The inquisition.* Trans. M. Carroll. [New York: Society of St. Paul, Alba House, 1966.] 176 p. Orig. publ. as *Que faut-il penser de l'inquisition?* (Paris, 1958).

1942 Heimpel, H., ed. *Zwei Wormser Inquisitionen aus den Jahren 1421 und 1422.* Abhandlungen der Akademie der Wissenschaften in Göttingen, Philol.-

hist. Klasse, 3rd ser., 73. Göttingen: Vandenhoeck und Ruprecht, 1969. 81 p.

Rev. M. Kaiser, *AHC*, 2 (1970), 431-433; G. May, *ZSSRG*, Kan. Abt., 88 (1971), 386-388.

1943   Jalby, R. "Les conciles provinciaux et la répression des doctrines hétérodoxes." *Revue du Tarn*, 87 (1977), 321-328.

1944   Jansen, H. P. H. "De oorsprong van de inquisitie." *Spiegel historiael*, 2 (1967), 279-287.

1945   Karlen, A. "The homosexual heresy." *The Chaucer review*, 6 (1971), 44-63. Revision of ch. 5, "The capital sin," in his *Sexuality and homosexuality: a new view* (New York: Norton, c1971), p. 85-99.

1946   Kieckhefer, R. *Repression of heresy in medieval Germany*. Philadelphia: University of Pennsylvania Press, 1979. xiv, 161 p.

1947   ——. "Repression of heresy in Germany, 1348-1520." Diss. Univ. of Texas, Austin. *DAI*, 34A (1973), 691.

1948   Koch, J. "Der Kardinal Jacques Fournier (Benedikt XII.) als Gutachter in theologischen Prozessen." *Die Kirche und ihre Ämter und Stände: Festgabe seiner Eminenz dem hochwürdigsten Herrn Joseph Kardinal Frings ... dargeboten*. Ed. W. Corsten, et al. Cologne: Bachem, 1960. p. 441-452.

1949   Kreuzer, J. "Inquiry into the inquisition." *Liguorian*, 50, no. 10 (1962), 11-13.

1950   Kriegel, M. "Prémarranisme et inquisition dans le Provence des XIIIe et XIVe siècles." *Provence historique*, 27 (1977), 313-323.

1951   Kulcsár, Z. *Inkvizíció és boszorkánypörök*. Budapest: Kossuth, 1960. 139 p. 3rd ed., enlgd. (208 p.), Budapest: Gondolat, 1968. [Inquisition and witch-trials]

1952   Kurze, D., comp. *Quellen zur Ketzergeschichte Brandenburgs und Pommerns*. Veröffentlichungen der Historischen Kommission zu Berlin, 45; Quellenwerke, 6. Berlin and New York: de Gruyter, 1975. xi, 390 p. ill.

Rev. R. E. Lerner, *CHR*, 63 (1977), 143-144; J. Petersohn, *HZ*, 224 (1977), 696-698; A. Patschovsky, *DAEM*, 34 (1978), 589-590; Anon., *BSSV*, 139 (1976), 90-93; V. Vinay, *BSSV*, 144 (1978), 85-87.

1953   Lea, H. C. *The inquisition of the middle ages*. Ed. M. Nicolson. New York: Macmillan, 1961. 906 p. [Abridged ed. of *A history of the inquisition in the middle ages*, 3 v. (New York, 1887)]

1954   ——. *The inquisition of the middle ages: its organization and operation*. With intro. by W. Ullman. London: Eyre and Spottiswoode, 1963; New York: Harper and Row, 1969. 326 p. [Abridged ed. of v. 1 of *A history of the inquisition in the middle ages* (New York, 1887)]

Rev. M. Bévenot, *HJ*, 5 (1964), 338-339; R. H. C. Davis, *JEH*, 15 (1964), 128-129; J. W. Gray, *History*, 48 (1963), 363-364; P. McGrath, *The tablet*,

217 (1963), 256-258; H. Mayr-Harting, *The month*, 215 (1963), 356-360; J. N. Hillgarth, *Estudios lulianos*, 11 (1967), 195-196.

1955   Leiber, R. "Die mittelalterliche Inquisition." *Stimmen der Zeit*, 170 (1962), 161-176.

1956   ——. *Die mittelalterliche Inquisition: Wesen und Unwesen*. Entscheidung, 33. Kevelaer: Butzon and Bercker, 1963. 30 p.

1957   Logan, F. D. *Excommunication and the secular arm in medieval England: a study in legal procedure from the thirteenth to the sixteenth century*. Studies and texts, 15. Toronto: Pontifical Institute of Mediaeval Studies, 1968. 239 p.

1958   [Lucchini, P.] *L'inquisition*. Paris: Perrin, c1969. 344 p. ill.

1959   Machilek, F. "Ein Eichstätter Inquisitionsverfahren aus dem Jahre 1460." *Jahrbuch für fränkische Landesforschung*, 34/35 (1974-75), 417-446.

1960   Maier, A. "Eine Verfügung Johanns xxii. über die Zuständigkeit der Inquisition für Zaubereiprozesse." *Ausgehendes Mittelalter: gesammelte Aufsätze zur Geistesgeschichte des 14. Jahrhunderts*. Rome: Storia e Letteratura, 1964-1967. II, 59-80. Orig. publ. in *AFP*, 22 (1952), 226-246.

1961   Maisonneuve, H. "Le droit romain et la doctrine inquisitoriale." *Études d'histoire du droit canonique dédiées à Gabriel Le Bras*. Paris: Sirey, 1965. II, 931-942.

1962   ——. *Études sur les origines de l'inquisition*. L'église et l'état au moyen âge, 7. 2nd ed., rvsd. and enlgd. Paris: Vrin, 1960. 386 p. Orig. publ. Paris, 1942. Rev. M. W. Baldwin, *Speculum*, 37 (1962), 141-143; A. Borst, *ZKG*, 75 (1964), 386-387; C. Lefebvre, *RHE*, 56 (1961), 528-529.

1963   Manselli, R. "De la *persuasio* à la *coercitio*." *Le crédo, la morale et l'inquisition*. Cahiers de Fanjeaux, 6. Toulouse: Privat, c1971. p. 175-197.

1964   Marchetti, V. "L'archivio dell'inquisizione senese (rendiconto di una ricerca in corso)." *BSSV*, 132 (1972), 77-83.

1965   Marchi, A. "Eresia ed inquisizione a Prato." *Archivio storico pratese*, 45 (1969 [1974]), 100-116.

1966   Maycock, A. L. *The inquisition from its establishment to the great schism: an introductory study*. Intro. R. Knox. London, 1927. Rpt. New York: Harper and Row, 1969. xxiii, 276 p. ill.

1967   Mayr-Harting, H. "The medieval inquisition." *The month*, n.s. 29 (1963), 356-360.

1968   Mazur, Z. "Powstanie i działalność inkwizycji dominikańskiej na Śląsku w XIV w." *Nasza przeszłość*, 39 (1973), 181-191, ill. [Origin and activity of the Dominican inquisition in Silesia in the 14th century]

1969   Merlo, G. G. "Sopravvivenze ereticali e nuovi fermenti eterodossi del trecento: disponibilità di ambienti sociali e repressione ecclesiastica nella diocesi di Torino." *Bollettino storico-bibliografico subalpino*, 74 (1976), 145-238. Abridged version publ. as "La repressione antiereticale in Piemonte nel secolo XIV," *BSSV*, 138 (1975), 3-13.

1970   Michaud-Quantin, P. "Textes pénitentiels languedociens au xiiie siècle." *Le crédo, la morale et l'inquisition.* Cahiers de Fanjeaux, 6. Toulouse: Privat, c1971. p. 151-172.

1971   Molinier, C. *L'inquisition dans le midi de la France au xiiie et au xive siècle: étude sur les sources de son histoire.* Paris, 1880. Rpt. Marseille: Laffitte, 1973. xxvii, 483 p.

1972   Nickson, M. A. E. "Locke and the inquisition of Toulouse." *The British Museum quarterly*, 36 (1972), 83-92.

1973   O'Brien, J. A. *The inquisition.* New York: Macmillan; London: Collier Macmillan, c1973. xiii, 233 p.
       Rev. W. A. Hinnebusch, *The Thomist*, 38 (1974), 670-672; J. A. Brundage, *America*, 130 (1974), 59-60; A. P. Lowe, *The sign*, February 1974, p. 49; J. M. Sánchez, *Review for religious*, 33 (1974), 247; C. Hollis, *The tablet*, 228 (1974), 1259-1260; A. C. Shannon, *CHR*, 63 (1977), 452.

1974   Ourliac, P. "La société languedocienne du xiiie siècle et le droit romain." *Le crédo, la morale et l'inquisition.* Cahiers de Fanjeaux, 6. Toulouse: Privat, c1971. p. 199-216.

1975   Padovani, A. "Disposizioni antiereticali negli statuti cittadini e nel contado di Imola nel secolo xiv." *Studi romagnoli*, 26 (1975), 137-162. —

1976   Paolini, L., ed. *Il 'De officio inquisitionis': la procedura inquisitoriale a Bologna e Ferrara nel trecento.* Bologna: Ed. Universitaria Bolognina, 1976. xlii, 166 p. ill.
       Rev. G. Barone, *SM*, 3rd ser., 17 (1976), 1029-1030; G. May, *ZSSRG*, 94, Kan. Abt. (1977), 354-356; A. Patschovsky, *DAEM*, 33 (1977), 612-613; G. G. Merlo, *RSLR*, 14 (1978), 305-306.

1977   Parwew, G. "*Podrecznik inkwizytora* Bernarda Gui jako zródlo do ruchów heretyckich w xiii i xiv wieku." *Universitas Iagellonica.* Prace historyczne zeszyt, 56. Kraków: Jagellonian University, 1977. p. 7-17. [Incl. summary, "*Manuel de l'inquisiteur* par Bernard Gui, source des mouvements hérétiques aux xiiie-xive siècles"]

1978   Patschovsky, A. *Die Anfänge einer ständigen Inquisition in Böhmen: ein Prager Inquisitoren-Handbuch aus der ersten Hälfte des 14. Jahrhunderts.* Beiträge zur Geschichte und Quellenkunde des Mittelalters, 3. Berlin and New York: de Gruyter, 1975. xviii, 319 p. ill.
       Rev. F. Graus, *SZG*, 25 (1975), 581-582; P. W. Knoll, *CH*, 45 (1976), 252; E. Winter, *ZG*, 24 (1976), 356; W. Ullman, *JEH*, 27 (1976), 423-425; H. S. Offler, *JTS*, 28 (1977), 219-221; E. Potkowski, *Kwartalnik historyczny*, 83 (1976), 921-923; K. Langosch, *Mittellateinisches Jahrbuch*, 12 (1977), 290; F. Seibt, *Zeitschrift für historische Forschung*, 5 (1978), 487-488; P. T. Stella, *Salesianum*, 39 (1977), 165-166; H. Kaminsky, *Speculum*, 53 (1978), 180-181; B. Llorca Vives, *Revista española de derecho canónico*,

32 (1976), 463-465; J. Kejř, *zssrg*, Kan. Abt., 93 (1976), 445-448, and *Právněhistorické studie*, 20 (1976), 266-268; Anon., *bssv*, 139 (1976), 87-90.

1979 Pellegrini, L. "L'inquisizione francescana sotto Alessandro IV (1254-1261)." *sf*, 64, no. 4 (1967), 73-100.

1980 Pennington, K. "'Pro peccatis patrum puniri': a moral and legal problem of the inquisition." *ch*, 47 (1978), 137-154.

1981 Peters, E. M. "Editing inquisitors' manuals in the sixteenth century: Francisco Peña and the *Directorium inquisitorum* of Nicholas Eymeric." *Bibliographical studies in honor of Rudolf Hirsch = The library chronicle* (Univ. of Pennsylvania), 40 (1974), 95-107.

1982 Petrika, A. *Apie šventrašţį, erezijas ir inkviziciją*. Vilnius: Valstybinė politinės ir mokslinės literatūros leidykla, 1964. 135 p.

1983 Potkowski, E. *Heretycy i inkwizytorzy*. Warsaw: Państwowe Zakłady Wydawnictw Szkolnych, [1971]. 167 p. ill. [Heretics and inquisitors]

1984 Reyes, A. "La confesión y la tortura en la historia de la iglesia." *Revista española de derecho canónico*, 24 (1968), 595-624.

1985 Richtmann, F. P. *A inquisição: breve ensaio crítico*. São Leopoldo: [Mensageiro da Fé], 1960. 62 p.

1986 Sacchetti Sassetti, A. "I paterini a Rieti nel secolo XIII." *Archivio della Società romana di storia patria*, 89 (1966), 87-99.

1987 Sancassani, G. "Un eretico veronese del primo '400: Luchino Pocapovina." *Atti e memorie dell'Accademia di agricoltura, scienze e lettere di Verona*, 137 (1960-61 [1962]), 215-238.

1988 Selge, K.-V. "Heidelberger Ketzerprozesse in der Frühzeit der hussitischen Revolution." *zkg*, 82 (1971), 167-202.

1989 ——, ed. *Texte zur Inquisition*. Texte zur Kirchen- und Theologiegeschichte, 4. Gütersloh: Mohn, c1967. 88 p.

1990 Severino, G. "Note sull'eresia a Siena fra i secoli XIII e XIV." *Studi sul medioevo cristiano offerti a Raffaello Morghen*. Rome: Istituto Storico Italiano per il Medio Evo, 1974. II, 889-905.

1991 Shatzmiller, J. "L'inquisition et les juifs de Provence au XIIIe s.." *Provence historique*, 23, nos. 93-94 (1973), 327-338.

1992 Silvestre, H. "Notules à propos d'une histoire de la tolérance." *rhe*, 58 (1963), 531-544.

1993 Sorgia, G. *Studi sull'inquisizione in Sardegna*. Università di Cagliari, Facoltà di lettere e di magistero, 5. Palermo: Palumbo, 1961. 93 p.

1994 Tanner, N. P., ed. *Heresy trials in the diocese of Norwich, 1428-31*. Camden fourth series, 20. London: Royal historical society, 1977. vi, 233 p.
Rev. R. Lerner, *Speculum*, 54 (1979), 429-430; R. G. Davies, *ehr*, 94 (1979), 629; J. C. Schmitt, *bec*, 137 (1979), 171-174.

1995 Testas, G., and J. Testas. *L'inquisition*. Paris: Presses universitaires de France, 1966. 128 p.
Rev. I. Cloulas, *SZG*, 17 (1967), 429-430; J. Jolivet, *RHR*, 175 (1969), 95-97.

1996 Thomson, P. van K. "The tragedy of the Spanish inquisition." *The bridge: a yearbook of Judaeo-Christian studies*, 4 (1961-62), 171-196.

1997 Thouzellier, C. "L'*inquisitio* et Saint Dominique." *AM*, 80 (1968), 121-130, ill. With reply to M.-H. Vicaire, p. 137-138.

1998 ———. "La repressione dell'eresia e gli inizi dell'inquisizione." *La cristianità romana (1198-1274)*. Ed. M. d'Alatri. Turin, 1968. —

1999 Triller, A. "Häresien in Altpreussen um 1390?" *Studien zur Geschichte des Preussenlandes: Festschrift für Erich Keyser*. Ed. E. Bahr. Marburg: Elwert, 1963. p. 397-404.

2000 Turberville, A. S. *Mediaeval heresy and the inquisition*. London, 1920. Rpt. Hamden, Conn.: Archon, 1964. vi, 264 p.

2001 Ullmann, W. "The inquisition: an explanation." *The listener*, 69, no. 1777 (18 April 1963), 671-673, ill.

2002 Vekené, E. van der. *Bibliographie der Inquisition: ein Versuch*. Hildesheim: Olms, 1963. viii, 323 p.
Rev. Y. Dossat, *AM*, 79 (1967), 232-233; B. A. Vermaseren, *TG*, 77 (1964), 472-477.

2003 ———. *Zur Bibliographie des "Directorium inquisitorum" des Nicolaus Eymerich*. [Luxembourg: B.W.U., 1961.] 14 p. ill.

2004 Vicaire, M.-H. "Un auxiliaire de la controverse: les *quaestiones ad decipiendum*." *Le crédo, la morale et l'inquisition*. Cahiers de Fanjeaux, 6. Toulouse: Privat, c1971. p. 65-73.

2005 ———. "Note sur la mentalité de Saint Dominique." *AM*, 80 (1968), 131-136. See 1997.

2006 ———. "La pastorale des mœurs dans les conciles languedociens (fin du xie – début du xiiie siècle)." *Le crédo, la morale et l'inquisition*. Cahiers de Fanjeaux, 6. Toulouse: Privat, c1971. p. 85-117.

2007 ———. "'Persequutor hereticorum' ou les 'persécutions' de saint Dominique." *Le crédo, la morale et l'inquisition*. Cahiers de Fanjeaux, 6. Toulouse: Privat, c1971. p. 75-84.

2008 ———. "La prédication nouvelle des prêcheurs méridionaux au xiiie siècle." *Le crédo, la morale et l'inquisition*. Cahiers de Fanjeaux, 6. Toulouse: Privat, c1971. p. 21-64.

2009 ———. "Saint Dominique et les inquisiteurs." *AM*, 79 (1967), 173-194.

2010 Villerot, D. *L'inquisition*. Paris: Grasset, c1973. 287 p. ill.

2011 Vourzay, M. J. "Les conditions de vie des émigrés cathares en Catalogne d'après le *Registre d'inquisition* de Jacques Fournier (1318-1325)." Diss. Univ. d'Aix-Marseille, 1969. —

2012   Wakefield, W. L. "Friar Ferrier, inquisition at Caunes, and escapes from prison at Carcassonne." *CHR*, 58 (1972), 220-237.

2013   ——. "Notes on some antiheretical writings of the thirteenth century." *FS*, 27 (1967), 285-321.

2013A ——. "Pseudonyms and nicknames in inquisitorial documents of the middle ages in southern France." *Names*, 27 (1979), 188-197.

2014   Walsh, W. T. *Characters of the inquisition.* New York, c1940. Rpt. Port Washington, N.Y.: Kennikat, 1969. xi, 301 p.

2015   Walther, H. G. "Häresie und päpstliche Politik: Ketzerbegriff und Ketzergesetzgebung in der Übergangsphase von der Dekretistik zur Dekretalistik." *The concept of heresy in the middle ages* (1976). p. 104-143. See 25.

2016   ——. "Haeretica pravitas und Ekklesiologie. Zum Verhältnis von kirchlichem Ketzerbegriff und päpstlicher Ketzerpolitik von der zweiten Hälfte des XII. bis ins erste Drittel des XIII. Jahrhunderts." *Die Mächte des Guten und Bösen.* Ed. A. Zimmermann. Miscellanea mediaevalia, 11. Berlin and New York: de Gruyter, 1977. p. 286-314.

2017   Yerushalmi, Y. H. "The inquisition and the Jews of France in the time of Bernard Gui." *Harvard theological review*, 63 (1970), 317-376.

Author Index

Molinier, Charles 1971
Mollat, Michel 127, 208
Molnár, Amedeo 51, 75, 95-96, 305, 715,
    717, 729, 747, 771, 790-812, 816, 822,
    830, 887, 1033, 1175, 1220, 1258,
    1349-1350, 1385-1392, 1414, 1416,
    1421, 1442-1443, 1451, 1454, 1456,
    1494, 1500, 1547, 1550, 1553, 1590,
    1596-1612, 1674, 1691-1694, 1697,
    1722-1723, 1727, 1746-1748, 1758,
    1763, 1782
Molnar, Enrico S. 718, 1221, 1463в
Mols, R. 75, 305, 374, 396, 454-455, 479,
    489, 550, 572, 575, 887, 1393, 1414,
    1420, 1422, 1704, 1907
Monfrin, Jacques 697
Montégut, Olivier de 473
Monter, E. William 1818, 1848-1849,
    1851
Montet, Édouard 813
Montgomery, Ingun 119
Moonan, Lawrence 1721
Moore, R. I. 71, 97, 178-182, 258, 1818
Moorman, John R. H. 1037
Moral, Alvaro del 545
Mordant, Louis 814
Mordek, Hubert 988
Moreau, Pierre-François 532
Morero, Vittorio 815
Morghen, Raffaello 98, 183, 190, 346, 405,
    627, 1801
Morrall, John B. 1183, 1226
Morris, Colin 178-179, 374, 503, 532,
    1011
Morrison, S. St. Clair 184
Morrissey, Thomas E. 1037
Mosteller, James D. 1325
Mosti, Renzo 1122
Mottu, Henry 995
Moulis, Adelin 538
Mouzat, Jean 474
Mráz, Milan 1732-1734
Mudroch, Vaclav 53, 99, 1222-1224
Mühlpfordt, Günter 210, 830, 1674
Müller, Georg 996
Müller, Gotthold 24
Müller, Wolfgang 1348, 1429
Mundy, John H. 71, 475, 503, 537, 645
Muñoz, A. S. 126, 683
Murray, Alexander 179, 1850

Musy, Jean 185
Myln'ikov, A. S. 1394

Nardi, Bruno 858, 879, 997
Năsturel, Petre 252
Nataf, André 349
Nazor, Anica 270
Nečas, Jaroslav 1395
Nechutová, Jana 1464-1465, 1613-1614,
    1707-1709, 1742-1744, 1752
Nelli, René 100-101, 246, 350-353, 470,
    476, 539, 623, 627, 646-655, 696
Nelson, Janet L. 186, 1818, 1862
Němec, Igor 1466
Nemec, J. 1553
Nemec, Ludvik 1414, 1416, 1547, 1553,
    1601, 1704
Neumann, Eva Gertrud 913
Nickson, Margaret 102-103, 1972
Nicolson, Margaret 1953
Niederländer, R. 1615
Niel, Fernand 353-354, 477, 540-542
Nigg, Walter 104-105
Nobluez, Y. 914
Nolan, David 343
Nolte, Josef 61
Noret, J. 1258
Nováková, Julie 1467
Nübel, Otto 915
Nuttall, Geoffrey F. 1396
Nyhus, Paul L. 72, 1162, 1704
Nyíri, Antal 1616

Oakley, Francis 1382
Oberdorffer, Kurt 1617
Oberg, Renato Emir 1397
Oberman, Heiko A. 75, 1177, 1226
Obolensky, Dimitri 259
O'Brien, John A. 656, 1973
Odierna, Antonino 1123
Odlozilík, Otakar 1414, 1416, 1420, 1422,
    1475, 1618-1619, 1758, 1763
Offler, H. S. 75, 109, 1162, 1500, 1978
Okič, M. Tăyyib 260
Olagüe, Ignacio 106
Oldenbourg, Zoé 543
Oldoni, Massimo 696
Oliver, A. 107
Olsen, Glenn 1862

Subject Index

Norbert of Xanten 56, 203
Northampton 1323
Norwich 1331, 1994
Nürnberg 1633, 1839

Ockham, William 1060, 1196, 1210
Oldcastle, John 71, 1214, 1284-1285, 1291, 1298, 1330, 1332
Oldřich of Rožmberk 1491, 1494, 1751, 1758
Oldřich of Znojmo 1666
Olivi, Peter 71, 75, 580, 891, 906, 946-947, 974, 979, 982, 989, 1003, 1011, 1028, 1040-1041, 1048-1065, 1070, 1072, 1074, 1075-1088, 1093-1119, 1123-1124, 1126, 1128, 1135-1154, 1673
Olivi, bibliography 1092
Opus arduum 1313
Ordinances, of Thoresby 1205
Orebites 1503, 1559, 1635, 1776, 1780
Orléans 53, 56, 71, 137, 141, 148, 156, 158, 178-180, 185, 190, 197-198, 208, 210-211, 1818, 1860, 1921-1922
Orthographia bohemica, of Hus 1476
Ortlibians 68, 102, 1182
Orvieto 178, 204, 535
Oxford 71, 75, 190, 1313
Oxford, university 71, 1200, 1226, 1252, 1259, 1332, 1645, 1649

Paesana 739
Páleč, Stephen 71, 75, 1354, 1382, 1414, 1416, 1420-1422, 1465, 1752-1755
Palmerio di Leonardo 1986
Pamiers 374, 455, 488, 490, 771, 842, 1889, 1919-1920
Pamiers, statutes of 488
Paris 895, 1839
Paris, university 909, 1125
Passagians 603, 1799
Passau 103, 1807
Passau Anonymous 56, 102-103, 816, 830, 1182, 2013
Passio domini nostri, attrib. to Hus 1452, 1543
Pastoureaux 24, 76, 1889
Patarenes 236, 240, 264, 277, 340-341, 553, 888, 1121, 1986
Pataria 17, 53, 71, 103, 119, 126, 136, 145-146, 153-154, 164, 168-171, 173, 176,

179, 190, 193, 197, 199-200, 202, 204, 208, 210, 374, 1990
"Pataria," name 126, 154, 193
Paulicians 71, 217, 251-252, 261, 272, 281, 340, 346, 399, 403, 411, 413, 659, 707
Payne, Peter 1242, 1305, 1329, 1494, 1500, 1510, 1574, 1666-1667, 1756-1757
Peachey, John 1322
The Pearl 1193, 1226
Pecock, Reginald 1283, 1286
Pedro II. *See* Peter II
Pelhřimov, Nicholas. *See* Nicholas of Pelhřimov
Pellegrini, Zulittina 880
Peña, Francisco 1924, 1981, 2003
Penitents 869, 878, 984, 1039, 1047
Penna 1879
Pentagon 651
Périgord 178, 443
Perkins, William 1284
Perrette 1825
Perugia 1793
Peter II, of Aragon 374, 377, 484, 499, 503
Peter Amiel 1922
Peter Aquila 1876
Peter Autier. *See* Autier, Peter
Peter of Bruys 42, 53, 56, 71, 134, 137, 151-152, 161-162, 166, 178-179, 190, 198, 397, 1962
Peter of Castelnau. *See* Castelnau, Pierre
Peter Damian 830
Peter Eugrini de Podiodanielis 561
Peter Lombard 1099
Peter Lombard, Hus' commentary on 1434, 1470
Peter Martyr of Verona 381
Peter of Mladoňovice. *See* Mladoňovice
Peter of Penna 1879
Peter Riga 688
Peter of Sicily 251
Peter de Trabibus 1091, 1099
Peter of Vaux-de-Cernay 126, 374, 381, 439, 455, 579, 2013
Peter the Venerable 55, 134, 151, 162, 166, 198, 329, 397
Peter of Verona 1983, 2013
Peter Waldo. *See* Valdes
Petrarch 1599
Petrobrusians. *See* Peter of Bruys

Manuscript Index